Elder Activities
for People Who Care

Volume Two
July through December

by Pat Nekola

Published by:
Applewood Ink
A division of: Catering by Design
P.O. Box 181
Waukesha, WI 53187

Picnics

Catering on the Move:
A Cookbook and Guide
by Pat Nekola

Learn to cater your own picnic for family and friends, for church or service club gatherings, or open a catering business. This cookbook has a variety of recipes designed especially for picnics. View buffet layouts, decorations, and various styles of picnics from simple to elegant. Recipes serve groups of 12-100, some up to 1,500!

Snacks and beverages, salads, grilled meats, hot vegetables, and dessert recipes are all designed for the picnicker's appetite.

From the owner of Pat's Party Foods, Caterers.

Pat Nekola has a long history of fine catering with her own business, Pat's Party Foods, in Wisconsin. She shares many delicious recipes in *Picnics, Catering on the Move*. Picnics were her favorite parties because she enjoyed watching families and friends relax and have fun.

242 pages, hard back with spiral binding.
ISBN: 0-9660610-0-4
®Copyright 2000, Catering by Design

Pat Nekola began writing *Picnics, Catering on the Move* when her mother was diagnosed with Alzheimer's disease. Alzheimer's is a progressive, degenerative disease of the brain causing confusion, personality, and behavioral changes. Eventually many people with Alzheimer's are not able to care for themselves. A family member loses them twice: first to Alzheimer's, then to death. Taking care of a person with Alzheimer's takes a lot of patience and love.

Pat is donating $3.00 of every book sold to the Alzheimer's Association. The funds are being used for research to find a cure for the disease and for educational programs that help caregivers.

- *Kitchen-tested recipes.*
- *Picnic ideas.*
- *Quantities shown for small to large groups.*
- *Decorations for theme parties.*
- *Diagrams to guide the reader.*
- *Buffet layout diagrams act as a learning tool.*
- *Heartwarming stories accompany recipes.*
- *Easy-to-follow instructions.*
- *Garnishes to make food attractive.*
- *Catering for crowds for fun and profit.*

Picnics
Catering on the Move:
A Cookbook and Guide
by Pat Nekola

Customer Name _____

Address _____

City State Zip _____

Phone _____ Fax _____

Mail or fax to:	**Catering by Design** P.O. Box 181 Waukesha, WI 53187 Ph: (262) 547-2004 Fax: (262) 547-8594

Thank you for your order!

Qty:	Price @	Ext.
	$27.95	$
Shipping	$4.50	$
Total		$

MasterCard and Visa accepted.

WI residents please add 5.5% sales tax.

Signature _____

Date _____

Invoice Number _____

An Alzheimer's Guide

Activities and Issues for People Who Care

When Pat Nekola's mother and aunt were stricken with Alzheimer's disease, she found help and information from a number of public and private sources. She also found that there were many others—families, caregivers, residential facilities' staff—just like herself, that could make use of the same types of information. With this in mind, Pat set out to accumulate the education and information to write this handbook to help others going through the same trying personal experiences.

This handbook is easy to read and to understand. Pat's writing approach is like a one-on-one conversation with a friend that has "been there and done that". Everyone needs to read this book, we are all dealing with the disease whether on a personal level, or as members of our local communities. It is an informative and warm approach to helping the Alzheimer's patient live to their fullest and enjoy each day—no matter what their present situation.

242 pages, soft cover.
ISBN: 0-9660610-8-X
®Copyright 2002, Catering by Design

Information included in Part One of this Handbook:

- Easy to understand information on each stage of the disease.

- How to deal with the different stages for families and caregivers.

- Coping strategies when caring for the patient at home.

- What to look for when selecting a care facility.

- Resources including telephone numbers, websites, and questions to ask.

Information and Activities Useful for the Care Facilities' Activity Directors included in Part Two of this Handbook:

- Directions for different craft activities.

- Color graphics for use with the activities.

- Recommended music for patient participation.

- Recipes.

- Patient assessment forms.

An Alzheimer's Guide
Activities and Issues for People Who Care

| | Customer Name _____ |
| Address _____ |
| City State Zip _____ |
| Phone _____ Fax _____ |

Mail or fax to:	**Catering by Design** P.O. Box 181 Waukesha, WI 53187 Ph: (262) 547-2004 Fax: (262) 547-8594

Thank you for your order!

Qty:	Price @	Ext.
	$34.95	$
Shipping	$4.50	$
Total		$

MasterCard and Visa accepted.

WI residents please add 5.5% sales tax.

Signature _____

Date _____

Invoice Number _____

As Pat Nekola travels the country visiting nursing homes and assisted living facilities, she hears so many heart-warming stories from residents, families, and staff. Pat has decided to share some of these stories in her latest publication, *Elderly Reflections for People Who Care*. The elderly have many stories and experiences to share and they are worth hearing.

Pat hopes these stories will help you feel good while dealing with the everyday "nitty gritty" of an elderly person in need of your care and love.

There are fifty-four short stories by Pat and passed on by friends. Enjoy the book yourself or bring it with you when visiting a family member or friend at home, in a hospital, or care facility.

Elder Reflections
for People Who Care
by Pat Nekola

64 pages, soft cover.
ISBN: 0-9660610-6-3
©Copyright 2003, Catering by Design

To order, mail or fax to:
Catering by Design
P.O. Box 181
Waukesha, WI 53187
Ph: (262) 547-2004
Fax: (262) 547-8594

Customer Name _____

Address _____

City State Zip _____

Phone _____ Fax _____ E-mail _____

Qty:	Price @	Ext.
	$14.95	$
Shipping	$4.50	$
Total		$

MasterCard and Visa accepted.

WI residents please add 5.5% sales tax.

Signature _____

Date _____

Invoice Number _____

v

Activities are the hub of the elderly care facility, with the residents looking for things to brighten their days and keep their minds and bodies fit. Activity Directors have the challenge of developing and delivering programs that meet residents' needs.

Elderly Activities for People Who Care Volume One includes many, many detailed themed activities for January through June. Caribbean themed parties, Valentine's Day, St. Patrick's Day, Easter, Cinco de Mayo, Kentucky Derby, Norwegian Independence Day, as well as activities that can be used any time of the year. Elderly Activities gives activity directors everything they need to enrich their programs with plans for a whole new set of detailed themed activities.

Pat Nekola began working on behalf of people with Alzheimer's disease when her mother became afflicted with the disease. She travels the country conducting seminars with activities staff in care facilities. Pat holds B.S. and M.A. degrees in education and has designed programs for the elderly, working as an Activity Consultant Trainer. She is a strong advocate for the elderly and gives a portion of her book sales to the Alzheimer's Association in honor of her mother.

Elder Activities *for People Who Care*
Volume One
January through June

292 pages, soft cover.
ISBN: 0-9660610-8-X
©Copyright 2003, Catering by Design

Pat Nekola was born in Akron, Ohio, and raised in Indiana. She holds B.S. and M.A. degrees in home economics education with a minor in music. Pat became interested in helping the elderly when her mother became afflicted with Alzheimer's. She completed the ACT (Activity Consultant Trainers) and Management program sponsored by the state of Wisconsin and has worked as an Activity Director.

She presently travels the country conducting seminars with Activity staff in care facilities; counsels families dealing with Alzheimer's; and trains Girl Scouts to entertain the residents in local care facilities. She presents programs in libraries on Alzheimer's and picnics having written two previous books, *An Alzheimer's Guide—Activities and Issues for People Who Care*, and *Picnics— Catering on the Move: A Cookbook and Guide*.

Pat has been a co-facilitator for the Alzheimer's patients and gives a portion of her book sales to the Alzheimer's Association in honor of her mother. She is a strong advocate for the elderly, and has designed many activity programs for the elderly. Pat uses her programs to work with the elderly on a personal level.

Elder Activities *for People Who Care*

Volume Two
June through December

292 pages, soft cover.
ISBN: 0-9660610-7-1
©Copyright 2004, Catering by Design

Mail or fax to: Catering by Design
P.O. Box 181 • Waukesha, WI 53187
Ph: (262) 547-2004 • Fax: (262) 547-8594

Customer Name _____

Address _____

City State Zip _____

Phone _____ Fax _____ E-mail _____

Qty:	Price @	Ext.
	$36.95	$
Shipping	$4.50	$
Total		$

MasterCard and Visa accepted.

WI residents please add 5.5% sales tax.

Signature _____

Date _____

Invoice Number _____

Acknowledgments

My sincere thanks goes to the managers, produce department, and employees at the BKT Sentry Foods Fox Run for supplying items I needed to prepare the recipes in this book. I'd like to thank Glen Victorey, the owner of Let's Celebrate for his kind support and encouragement in helping me select the party decorations for the photography in this book.

I also want to acknowledge all the librarians across the U.S. who have given me the opportunity to present my programs at their facilities. Thank you for your support and encouragement in my projects.

The various Alzheimer's associations have been supportive of my work to raise funds to help find a cure for this dreadful disease. I appreciate your efforts to encourage me and the opportunities you've given me as a presenter and exhibitor at your meetings.

As always, my special thanks to Marcia Lorenzen and Camin Potts of Graphic Liaisons for their diligent work to make this book happen.

My husband, Steve, is my biggest supporter. Thanks for loving me.

Dedication

I would like to dedicate this book to all the caregivers and families that are caring for their elderly loved ones. May this book bring families closer—whether in a home setting or in a care facility—and create beautiful memories.

"Give a dash of joy and love and receive it in return. It is in giving that a person receives. Remember love is the greatest gift of all."

—Pat Nekola

Elder Activities *for People Who Care*
Volume Two—July through December

Color Section of Projects:

Contents

July Activities:

August Activities:

September Activities:

October Activities:

November Activities:

December Activities:

Disclosure

I do not proclaim to be an expert on dietary needs. However, my career began as a Home Economics teacher with strong emphasis in foods and diet. I have combined my studies with 18 years as a professional caterer, and Activity Director training specializing in Alzheimer's patients, and practical hands-on experience providing activities to the elderly population.

I share my experience and creative ability to meet the elder population's emotional and psychological needs. My mother had Alzheimer's for five years prior to her death.

I have authored *Picnics, Catering on the Move* and *An Alzheimer's Guide, Activities and Issues for People Who Care*. I implement information from both books during my work at care facilities. The *Picnics* book is a great tool to use when reminiscing with both Alzheimer's and higher functioning elderly residents.

I plan to continue to help families and activity personnel enrich the lives of the elder population, and I hope your facility will add this book to your library and apply some of my ideas in your activity planning.

—Pat Nekola

Preface

Many families often admit they don't know what to do with their elderly family members. This book is designed with many crafts, recipes, poetry, music, and party ideas for the entire family. These activities are designed to involve family members of all ages and encourage the entire family to get involved in the activity.

This book is divided into six chapters covering the months of July through December with various theme and holiday parties for each month. It is an ideal book for inter-generational projects and will stimulate all who take part in the various activities.

It is wonderful to witness how children and adult family members bond together. The elderly love children. Grandparents love to brag about their grandchildren and great-grandchildren.

Have fun using all these creative ideas with your family.

Best wishes,
Pat Nekola

Introduction

Volume One of this set of Activity workbooks gives a very detailed introduction on several important subjects every Activity Director should be aware of. Please take a few minutes to review that information whenever you have questions about recipes, special diets, residents' histories, calendars, working with family members and volunteers, field trips, and community resources. There are copies of client surveys and a sample activity calendar in Volume One.

I would just remind you to try to make every day special for your residents. Little acts of kindness and simple projects or trips make them feel as though they are still a part of the community.

It is also important to keep your total facility staff involved with your activities whenever possible, and work with your cafeteria staff to make the parties an endeavor of the total facility. Remember—you are all one big family, all working together in the best interests of everyone! So work together, play together, and enjoy every day!

July Activities

The Twin-Letter Word Game

Complete the blanks with "twin letters".

The first set of "twin letters" is:

MM

Co _ _ ode	A chest of drawers.
Co _ _ ittee	A group of people assigned to a matter.
Co _ _ ission	A percentage paid to an employee.
Co _ _ ander	An officer in the armed services that is below Captain and above Lieutenant.
Co_ _ encement	A ceremony in which diplomas or degrees are awarded for graduation.
Co _ _ onplace	Something ordinary or trite.
Co _ _ erce	Exchange of goods on a large scale.
Co _ _ andments	Divine command. Think of Moses and the Bible; or honor your father and mother.
Co _ _ ercial	An ad on the radio or TV.
Co _ _ iserate	To express pity.
Co _ _ ent	To make a remark or criticize.
Su _ _ er	Dog days occur in this season.

SS

Trespa_ _ ing	Wrongfully entering someone's property.
Pa_ _ ed	You took a test and did not fail.
Cro _ _	Christ died on the_____.
Rece _ _	School children go out to play during a certain time of the day.
Po _ _ e _ _ ions	Material goods a person owns.
Pa _ _ ive	The opposite of aggressive.
Stre _ _	A demand made on the nervous system if a person is pushed too hard on a job.
Pa _ _ ion	An intense emotion—such as love.
Croi _ _ ant	A type of bread originating in France. A roll that curves slightly at each end.
Po _ _ um	An animal that plays dead.
Dre _ _	A garment worn by women.
Dre_ _ ing	A type of food used to top a salad, or stuffing for a turkey.
Pa _ _ age	Channel, lane, alley, or corridor.

Pa _ _ enger   A person traveling on a airplane, boat, bus, car, or train.
Ma _ _ acre   A ruthless killing of people.
Ma _ _ achusetts   One of the eastern states.

TT

Pla _ _ er   A serving dish used for meat.
Se _ _ ler   An early colonist.
Ma _ _ er   There is a song with the title "Oh Dear, What Can The _____ Be".
Le _ _ er   A part of the alphabet.
Li _ _ le   Small.
Bri _ _ le   A form of candy with peanuts. Older people's bones become _____.
Le _ _ uce   Crisp leaves used in a tossed salad.
Fa _ _ y   Found in body tissue.
A _ _ ire   Very fine clothes or formal evening wear, such as a dress worn by a bridesmaid for a wedding.
A _ _ empt   To try to do a task.
A _ _ ache   A small briefcase for carrying papers.
A _ _ ack   Someone becomes ill with flu-like symptoms, heart problems or failure.
Pu _ _ y   A substance used to fill holes in wood, or hold a window in its frame.
Pa _ _ ern   A plan on paper used in sewing, or when making a model airplane.
Pa _ _ y   A fried meat cake such as a hamburger.
Ma _ _ ress   A frame stuffed with foam rubber, feathers, or other padding and placed on a bed frame.
Pu _ _   One type of shot in the game of golf.

PP

Pe _ _ er   A seasoning used on food, usually accompanied by salt.
Pu _ _ et   A doll or model with strings and wires.
Pu _ _ y   A young dog.
Po _ _ y   A red flower often given to a donor on Memorial Day.
Po _ _ le   To toss in choppy water.
A _ _ rove   Give an agreeable judgment on a person or event.
A _ _ etite   Hunger.
A _ _ ly   Someone looking for a job must _____.
A _ _ le   A fruit grown on a tree, picked in the fall, and used in pie.
A _ _ earance   How a person looks or dresses.
A _ _ laud   Clapping of hands to show approval.
Zi _ _ er   A closure on clothing.
Kidna _ _ er   To steal another person.
Sli _ _ ers   A type of shoe worn when lounging.
Sna _ _ le   A brand name of iced tea with flavoring, or a fruit drink.
Sna _ _ er   A fish that is two to three feet long and found in warm seas.

OO

C _ _ perate   To work together in a helpful manner.
N _ _ dle   A type of pasta served in soup.
N _ _ n   Middle of the day, or lunchtime.
N _ _ se   A loop in a rope.
M _ _ se   An animal with big branched antlers, part of the deer family.
M _ _ diness   A feeling of bad temper.
M _ _ n   A source of light in the sky at night.
P _ _ dle   A small French dog.
Sc _ _ p   To dip ice cream use a _____.
Fl _ _ d   An excessive amount of water.
G _ _ se   A web-footed, long-necked waterfowl.
L _ _ se   The opposite of tight.
Baref _ _ t   Not wearing shoes or socks.
S _ _ t   A black carbon susbstance found in chimneys.
Br _ _ m   Used to sweep.
Bl _ _ m   Flowers do this.

EE

Sp _ _ d   You'll get a ticket if you are driving too fast.
Sp _ _ ch   To speak in front of an audience.
Ch _ _ k   A part of your face or derrière.
Ch _ _ se   A food made from curd of milk that is high in protein.
Ch _ _ rful   A happy person.
Ch _ _ rio   An English expression meaning goodbye.
Proc _ _ d   To go forward on a project.
Ch _ _ secake   A dessert made with eggs, cream cheese, flavoring, and a graham cracker crust.
Fl _ _ t   A group of ships under one command.
Sh _ _ p   This animal's hair is called wool.
Sl _ _ p   Rest in bed overnight, or a nap.
Str _ _ t   An avenue or road.
Bl _ _ d   If you cut yourself you will do this.
Cr _ _ k   A squeaky sound a floor, or door, makes.
Sh _ _ ts   Pieces of paper, or fabric used on a bed.
P _ _ l   Remove the outer skin from a fruit or vegetable.
Tur _ _ n   A large serving dish used for soup.
B _ _ t   A root vegetable that is deep red.
Parak _ _ t   A small bird that lives in a cage as a pet.
Fr _ _ dom   The liberty to live as you choose.
Tr _ _   They grow in a forest.
Squ _ _ ze   How you get the extra moisture out of something.

LL

Ce _ _ ar	The bottom level of a building, sometimes used to store wine.
Se _ _ out	Tickets all sold for a game, or event.
Co _ _ ector	If you don't pay your taxes or bills this person may come to your door to collect, or a person that accumulates pretty things for pleasure.
Co _ _ ege	A school for education after high school where you can earn a professional degree.
Co _ _ ison	When two vehicles crash together.
Co _ _ arbone	The clavicle.
Co _ _ een	An Irish girl's name.
Co _ _ ie	A dog named Lassie.
Co _ _ inear	Sharing the same straight line.
Para _ _ el	Two lines in the same direction, the same distance apart.

RR

Mi _ _ or	Glass with mercury backing that reflects images.
Ca _ _ iage	A type of buggy pulled by a horse.
Ca _ _ ier	A shipping company that transports merchandise.
Ca _ _ ot	An orange vegetable supposedly good for your eyes. Rabbits and horses love these.
Strawbe _ _ y	A red fruit served with shortcake.
Ch _ _ ry	A red fruit that grows on trees. Some are maraschino.
Me _ _ y	The first word in a Christmas greeting.
Me _ _ y-go-round	An amusement ride with horses that go up and down and around.
A _ _ est	To seize someone for breaking the law.
A _ _ angements	Making plans for an outing or special celebration.
A _ _ aign	To be called into court to answer a charge.
Ma _ _ iage	A legal institution making a man and woman legally attached.

DD

Da _ _ y	The father of a child.
Mu _ _ y	Heavy rain makes the ground _____.
Pu _ _ ing	A sweet, soft dessert made with milk, eggs, and cornstarch and served in a parfait glass.
Sa _ _ le	A seat made of leather used for riding a horse.
Sa _ _ le soap	A mild cleaning agent for cleaning leather.
Pu _ _ le	A pool of water after it rains.
Ki _ _ le	A dam in a river.
Ki _ _ ing	Teasing someone in fun.
Ki _ _ minister	Ingrain carpet originally made in Worcestershire, England.

FF

Ta _ _ eta	A stiff, glossy fabric that is quite light weight.
Ta _ _ y	A candy made with brown sugar or molasses and pulled until it is light.
A _ _ ect	Saying some words that might make an impression. Example: He moved me greatly with his kind words.
A _ _ idavit	A statement in writing under oath stating the statement is true (usually notarized).
A _ _ ectionate	Having tender feelings toward another person.
A _ _ air	Some form of business, or a relationship out of marriage.
A _ _ ord	Having the money, or means, to purchase something.
A _ _ iliation	To associate with someone, or a member of a group.
A _ _ irmative	Answering with a firm yes that a statement is true.
A _ _ ix	To attach, like an appendage.
Ga _ _ er	A boss.
Sa _ _ lower	A thistle-like plant especially found in Asia. It has orange or red flowers used for red dye.
E _ _ icient	Very competent.
E _ _ ace	Cancelled or forgotten.
E _ _ ete	All worn out with no vitality, very exhausted.

GG

So _ _ y	Soaked with rain.
Gi _ _ le	Laugh like school girls.
Go _ _ les	Something worn on the face to cover the eyes, such as while swimming.
Ga _ _ ed	To choke.
Ga _ _ le	A flock of geese.
Sa _ _ ed	Past tense for bending under excess weight.
A _ _ ression	Anger displayed verbally or physically toward someone.
A _ _ ravate	To instigate trouble.
Su _ _ estion	If you have an idea on how to make something better, you write it down and put it in the _____ box.

ZZ

Da _ _ le	To impress someone with a brilliant display.
Me _ _ anine	An extra floor, or balcony, between two main floors.
Me _ _ o forte	Fairly loud (moderate).
Me _ _ otint	A way of engraving on copper. A rough plate is worked until it is smooth.
Dri _ _ le	A steady rain.
Fri _ _ le	Roasting, frying, or grilling.
Fri _ _ y	Extra-curly hair.
Qui _ _ ical	Gently make fun of something, or someone.
Bli _ _ ard	A bad snowstorm.
Si _ _ ling	Very hot temperature.

Answer Key for "Twin Letter" Word Game

MM
Commode
Committee
Commission
Commander
Commencement
Commonplace
Commerce
Commandments
Commercial
Commiserate
Comment
Summer

SS
Trespassing
Passed
Cross
Recess
Possessions
Passive
Stress
Passion
Croissant
Possum
Dress
Dressing
Passage
Passenger
Massacre
Massachusetts

TT
Platter
Settler
Matter
Letter
Little

Brittle
Lettuce
Fatty
Attire
Attempt
Attache
Attack
Putty
Pattern
Patty
Mattress
Putt

PP
Pepper
Puppet
Puppy
Poppy
Popple
Approve
Appetite
Apply
Apple
Appearance
Applaud
Zipper
Kidnapper
Slippers
Snapple
Snapper

OO
Cooperate
Noodle
Noon
Noose
Moose
Moodiness

Moon
Poodle
Scoop
Flood
Goose
Loose
Barefoot
Soot
Broom
Bloom

EE
Speed
Speech
Cheek
Cheese
Cheerful
Cheerio
Proceed
Cheesecake
Fleet
Sheep
Sleep
Street
Bleed
Creek
Sheets
Peel
Tureen
Beet
Parakeet
Freedom
Tree
Squeeze

LL
Cellar
Sellout

Collector
College
Collision
Collarbone
Colleen
Collie
Collinear
Parallel

RR
Mirror
Carriage
Carrier
Carrot
Strawberry
Cherry
Merry
Merry-go-round
Arrest
Arrangements
Arraign
Marriage

DD
Daddy
Muddy
Pudding
Saddle
Saddle soap
Puddle
Kiddle
Kidding
Kiddminister

FF
Taffeta
Taffy
Affect

Affidavit
Affectionate
Affair
Afford
Affiliation
Affirmative
Affix
Gaffer
Safflower
Efficient
Efface
Effete

GG
Soggy
Giggle
Goggles
Gagged
Gaggle
Sagged
Aggression
Aggravate
Suggestion

ZZ
Dazzle
Mezzanine
Mezzo forte
Mezzotint
Drizzle
Frizzle
Frizzy
Quizzical
Blizzard
Sizzling

Colonies Party with Scouts

The elderly love to interact with children so invite the Scouts to the party and use the following games as entertainment.

Marble games.

Bowling.

Ring Toss.

Gunnysack race.

Each Scout can take a turn telling about life in colonial America. Have a map available so each one can point out the state they are talking about. If a Betsy Ross flag example is available use it during the program.

Following is information you can use for each Scout to practice to use in their presentation about colonial life. Take time prior to the party to work with the children to make them feel comfortable with the information they will present.

★ Approximately four hundred years ago people came to America in small groups from Europe. Some were looking for religious freedom, while others were looking for a new life. Some even thought they would strike it rich in a land of plenty.

★ Settlers came, not only from England, but also from other countries such as: Holland, Spain, France, and Sweden. The people formed separate groups called colonies, eventually totaling 13, along the eastern coast of this country.

★ The early colonists were very independent and self-sufficient. They built their own homes, sewed their own clothes, and grew their own food in gardens. They even made their own shoes.

★ Although they washed themselves daily, most colonists only bathed a few times a year. They did not brush their teeth, and as a result there were many cavities. When the tooth became infected and sore the doctor would pull it. Of course, there was no Novocain at that time, so the procedure was very painful for most people.

★ There was no refrigeration, so food was stored in cellars or in a cool stream.

★ If a building should catch on fire, which happened regularly, the people would bring their buckets and form a line to pass the filled buckets to the person nearest the fire, who would pour the water on the fire. Needless to say not many buildings were saved with this method.

★ The town crier passed along news of the day. He walked through the main part of town and cried out the news as he rang his bell to alert the people he was coming through.

★ It was the law that every person must build a fence around their property. This was to keep strange animals from wandering onto neighboring properties.

★ The colonists tended to have large families, and families stayed together in one large house—or two adjoining houses. Of course, many hands were needed to do all the backbreaking work connected with early colonial life. Grandparents, Aunts, Uncles, and Cousins all lived together.

★ The children all had to work to complete all the chores. Girls were taught to sew and do housework; while boys learned to farm and most also learned a "trade". Children were taught that not working was sinful.

★ Slaves were brought on ships from Africa and sold to large landholders who had the funds to pay for them. They picked tobacco and did other farm work, as well as taking care of the livestock and household. The slave's day was very long with little time for rest. Some slave owners took good care of their workers and treated them with kindness, while other owners were very cruel. Quite often individual slaves would be sold to other owners. It was very hard for the slaves to see their families split up in this manner.

★ The colonies had one-room schoolhouses with one teacher, a schoolmaster. He taught the children of all grades and school was held six days a week. If you could not afford to pay for your education, you did not attend school. There were very few books in the early days. Two books used were the Bible and a primer with poems and the alphabet. Students used a wooden ruler to draw lines on blank sheets of paper for writing. A feather quill pen and ink was used for writing. The ink was kept in a bottle in a hole in the desktop called an ink well. Pigtails of girls always seemed to find their way into the ink well! Some boys were fortunate enough to go on to higher learning after the first six grades, but most didn't have enough money for higher education, and, of course, girls were never allowed to go any further than sixth grade. Girls were needed at home, and the feeling was they were only going to be housewives and mothers so they didn't need higher education for that—they could learn that at home.

★ Some games children played included: outdoor bowling, marbles, fishing, walking on stilts, spinning tops, and sack races. One game they played was Blindman's Bluff. They also enjoyed a game called "quoits" where they threw a ring on a stake.

★ Some of the large plantation homes had a swing on the porch where anyone could sit and relax, or talk to a friend. It was a cool place, as there was no air conditioning!

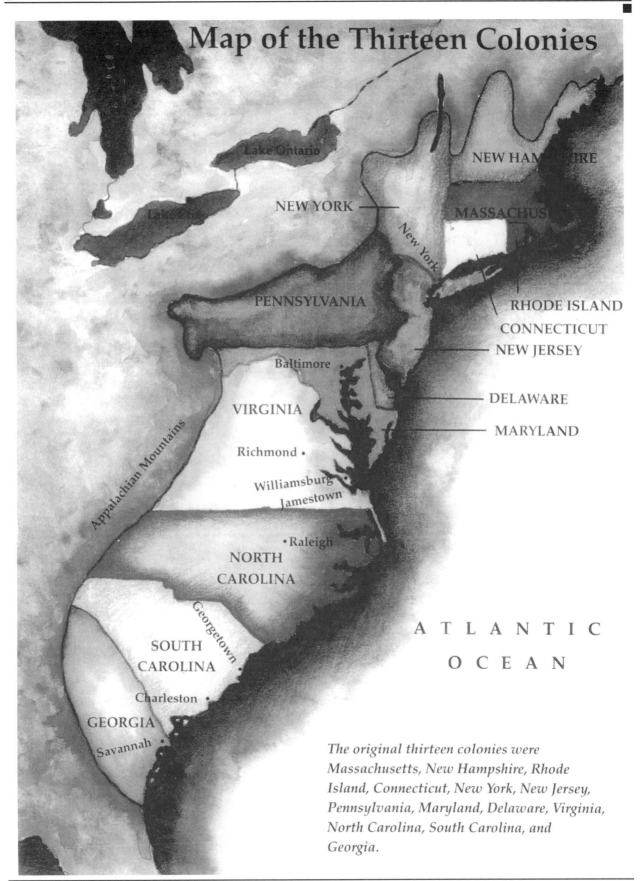

Map of the Thirteen Colonies

Lake Ontario

Lake Erie

NEW HAMPSHIRE

NEW YORK

MASSACHUSETTS

New York

PENNSYLVANIA

RHODE ISLAND

CONNECTICUT

— NEW JERSEY

Baltimore

— DELAWARE

VIRGINIA

— MARYLAND

Richmond •

Williamsburg

Jamestown

Appalachian Mountains

• Raleigh

NORTH
CAROLINA

ATLANTIC

OCEAN

Georgetown

SOUTH
CAROLINA

Charleston •

GEORGIA

Savannah •

*The original thirteen colonies were
Massachusetts, New Hampshire, Rhode
Island, Connecticut, New York, New Jersey,
Pennsylvania, Maryland, Delaware, Virginia,
North Carolina, South Carolina, and
Georgia.*

```
G E O R G I A L G H E T V I R G I N I A K G U
R E E D O Y B N C O N N E C T I C U T O I D O
A J A M T Y R H N M N M V I N E V I S T O M J
R M A T N V B Q A E R I U H N E S I T N N H O
I M R M N V I T A J V I R G I N I A O V V I O
N A H Q A N G U N V T E W O O D T U M M Q W S
O U O R E I E I O P E N N S Y L V A N I A V O
D A D P A C C N T O C M M A I N Y V N N N B U
A M E P P Y A O A N S A T P B N G O W E I E T
M E I V I S O R K J C A R N I A C O P W I I H
A P S K K O M T N O C A N G E P F B L H R M C
S T L O M A S H I N I Q W E O I U P Q A D A A
S T A H I T O C T O L A B A U B O D A M E R R
A S N I T H I A W A M A T C A M U I C P L Y O
C V D I I O Y R E Q C S W U U F A B A S A L L
H Q I T H I A O I H H A U W E B D T Y H W A I
U O K L H H V L I A A D E W E G A E D I A N N
S I P O Q X U I S O M E N I C A E Q D R R D A
E D U K L J N N F D S A Z X Y T E U I E E G U
T U N V I U M A U I N E W Y O R K Z I T G R S
T R B V E W Q A N E W J E R S E Y E Y N E R E
S A B A U O P Q S S U L Z T E A A V E H I E D
T P H L I P M O N L S E W R A T D T I R T K A
```

Thirteen Colonies Word Search

MASSACHUSETTS	NEW JERSEY	NORTH CAROLINA
NEW HAMPSHIRE	PENNSYLVANIA	SOUTH CAROLINA
RHODE ISLAND	MARYLAND	GEORGIA
CONNECTICUT	DELAWARE	
NEW YORK	VIRGINIA	

```
G E O R G I A L G H E T   V I R G I N I A K G U
R E E D O Y B N C O N N E C T I C U T O I D O
A J A M T Y R H N M N M V I N E V I S T O M J
R M A T N V B Q A E R I U H N E S I T N N H O
I M R M N V I T A J V I R G I N I A O V V I O
N A H Q A N G U N V T E W O O D T U M M Q W S
O U O R E I E I O P E N N S Y L V A N I A V O
D A D P A C C T O C M M A I N Y V N N B U
A M E P P Y A O A N S A T P B N G O W E I T
M E I V I S O R K J C A R N I A C O P W I H
A P S K K O M T N O C A N G E P F B L H R E C
S T S L O M A S H I N I Q W E O I U P Q A M A
S T A H I T O C T O L A B A U B O D A P D R
A S C I T H I A R W A M A T C A M U I C S E O
C V A I I O Y O R E Q C S W U U F A B A H L L
H Q R Q I T H I A L I H H A U W E B D T Y I A I
U O O K L H H V I A A D E W E G A E D R R N
S I L P O Q X U N S O M E N I C A E Q D E E G A
E D I U K L J N A F D S A Z X Y T E U I E U
T U N A V I U M A U I N E W Y O R K Z I T G R S
T R B V E W Q A   N E W J E R S E Y E Y N E R E
S A B A U O P Q S S U L Z T E A A V E H I E D
T P H L I P M O N L S E W R A T D T I R T K A
```

Thirteen Colonies Word Search

MASSACHUSETTS	NEW JERSEY	NORTH CAROLINA
NEW HAMPSHIRE	PENNSYLVANIA	SOUTH CAROLINA
RHODE ISLAND	MARYLAND	GEORGIA
CONNECTICUT	DELAWARE	
NEW YORK	VIRGINIA	

Clothing

Men wore knee socks and knee-length trousers called breeches. They wore powdered wigs and hats. The shirts were long sleeved and loose fitting with a long vest over the top. The coat that went over all this was called a frock coat. Every garment had buttons because zippers had not been invented.

Women also wore wigs, and wealthy folks would pay to have their wigs maintained. Most women wore layers of petticoats under their dresses. It you were wealthy the dresses would be made of silk, brocade, and lace. Dresses never had pockets, as we know them. Rather, pockets were separate and attached to a belt worn under the dress. The dress would have a slit in the seam so a woman could reach her hand inside the dress to the pocket. Many times the skirt of the dress was not attached to the bodice and the bodice was made to overlap the top of the skirt (like an overblouse). Women wore aprons whenever they were working to protect the dress from being soiled. Aprons also were good for gathering eggs, picking apples, and wiping a child's runny nose.

Clogs were worn over shoes to protect the shoes from dirt and mud. Women always wore hats or bonnets.

B	I	N	G	O
AMERICA	AMERICA THE BEAUTIFUL	YOU'RE A GRAND OLD FLAG	BATTLE HYMN OF THE REPUBLIC	ANCHORS AWAY
THE MARINE'S HYMN	THIS IS MY COUNTRY	AMERICAN PATROL	YANKEE DOODLE DANDY	WHEN JOHNNY COMES MARCHING HOME
STARS AND STRIPES FOREVER	WASHINGTON POST MARCH	**FREE**	DIXIE	THE BATTLE CRY OF FREEDOM
GOD BLESS AMERICA	THIS LAND IS YOUR LAND	CASISSONS SONG	STAR SPANGLED BANNER	YELLOW ROSE OF TEXAS
HOME ON THE RANGE	THIS IS A GREAT COUNTRY	OUR DIRECTOR MARCH	WHEN THE SAINTS GO MARCHING IN	76 TROMBONES

How the Colonies Came to Be

The first ship from England landed at what we now call Virginia in 1607. The settlers hoped to gain freedom and a better life. There was much to do. They had to clear forestland for wood to build their small huts and for cooking and heat. This first settlement was called Jamestown after King James. This colony belonged to England. The pilgrims that settled in Massachusetts were seeking religious freedom. There is more information about pilgrims in my book *An Alzheimer's Guide Activities and Issues for People Who Care* page 280-282.

The Quakers settled in Pennsylvania. Did you know Betsy Ross was a Quaker? Betsy Ross made the first flag in 1776. It had 13 stars and 13 stripes. The Quakers were peace-loving people looking to be able to practice their faith and have a better life in this country.

Bitter cold winters killed the crops. The colonists clung to their old ways of farming, but eventually they learned new ways in the new land. They began to eat fruits and vegetables, and the Indians showed them how to farm, fish, and hunt.

When the settlers first arrived many did not have medicines to help fight off disease and fevers and many died the first year. The Indians taught them different techniques for curing disease like using the bark of the willow tree to cure a headache. (Aspirin is made from the willow bark.)

Unfortunately, the colonists brought over diseases not known by the Indians and the natives became very sick and many died. Indian life on the East coast basically disappeared over a hundred-year time span.

The thirteen colonies were:

★ New Hampshire ★

★ Massachusetts ★

★ New York ★

★ Pennsylvania ★

★ Rhode Island ★

★ Connecticut ★

★ New Jersey ★

★ Delaware ★

★ Maryland ★

★ Virginia ★

★ North Carolina ★

★ South Carolina ★

★ Georgia ★

These colonies banded together and formed the first government in 1775. The first leaders in Virginia were George Washington, Thomas Jefferson, and James Madison.

Most of the colonies were carved out of thick forest. The Indians taught the settlers how to girdle a tree by stripping off a strip of bark all around the trunk. This would cause the tree to die and then it was used for firewood.

Fruit trees were planted and barns were built. The settlers ground their own grain for flour. Each settlement had carpenters, silversmiths, shoemakers, and blacksmiths.

Ships from Europe would come along the coast and deliver goods including cloth and spices. Boston was an unusually busy port.

The people cooked in the fireplace. The fireplaces accumulated a lot of soot from the wood and a broom was used to clean out as much as they could reach from the bottom of the chimney. To clean the rest of the chimney, a goose would be lowered into the chimney, and, as he flapped his wings he would break the soot loose.

Cabins had steep roofs so the snow would slide off. The windows were very small as glass as very expensive. Most cabins were made of logs with mud and grass filling the spaces between logs.

For the most part the settlers stayed fairly healthy by raising gardens and eating fruits and vegetables and meat from hunting and fishing.

They would tap maple trees for sap to make syrup and find beehives for honey to make sweet treats. They liked rock candy and Marzipan, which is made from eggs, almond flavor, and sugar.

Even though people were busy they took time for each other and fun. Children played Hide and Seek and Hopscotch. In the winter families went ice skating and sledding. The Dutch played a game called 9 Ball. It was similar to bowling.

The 4th of July

Parades were a common occurrence on the 4th of July, with waving flags, bands, and booming cannons. People would salute "old glory" as it went by in the parade. Families enjoyed picnics. Some of the foods for the picnics were: hen stew, baked beans, jackrabbit, pot pie, Irish potatoes, rice, pickles, bread, biscuits and preserves, pies, pound cake, and ice cream.

Uncle Sam's Birthday Party

See page 1 in the color section for finished project.

I remember doing an Uncle Sam's Birthday Party with my friend in her home. Everyone was supposed to come in costume. They were also to recite a poem or tell something about an event in the spirit of 1776.

One of the guests, a very tiny lady, came all dressed up like Mrs. America. She wore padding to make her look very pregnant. What made us laugh was she was a very quiet person of few words. This costume made her come to life. She moaned and carried on. When it was time to judge the best costume she was given first prize for being the most creative. She exclaimed, "I have waited so long for this joyous occasion. My baby is finally born. His name is Sam after Uncle Sam, of course!"

I sponsored a "birthday bash" in honor of Uncle Sam at the care facility. I told the residents that Uncle Sam wanted them to have fun at his birthday party.

We played music bingo. The previous day we had made the 11 x 17-inch birthday cake from cake mixes. (It takes two mixes to make a cake of this size.) Follow the directions on the box, doubling it for two mixes. Bake at 350 degrees for 30-35 minutes and frost with your choice of frosting. Decorate your cake to look like a flag by drawing a circle in the upper left-hand corner of the cake. Place 13 flags in the circle (you can purchase the flags at a specialty party shop). Place 50 candles (representing the 50 states) in lines across the cake to represent the stripes on the flag. I used candles that would re-light when blown out, which the residents enjoyed very much.

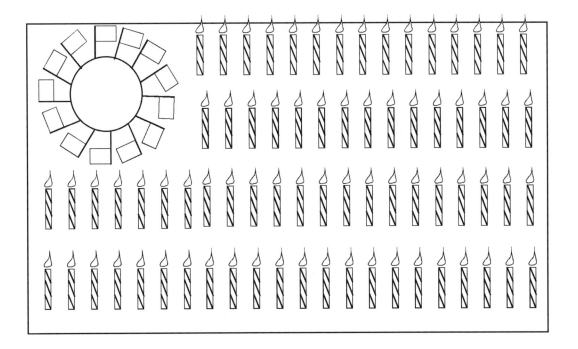

```
S P I R I T O F S E V E N T Y S I X I I K D W
O T E O O Y B N L O L I B E R T Y B E L L M A
L H A C T Y R H N A N M V I N E V I S T N U S
D I A K N V B Q A E G I U H N E S I T N V N H
I R M E N V I T A J E E F R E E D O M V Q C I
E T L T A N G U N V T E W O L O Y A L M P L N
R E A S E I E B A T T L E E W Q B T L P N E G
S E I P A C C I T O C P A T R I O T I C I S T
D N C A I S S O N S S O T P B N G O N M I A O
A C R M I S O P K J C L R N I A C R U M R M N
P O A E K O M I N O C I N G E P F E N G C H I
O L M R M A S M I N I T W E O I U V I I V I H
S O Q I I T O R T O L I B A U B O O T I F N T
S N S C T H I O W A M C T C A M U L E U I E E
E I L A N D Y T E Q C S W U U F A U D A F U M
K E I T H I A E I H H A U W E B D T S N T H A
I S K L H H V E I R E D C O A T S I T U Y A R
S T R I P E S H S O M E N I C A E O A E S G C
T D U K L J N G S E T T L E R S E N T R T R H
A U N V I U M A U I O P G R E X A A E T A R I
R R B V E W Q G O V E R N M E N T R S N T E N
S T A T E S P Q S C O U N T R Y A Y Y H E T G
R B O S T O N T E A P A R T Y T D V E R S U Z
```

Uncle Sam's Word Search

STARS	GOVERNMENT	FLAG	BOSTON TEA PARTY
STRIPES	COUNTRY	ROCKETS	THIRTEEN COLONIES
BATTLE	AMERICA	RED COATS	SPIRIT OF SEVENTY SIX
FIFTY STATES	POLITICS	REVOLUTIONARY	MARCHING
FREEDOM	WASHINGTON	LIBERTY BELL	UNITED STATES
LOYAL	LAND	SETTLERS	STATES
PATRIOTIC	UNCLE SAM	CAISSONS	SOLDIERS

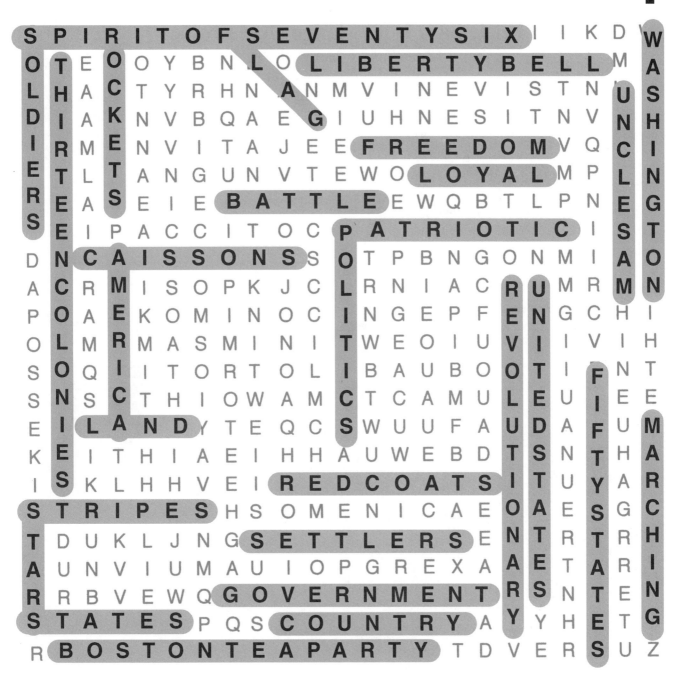

Uncle Sam's Word Search

STARS
STRIPES
BATTLE
FIFTY STATES
FREEDOM
LOYAL
PATRIOTIC

GOVERNMENT
COUNTRY
AMERICA
POLITICS
WASHINGTON
LAND
UNCLE SAM

FLAG
ROCKETS
RED COATS
REVOLUTIONARY
LIBERTY BELL
SETTLERS
CAISSONS

BOSTON TEA PARTY
THIRTEEN COLONIES
SPIRIT OF SEVENTY SIX
MARCHING
UNITED STATES
STATES
SOLDIERS

Uncle Sam Door Hanger Art Project

See page 1 in the color section for finished project.

Note: This project can be hung on the door of each resident's room, or on the wall. The facility donat - ed the tongue depressors and my husband cut the wood and drilled the holes. The remainder of the supplies can be purchased at a craft store. If you have donated funds for projects this would be a good use of those funds. The residents enjoyed this project. We sold some of the door hangers for $5 each and the money was used for snacks at the Uncle Sam Birthday Party.

Supplies needed: (for one finished project)
1 3 x 7-inch board 1/4- or 3/8-inch thick
1 3 x 7-inch piece of tan felt
4 6-inch tongue depressors
1 ice cream stick
2 3 x 3-inch patriotic fabric for the hat
1 1/2-inch star
1 3/4-inch star
Silver or gold glitter
2 eyes
1 knob for the nose
2/3 yard of wire
1 pencil
Art paint brushes
Newspaper
Water
Throw-away container for water for cleaning brushes
2/16-inch drill bit
Glue gun
Glue stick

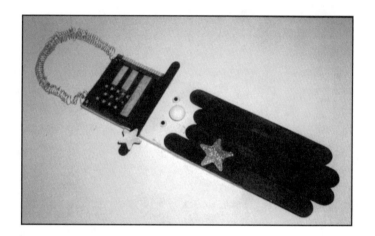

Water Base Paint:
Blue paint for the ice cream stick
Burgundy-red paint for the tongue depressors
Silver paint for the stars
Tan paint for the board and nose

Cut all the boards.
Paint the nose, board front and back, tongue depressors, ice cream sticks, and stars with two coats of paint and let them dry.
Sprinkle glitter on the large star when doing the second coat of paint.
Cut out the patriotic fabric for the hat and felt for the back.
Using the glue stick, glue the patriotic fabric on for the hat.
Glue felt onto the back of the board.

Drill evenly-spaced holes at the top of the board for hanging.

Hot glue the ice cream stick across the bottom of the fabric hat to form the brim of the hat.

Hot glue eyes and nose.

Place tongue depressors around the chin to form the beard. Place the two middle pieces lower than the end pieces so it forms a curve for the chin.

Cut the wire and wind around a pencil to form the hanger.

Pull the hanging wire through the holes you drilled and twist to secure.

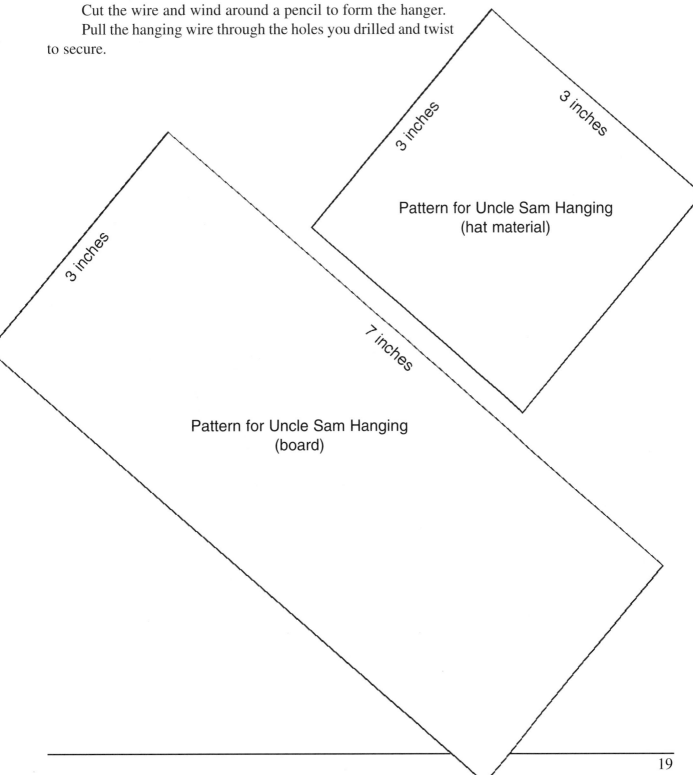

3 inches
3 inches
3 inches
7 inches

Pattern for Uncle Sam Hanging
(hat material)

Pattern for Uncle Sam Hanging
(board)

Fire Cracker Art Project

See page 1 in the color section for finished project.

You can use this for a bingo prize, a card party, or a door prize at the 4th of July Party, or use as centerpieces.

Note: There are two different sizes of Pringle cans and I also used a small-size shoestring potato can. Select the size you prefer. I like the combination of sizes. Some facilities prefer to make them all the same so residents won't bicker over which size is best. It is fun to see the residents swap sizes and I haven't had problems with the different sizes.

Supplies needed:

1 bottle (8 ounces) silver or gold (or both) washable glitter glue
1 package 9 x 12-inch red construction paper (30-50 sheets
     per package)
1 can (7 ounces) Pringle chips
1 can (1 2/3 ounces) Pringle chips
1 can (small size) shoestring potatoes
1 package blue confetti stars (or your choice of colors and sizes)
1 package each (12 feet) gold and red wire garland
Scotch tape
Paper punch
Newspaper to cover work surface

Pattern sizes for different size cans:

Tall Pringle can—9 x 10 inches
Short Pringle can—3 1/8 x 10 1/2 inches
Small shoestring potato can—4 1/2 x 9 1/4 inches

Make a pattern out of newspaper (that fits each can size, see sizes above) and cut the pattern out of red construction paper. At random, make a design with the glitter glue on the red construction paper. Do not squeeze the glue too hard because you don't want heavy lines. Place stars at random on the glue lines while wet. You can use two different sizes of stars if you wish, **but don't use small stars as they are too difficult for the elderly to pick up**. Set your papers aside and let dry overnight. (If you don't want to use glitter glue due to the drying time, just glue the variety of stars onto the construction paper with a glue stick. I find it is less expensive to not use the glitter glue.)

Punch a small hole in the center of the can lid. Cut three strips of wire garland 7, 8, and 9 inches in length. Make two of the strips red and the third strip should be gold or silver. Bend the wire into desired shapes and place all three strips in the hole in the lid to form the sparks of the firecracker. Secure the wire with tape on the underside of the lid.

The next day glue the red construction paper to the cans and place the lid on top of the finished fire cracker.

A Picnic with Head Start Students in the Park

We reserved a shelter in the park and packed sack lunches for each resident. The children brought their own sack lunch. You will also need to arrange handicapped transportation for residents in wheelchairs. Make sure you are near a bathroom and bring CNAs with you to assist the residents.

The facility furnished watermelon and the beverages.

We invited the children to sing songs and play games for the residents (they always enjoy the children). It is relaxing for the residents to be outside and enjoy the breeze and sunshine so you don't need to plan too much entertainment. If you have card players in the group, you might bring cards along for them to spend the time in a game.

The July day was sunny and pleasant and everyone enjoyed the day out. The park was only one mile from the facility so it was a very simple event to plan and the residents talked about it for several days.

Butterfly Program

Butterflies represent life to the elderly and to young people. Butterflies are multicolored insects that attract many people. There are 20,000 species living all over the world, except for Antarctica. Due to the frigid temperatures butterflies cannot survive in that climate. Arizona has the largest number of varieties of butterflies in the United States.

Butterflies begin their flight to mate in the air and often fall to the ground. The male carries the female to a tree after the mating process. Once the mating is complete, the male dies. The female has many eggs and prefers to lay them on milkweed. Once the female has laid all the eggs, she will also die. There are exceptions however, some butterflies live only for two weeks, while others can live up to a year.

Then the cycle begins all over again. Butterfly eggs are the size of a pinhead. They are white and shiny. It takes about two weeks to produce a caterpillar, and in a few weeks more it becomes a butterfly. The yearly second generation can be found in California, Missouri, Iowa, Delaware, and Virginia. In the summer the third generation will migrate back to the Great Lakes area, southern Canada, and the bays of the eastern United States. The process of flying back and forth is called migration. Butterflies fly with the wind, and some can fly up to 80 miles in a day's time, while others, like the Monarch, fly 35 miles per hour and travel up to 260 miles a day. Some Monarchs can fly 2,500 miles in six weeks and most fly in a large group. The beautiful colors of all these butterflies migrating at once is one of nature's treasures for all spectators to witness and enjoy.

Butterflies cannot function in the cold. If temperatures get below 55 degrees the butterfly will not be able to fly. In the winter butterflies sleep and stay dormant.

Butterflies Are Free Party

Recipes:

Garden Vegetable Cheese Ball

Yield: serves 18-20.

1	package (15 ounces) Garden Vegetable Cream Cheese Spread
1	package (8 ounces) cream cheese
1/2	cup finely chopped broccoli flowerets
1/2	cup finely chopped celery
1/2	cup finely chopped water chestnuts
1	teaspoon chives
2	teaspoons horseradish sauce (optional)
1	cup natural shredded, low-moisture mozzarella cheese
1	cup natural shredded cheddar cheese
1	piece of waxed paper

Garnish:

1   tablespoon chopped chives

Beat vegetable spread and cream cheese together. Add broccoli, celery, water chestnuts, chives, and horseradish sauce. Form into a ball. Place waxed paper on counter and sprinkle cheeses into center of paper. Roll cheese ball in the shredded cheeses. Serve cheese ball on 8-or 9-inch plate garnished with chopped chives. Serve with butterfly shaped crackers.

Lime Bars

Yield: 16 two-inch bars.
Use one 8 x 8 x 2-inch pan.

Crust:

1	cup flour
1/4	cup powdered sugar
1/2	cup (1 stick) butter, melted

Preheat oven to 350 degrees.

Stir flour and powdered sugar together in a bowl. Thoroughly blend in butter. Press crust evenly into ungreased pan and bake for 12-15 minutes.

Filling:

2	eggs
1	cup granulated sugar
1	teaspoon baking powder
1/2	teaspoon salt
2	tablespoons lime juice
1	scant drop green food coloring

Beat eggs, sugar, baking powder, salt, and lime juice together in a mixing bowl. Add food coloring at the end and mix thoroughly. Pour over baked crust and bake for 25-30 minutes more. Cool and cut into bars.* Refrigerate overnight.

Glaze:

1	cup powdered sugar
	dash of salt
1/2	teaspoon almond flavoring
1	tablespoon cold water
2	tablespoons slivered almonds

In a mixing bowl add water and almond flavoring to powdered sugar and salt. Mix until smooth. Drizzle glaze over the top of the baked bars to form a pattern of your choice. Sprinkle almonds over the glaze.

For a yield of 30 bars use 9 x 13-inch pan.

Crust:

2	cups flour
1/2	cup powdered sugar
1	cup (2 sticks) butter, melted

Filling:

5	eggs
3	cups granulated sugar
3/4	teaspoon baking powder
1/2	teaspoon salt
1/3	cup lime juice
1	drop green food coloring

Glaze:

1 1/2	cup powdered sugar
2	tablespoons plus 1 teaspoon cold water
3/4	teaspoon almond flavoring
1/2	cup sliced almonds

For a yield of 50 bars use a half-sheet (5 x 10 inches) pan.

Crust:

3	cups flour
3/4	cup powdered sugar
1 1/2	cups (3 sticks) butter, melted

Filling:

8	eggs
4	cups sugar
2/3	cup lime juice
1	teaspoon baking powder
1/2	teaspoon salt
1/2	cup lime juice
2	drops green food coloring

Glaze:

2 1/2	cups powdered sugar
1/2	cup cold water
	dash of salt
1	teaspoon almond flavoring
1/2	cup sliced almonds

* *If you want information on cutting bars and size refer to page 145 in* Picnics Catering on the Move *by Pat Nekola.*

*Lime bars are very simple and economical to make. I prefer using butter in the crust instead of mar - garine, but you can use half butter and half margarine—or all margarine, if you prefer. **Do not over bake.** The filling puffs during baking, but flattens when cooled. I have given you measurements for powdered sugar for the glaze topping, but you may need to use more, or less, according to your taste.*

I use two half-sheet pans nestled together for more strength and stability. You are less likely to have the pan bend or spill with the double pan method.

On a hot day serve with lemonade or limeade and iced tea. However, you may want to poll the resi - dents as many elderly like coffee even when the weather is very hot.

The Four States of Butterfly Metamorphosis

Stage One:

The egg stage. Many butterflies have as many as 1,500 eggs, while others have very few. Butterflies lay their eggs on the milkweed.

Stage Two:

The larvae stage. The egg grows into a caterpillar and the caterpillar eats and eats and eats growing quickly and outgrowing and shedding its skin four to five times, during this molting process, before become a caterpillar.

Stage Three:

The pupa stage called chrysalis. The chrysalis is a hard, green shell with gold dots and is found hanging on the milkweed plant. The butterfly grows inside this chrysalis. In this stage (pupa) the insects rest while changing into an adult butterfly.

Stage Four:

When the adult butterfly is fully grown the shell of the chrysalis cracks, releasing the insect. The butterfly has wet wings and will hang upside-down until the wings are dry. Then the butterfly is ready for flight.

This entire process is known as a metamorphosis, coming from the Greek word meaning change of form. This process is very fascinating to all generations. Both children and adults gain much pleasure by watching the process. It takes up to 15 days to complete the metamorphosis.

Note: You can buy a kit called Butterfly Jungle (Habitat) from a learning store, or order it from the address referenced at end of article. Follow the directions and watch the four stages. It is wonderful to watch the children's and elderly's faces as they see each stage. This activity can keep the resident's attention the entire time and they will have a conversation topic during the process.

Pacific Grove, California, is known as "Butterfly U.S.A." On the second Saturday of October, Pacific Grove holds a butterfly parade. Small children dress up like Monarch butterflies with headbands with antennae.

Pacific Grove also has an association called Friends of the Monarch Butterfly. They work diligently to preserve the milkweed fields and the forest. In fact, the entire town voted unanimously to buy up the land to preserve the butterfly area. Pacific Grove is a wealthy community that appreciates nature and can afford to preserve this land for the butterflies.

On the other hand, there is a town in Mexico called El Rosario. This town is very poor with few roads. The Monarch butterflies come to this area every year in the spring due to the warm weather. People believe there are at least 30 million butterflies in El Rosario due to the 3,500 trees in the area. Many people visit the area to see the butterflies and the villagers hope to make a few dollars from all the visitors.

For more information on the various species of butterflies read the book *The World of Butterflies* by Patrick Hook. There are colored illustrations and descriptions of each one.

Facts About Butterflies, Moths, and Caterpillars

The butterfly has tiny scales on its wings, which produce the color and patterns. Butterflies are insects with very delicate wings. Predators don't often harm the butterfly due to a poison they leave on the leaf. Butterflies do not eat solid foods, for they cannot chew. They drink water and nectar through their proboscises. Nectar is the sweet liquid found in flowers. If people put pesticides on the flowers it harms the butterflies.

Butterflies carry pollen to the trees, which helps the fruit trees to pollinate and produce fruit.

Butterflies do have enemies such as birds, mice, and lizards. The color of the caterpillar alerts predators not to eat them because caterpillars eat poisonous plants. Because the caterpillar is green, sitting on a leaf, and it is easily camouflaged for safety. Often the chrysalis is not eaten by predators because it looks like a dead leaf.

Some moths and butterflies look alike, but they are very different. Butterflies generally have little hair and fly in the daytime. Moths, on the other hand, are hairy and fly at night. Butterflies have spiracles, which are tiny holes for breathing. The spiracles are found on the abdomen and thorax (the wings grow out of the thorax). Each butterfly has three pairs of legs located on the thorax also. The tube located on the butterfly's head is called the proboscis and is actually a tongue.

There are all sizes of caterpillars. Some are long while others are short. Some are fat, while others are thin and long. Some are very hairy, and some have bumps. The majority of caterpillars have three pairs of legs. The front legs are called legs, while the back legs are called prolegs. The caterpillar's body is divided into twelve segments. Some caterpillars change into moths, while others change into butterflies.

A gypsy moth caterpillar is one you do not want to touch—for it can make your skin itch. A wooly bear caterpillar becomes a moth and will roll into a ball if you disturb it. A puss moth caterpillar is so hairy you cannot see its head. Don't touch this caterpillar either for it will make you itch. Some moth caterpillars are spiny and have bumps. The hickory horned devil has horns and spins.

There is also a prominent moth caterpillar that has a tail.

The silk caterpillar lives in Asia. It can form a single thread of silk one-mile long.

People try to keep moths out of their houses because they will chew holes in wool clothing, feathers, and fur. As the eggs hatch the caterpillars eat the holes for food.

The butterfly caterpillar has spines. The monarch butterfly caterpillar has horns at both ends of the striped body. Spicebush swallowtail caterpillars eat leaves from the sassafras tree, while black swallowtail caterpillars eat parsley. Most caterpillars eat leaves. The white butterfly caterpillar is green with a white stripe the entire length of the body.

You can tell a moth caterpillar from a butterfly caterpillar because the moth will spin a cocoon, while the butterfly caterpillar will become hard and change into a chrysalis. There is a big difference between a cocoon and a chrysalis.

If you want to see how caterpillars live take a big jar, poke some holes in the lid, and place some plants in the jar with the caterpillar and watch it feed.

Where to order the butterfly jungle:
Butterfly Farm
Department C
5717 Corsa Avenue
Westlake Village, CA 91362

Butterfly Spelling Bee

Simple Words:

Legs	Insect	Pupa	Patterns
Eyes	Nectar	Climate	Colorful
Feet	Plants	Shell	Milkweed
Front wings	Flowers	Adult	Tree
Food	Egg	Tongue	Mating
Body	Molt	Skin	Scales
Rear wings	Crack	Tube	

Challenging Words:

Antarctica	Spiracles	Fertilize	Breathing
Abdomen	Hemisphere	Beautiful	Butterflies
Proboscis	Wildflowers	Caterpillar	
Chrysalis	Thorax	Predator	
Antennae	Migrating	Sunshine	

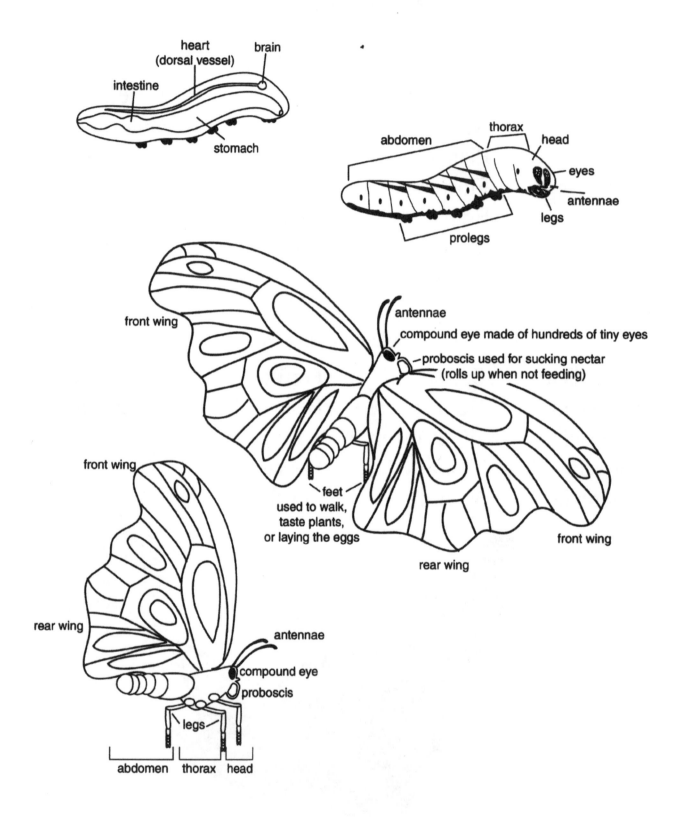

Note: Read Fun with Nature *published by North Word Press, Minnetonka, Minnesota, pages 37-43 and* The World of Butterflies *by Patrick Hook to gain more knowledge about some of the butterflies listed in the Word Search.*

```
Q U E E N A L E X A N D R A S B I R D W I N G
R E A M Q M A R B L E D W H I T E W M O O M R
A J S E T Y R H A U S T R A L I A N B E A K E
P M T R L V B Q A E R I U H V M S I T N V I E
I A E A Q O I T A J E E P G E O A P O L L O N
P L R L R N N U N V T E W O R N T U M M P V S
E A N D P I E G O T P I C E S A B T G P N B P
V Y T S E C C I T O C A M A P R Y V N M I E O
I L I W A Y S A A A S A I P O C G O W M I I T
N A G A R S M M R J I A R N T H C O P G R L T
E C E L L O A I A E C L N G T P O S T M A N E
S E R L Y A L M I L D Q E Y E E U P Q I V I D
W W S O H T L R C O L A B D D B D D A U A E T
A I W W E H H O A A M C D C S M U L C A K M R
L N A T A O E T B Q C S O M K K A B A N G P I
L G L A T I A E B H H A U P I B I T Y D I E A
O O L I H H T E A A A D E W P R A P D E Y R N
W I O L K X H H G O M E N I P E A Q P R T O G
T D W V V J N G E D S A Z X E T R L I E G R L
A U T V B U C K E Y E P G R R X A Z I N R R E
I R A A A W Q G I A N T S W A L L O W T A I L
L A I L L O P Q G R E E N D R A G O N T A I L
A P L N N S M S C A R C E B A M B O O P A G E
```

Butterfly Word Search

SMALL COPPER	APOLLO	MARBLED WHITE
AUSTRALIAN BEAK	RED ADMIRAL	EASTERN TIGER SWALLOWTAIL
MONARCH	PAINTED LADY	LONG-TAILED SKIPPER
CABBAGE	BUCKEYE	SILVER-SPOTTED SKIPPER
PEARLY HEATH	SMALL HEATH	QUEEN ALEXANDRA'S BIRDWING
EMERALD SWALLOWTAIL	EMPEROR	GREEN SPOTTED TRIANGLE
MALAY LACEWING	POSTMAN	GREEN DRAGONTAIL
PIPE-VINE SWALLOWTAIL	GIANT SWALLOWTAIL	SCARCE BAMBOO PAGE

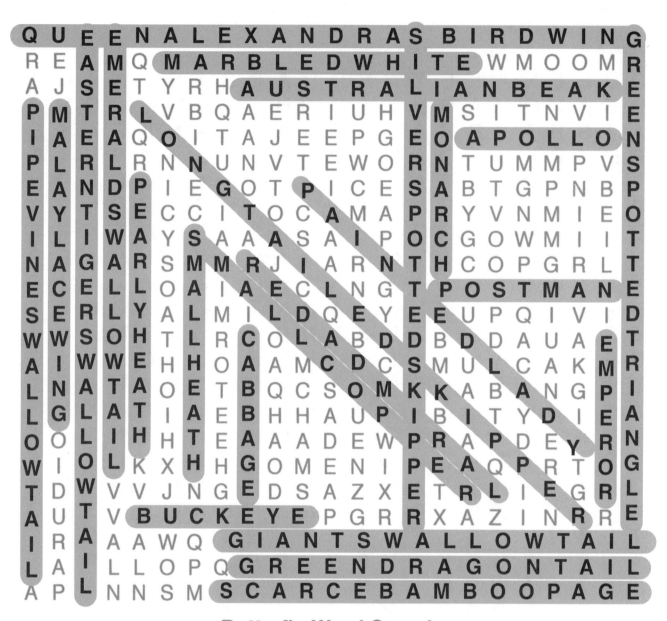

Butterfly Word Search

SMALL COPPER	APOLLO	MARBLED WHITE
AUSTRALIAN BEAK	RED ADMIRAL	EASTERN TIGER SWALLOWTAIL
MONARCH	PAINTED LADY	LONG-TAILED SKIPPER
CABBAGE	BUCKEYE	SILVER-SPOTTED SKIPPER
PEARLY HEATH	SMALL HEATH	QUEEN ALEXANDRA'S BIRDWING
EMERALD SWALLOWTAIL	EMPEROR	GREEN SPOTTED TRIANGLE
MALAY LACEWING	POSTMAN	GREEN DRAGONTAIL
PIPE-VINE SWALLOWTAIL	GIANT SWALLOWTAIL	SCARCE BAMBOO PAGE

Butterfly Memory Art Project

See page 1 in color section for finished butterfly project.

Supplies needed for simple butterfly:
1 butterfly pattern (on page 33)
1 piece of brightly colored construction paper or
  brightly colored fabric to fit the pattern
1 straight clothespin
1 pipe cleaner
1 leaf pattern
1 sheet green construction paper
1 pinking shears to make pointed edge (optional)
1 sheet white paper 8 1/2 x 11
1 glue stick

Place pattern on construction paper or fabric and cut out butterfly. Pleat the middle of the butterfly in a back and forth fold. Place clothespin in the middle of the butterfly to hold the folds. Tie the pipe cleaner on the top crease of the clothespin to shape into antennaes.

Using the leaf pattern cut the leaf out of the green paper. Type the sayings on the white paper (you can use your own, or the ones following these instructions), cut out and glue the white saying pieces on the green leaf pieces. Glue the completed leaf on the bottom edge of the clothespin. Residents can use in their room for reminders or just nice thoughts.

Butterfly Option 2:
Supplies in addition to list above
Brown or white paper grocery bag or 1 piece of brightly colored paper or fabric
All purpose glue
Glitter of your choice
Colored pipe cleaner

Cut the butterfly pattern out of the paper bag. Make a pattern with the glue and glitter on the wings of the butterfly and set aside to dry. Pleat the middle of the butterfly in a back and forth fold and place the clothespin down the center of the butterfly. Tie the pipe cleaner around the top crease of the clothespin for the antennae. Use the same green leaf pattern with the typed saying as in example one and glue the saying to the end of the clothespin.

Decorative Butterfly Option 3:
Supplies in addition to list in option 1
Wallpaper of your choice—use paper wallpaper, not any that is too shiny or heavy as the glue won't stick.
Variety of colors of glitter glue

Cut the butterfly pattern out of the wallpaper and outline with glitter glue of your choice. Draw an egg-shaped oval in the center of each butterfly wing and fill in with glitter glue. Use glitter glue to paint the top of the clothespin and another color of glitter glue for lines on the butterfly wings. Set aside to dry overnight.

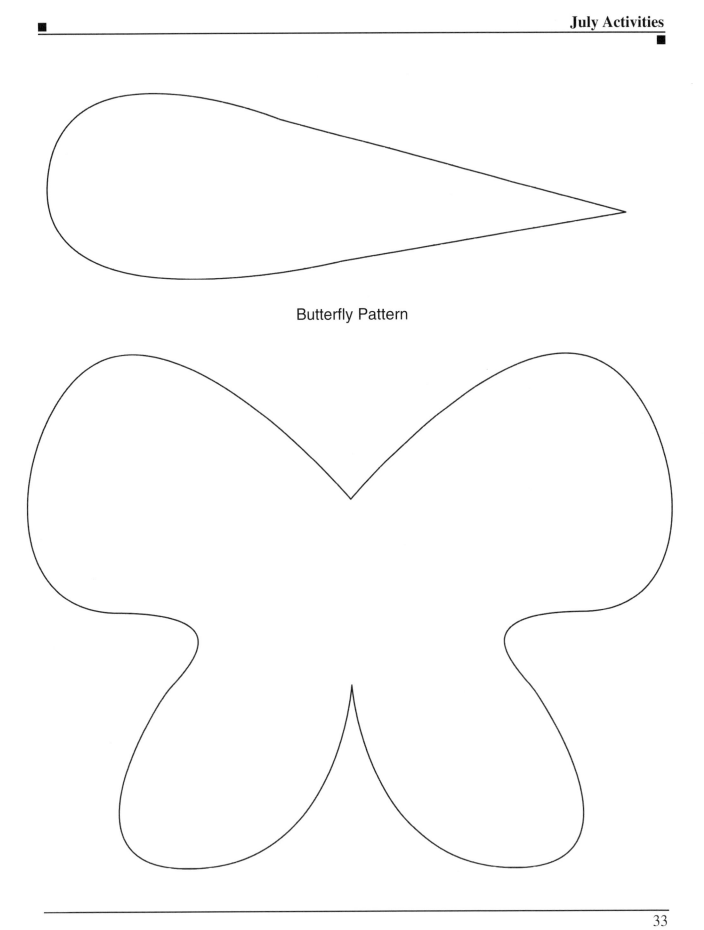

Butterfly Pattern

Sayings for Butterfly Projects Leaves

Here some examples of sayings, but you can do your own.

Remember attitude is everything!

Remember to say a prayer for a special person in your life!

Remember to brush your teeth after each meal.

Remember to be ready by 1:15 for art class!

Remember today is Sunday Family Visitation Social!

Remember Dr. Frank is our guest speaker at 2:00 p.m. on maintaining healthy bones.

Remember to walk with your walker!

Remember to bring your wedding picture today for social hour!

Remember today is shower day!

Remember your hair appointment today!

Remember to celebrate with Saddie today. She's 100 years young!

Remember the petting zoo is on 2nd floor patio today!

Remember pet day today!

Remember to clean your dentures every night!

Remember the picnic lunch at noon today!

Remember your daughter will pick you up today for an eye appointment at 9:30 a.m.

Remember your last pill at 6 p.m.

Activity Suggestions for the Butterfly Program

Take a field trip to the local zoo when they have a butterfly exhibit.

Invite a person who has a butterfly collection to come and talk to your residents and show their collection.

Discuss the metamorphosis process.

Show pictures of butterflies and serve butterfly-shaped crackers with cheese dip.

Purchase the butterfly kit and set it up so the residents can witness the metamorphosis process.

Decorating with Butterflies

My little friend just loves butterflies. Her whole room is filled with them and she has many books on the various butterflies.

My lady friend collects butterfly pins from all over the world.

My elderly friend has hundreds of butterflies mounted and placed on the walls throughout her home.

The assistant youth minister at our church has her entire office decorated in a butterfly theme.

Many people tell me that color attracts people to butterflies.

Butterfly Poem
by Pat Nekola

Butterfly, Butterfly, fly away with the wind,

Fly in the sunny days and rest by night,

Stay warm as you migrate south.

Return to the north in the spring,

Taste the sweet nectar of the colorful flowers,

Mate in the air,

So you can bear an egg on the milkweed plant.

Life will begin again

From a tiny pinhead egg, almost unnoticed.

A caterpillar will be born,

And then a beautiful new butterfly.

A butterfly's life is short,

But all so beautiful and precious

For the gifts it gives Nature and mankind!

Strawberry Fest

When I was young I used to pick strawberries at a neighboring farm. There was a large woman there with a big bullhorn. She would go up and down the rows with her bullhorn and say very loudly, "Pick the little berries, too, not just the big ones. Pick your row clean in my berry patch or there will be a big penalty." I never did learn of the penalty, but her bark was bigger than her bite!

She actually had a kind heart. She worked the land all her life and it was hard work. Her berries were so wonderful and made excellent freezer jam. Year after year we would pick the berries at her farm. But one day she passed away at age 85 and the farm closed down because her family did not want to farm the land. I still think of her and those wonderful strawberries.

Actually, the strawberry is one of my favorite berries. There are other kinds of berries. Can you name them?

Cranberries, Boysenberries, Blackberries, Blueberries, Raspberries, Wild Strawberries, Elderberries, Currants, and Holly berries.

Berry Trivia

Which berry is associated with Christmas? (Holly berry)

Which continent cannot grow berries? (Antarctica)

How long have berries been in existence? (Millions of years)

Which two animals whose name starts with "B" like berries? (Bears and Birds)

Did you know that the Indians taught the early American colonists all about berries?

How many of you grew raspberries or strawberries or some other type of berry in your garden?

How many of you went to a farm and picked berries and made jam?

Can you name some products made from berries? (Jam, Yogurt, Juice)

What time of the year do the strawberry plants start to bloom? (May-June)

What type of process is needed to set the berries? (Pollination by the wind or insects)

Do the petals of the plant die off? (Yes)

What color are the berries when they begin to grow? (Green)

The majority of strawberries are grown in which state? (California)

Name the two countries that grow the majority of strawberries. (Canada and the U.S.)

Berries are very tasty with ice cream.

Strawberries have roots with tiny hairs. The hairs allow the water in to help the plant grow. The strawberry has green leaves. Like most plants, the strawberry plant sets buds, which turn into flowers. Once the pollination has occurred the strawberry starts to grow. Strawberries have seeds, which are in the skin of the fruit. The fruit starts out green, but turns from green, to yellow, to white, to pink, to red color. If the strawberries are not harvested they will rot on the plant.

Berry plants grow runners, which is a long stem that starts a new plant. Every runner has a bud with tiny hairs to protect the bud. A new strawberry plant grows when the bud opens with the leaves beginning to unfold.

The day before the Strawberry Fest party make up some strawberry desserts and set up a display of them in the dining room. Let the residents choose the dessert they prefer. If it is easier for the resi - dents you can display the desserts on a tray that you carry from table to table for them to choose the dessert of their choice.

Also have a couple of baskets of cleaned whole strawberries with the stems still on. Some of the res - idents may just like plain fresh strawberries just like they'd be from the patch!

I have several strawberry desserts in my Picnics, Catering on the Move *book. See pages 135-136.*

Strawberry Trifle

Yield: 10 servings.

    1/2   10-inch angel food cake, torn into bite-size pieces
     5   cups fresh strawberries
     1   pint blueberries
     1   can (15 ounces) vanilla pie filling

Here's a dessert the English are very fond of. If you have diabetic residents you can substitute a 1-ounce package of vanilla sugar-free instant pudding and pie filling.

Place the angel food cake pieces in the bottom of a deep, glass bowl. Reserve 1/4 cup of the blueberries and 1/2 cup of the strawberries. Place the remaining blueberries and strawberries over the cake pieces. Spread the pudding over the berries. Garnish with the reserved blueberries and strawberries. Chill until serving time.

Strawberry Sundaes

1 quart diabetic vanilla ice cream
1/2 gallon regular vanilla ice cream
3 quarts fresh strawberries
1 package (12 ounces) non-dairy whipped topping

Clean and slice strawberries. Reserve some strawberries without sugar for the diabetic guests, and sugar the remainder for the group. Place one or two scoops of ice cream in a bowl and top with prepared strawberries and whipped topping.

Strawberry Pound Cake Dessert Sandwich
Yield: one Bundt cake, or one 9 x 5-inch loaf cake.

1 cup solid vegetable shortening
1 1/2 cups sugar
1 teaspoon vanilla
2 teaspoons lemon extract
6 eggs
2 cups flour
1 teaspoon baking powder
1 cup fresh or canned blueberries, drained
1 quart fresh strawberries
1 container (12 ounces) non-dairy whipped topping
mint leaves for garnish

Note: You can purchase a box mix pound cake if you wish, but I like to make mine from scratch. If you'd like biscuits instead of pound cake please refer to Picnics, Catering on the Move, *page 138 for the Pan Shortcake recipe.*

Preheat oven to 350 degrees. Grease and flour the baking pan.

Cream shortening, sugar, vanilla, and lemon extract together until fluffy. Add eggs and beat well. Add flour and baking power and mix well again. Gently fold in the blueberries and pour the batter into the prepared pan. Bake for 1 hour to 1 hour and 15 minutes or until a wooden toothpick inserted in center of cake comes out clean.

Cool cake in the pan for 15 minutes. Loosen edges with a knife and remove cake from the pan to cool completely on a wire rack. Thinly-slice the cake.

To serve place a slice of cake on the dessert plate, spread with whipped topping, top with a spoonful of strawberries, and top with a second piece of thinly-sliced pound cake. Top with a spoonful of strawberries and garnish with topping, mint leaf, and strawberry half.

Homemade Strawberry Jam and Toast

2   quarts strawberries
1   bottle (6 ounces) Certo liquid fruit pectin
4   tablespoons lemon juice
8   cups sugar

Discard tops of strawberries. Mash berries a little at a time with a potato masher. **Measure the exact amount of strawberries**. Add sugar to berries and let stand for 10 minutes, stirring occasionally. Stir pectin and lemon juice together in a small bowl and then stir into strawberries. Continue stirring until the sugar is dissolved (3-4 minutes). Pour jam into freezer containers and let stand for 24 hours until set. You can keep this jam up to three weeks in the refrigerator, or one year in the freezer.

```
R T P P L I T U R N I P S W R A T O N I O N S
G E T E H I A L G H E T V I P O T A T O E S J
O K R A O Y B N O O N S T E R H I W M O O M B
A J A S T T O M A T O E S I B S V I S T N H R
R M A T W V B Q A E R I U H E O S I T N V L U
I M M M N E I T A J E E P G E P S O R V Q E S
N A L Q A N E U N V T E W O T E T U U M P A S
O U A R E I E T O T Q A C E S P B T T P N F E
C A R R O T S I C O C C M A I P Y V A M I L L
A M C P P Y A A A O S O T S B E G O B M I E S
P R R V I S O P K J R R R P I R C O A G R T P
O O A K K O M D N O C N N A E S F B G I C T R
S S M O C A S M I N I S W R O I U P A I V U O
S E Q H I H O R T L L Q B A U B O D Q U A C U
E M S I T H I O W A L U T G A M U I A A R E T
K A Y I I O Y V E Q C A W U U F A B C N A H S
I R I T H I A E E H H S U S E B D T Y U D A U
P Y K S H H V E I S A H E W E G A E A E I G S
C D P A Q X U H S O M E N W C A E Q M R S R E
O L U G L J N G F D S A L E E K E U S T H R P
N U N E I U M A U I O P G R E X A Z Y N E E E
T R B V E W Q A S E Z U C C H I N I E H S K D
T A B A U G R E E N B E A N S A A V K R T U A
```

What's In Your Vegetable Garden Word Search

SWEET CORN	POTATOES	TURNIPS
PEAS	GREEN BEANS	RUTABAGA
ACORN SQUASH	OKRA	LEEK
CARROTS	BRUSSEL SPROUTS	LEAF LETTUCE
BEETS	ZUCCHINI	CHIVES
PEPPERS	RADISHES	DILL
TOMATOES	YAMS	SAGE
ASPARAGUS	ONIONS	ROSEMARY

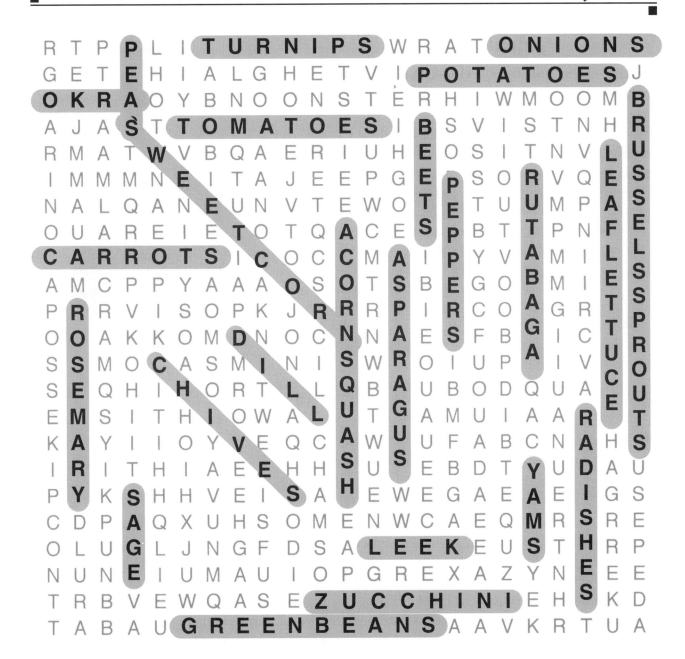

What's In Your Vegetable Garden Word Search

SWEET CORN	POTATOES	TURNIPS
PEAS	GREEN BEANS	RUTABAGA
ACORN SQUASH	OKRA	LEEK
CARROTS	BRUSSEL SPROUTS	LEAF LETTUCE
BEETS	ZUCCHINI	CHIVES
PEPPERS	RADISHES	DILL
TOMATOES	YAMS	SAGE
ASPARAGUS	ONIONS	ROSEMARY

Men's Lunch
Discussion of the Civil War

Invite the men to meet in the activity room, or a quiet area. Arrange with the kitchen in advance to bring the men's meals to the room. If you can acquire a Civil War uniform, some war books or memorabilia, it is nice for a hands-on discussion. The museum in Waukesha, Wisconsin, has a display about the Civil War. I'm sure you probably have some resources in your area, too.

The men always seem to enjoy their lunch meeting as there are so few men versus women residents. It's nice to show them some special thought.

All through the country people are interested in accounts of the Civil War. The history channel has presented programs on the topic. There are a lot of people that consider themselves "history buffs" and may be willing to help you present a program on the topic.

For a field trip you might want to take the men to the museum to see a Civil War display. They will find it very interesting.

Whatever you do—make the men feel special for participating. Make the topic interesting and always include the men in the conversation. Some men will have fought in a war and will want to share their experiences, too. Encourage them to do so.

A Little About the Soldiers

The Confederate soldiers wore gray woolen shirts with decorative gold buttons, wool pants, and hat. A big belt with a square buckle held their sword. A strap over the shoulder held their canteen with the confederate star and bar flag imprint. A leather pouch, called a haversack, held their bullets. It had a waterproof lining and a flap that buckled. Some soldiers felt the bag was too clumsy to carry, so they often carried their things in a rolled blanket.

The shoes of the Union soldiers were known as the Jefferson Borgars, the heel of these shoes had a horseshoe-like heel plate. Shoes were hard to come by at this time and some soldiers went barefoot because of the scarcity.

During the Civil War the men used the bugle horn. The gunshots and cannons were so loud no one could hear, or even talk, to the man next to you. With the bugle they could amplify the orders of the commanders. A bugle is a no-valve trumpet. Before the Civil War they used a fife and drums to signal the troops.

The men slept in a shelter tent commonly known as a dog tent by the veterans. You had to crawl into the tent on hands and knees like a dog. It was basically canvas hung over wooden sticks. But many men preferred sleeping under the stars. They used a gum blanket. It was made of a piece of material backed by a thin coating of rubber with a wool top layer. It not only was used as a blanket, but a ground cloth, tent flap, and a tarp to transport straw used by the soldiers.

The Confederates had three flags. (Try to have all three examples to discuss with the men.)

CSA Third National Flag

The confederates adopted the flag on March 3, 1865. This flag was not used much, not even at Fort Sumter. Probably this was to reduce the possibility of being mistaken for a surrender flag, as the top was white with a red strip across the bottom. In the right-hand corner were four triangles in red with a blue cross with 13 white stars to represent the 13 colonies.

The Confederate Battle Flag

The best know confederate battle flag was the flag with the Southern Cross. It was carried by the confederate troops in the field. Eleven stars represented the eleven states in the confederacy.

Confederate Stars and Bars

The stars and bars was the first official flag of the confederacy dating from March 1861 to May 1863.

Diseases such as dysentery, typhoid fever, malaria, pneumonia, arthritis, measles, mumps, and malnutrition killed many solders. A total of 364,000 union soldiers lost their lives in the war. A third were killed, or died from their wounds, and two-thirds died of disease.

Questions to Ask the Men:

What is meant by Civil War? (When two groups of people from the same country fight each other.)

So who fought in the Civil War? (North and South.)

When did the Civil War begin and when did it end? (April 1861 to April 1865. It lasted for four years.)

What was the fight about? (Leaders could not agree on how to run the country. President Abraham Lincoln thought it was worth fighting for unity, and the union felt the slaves should be freed by their owners.)

What were some of the disagreements between the North and South? (Slavery and Free Public Schools. The North thought there should be free schools, but the South said people should pay for their education. Many children didn't learn to read in both the North and the South because of the cost. The masters of the slaves did not permit the slaves to learn to read or write.)

Were there slaves in the South working on plantations? (Yes.)

What kind of crops did they grow in the South? (Rice, cotton, and tobacco.)

Were the slaves paid for their work? (No. They were considered property of their masters. The slaves helped their owners make money and keep the large plantations running.)

What type of work was in the North? (The North had factories and machines, and smaller farms.)

How did the war affect families? (Families were divided and many wanted the slavery to end. Very young boys joined the army as the drummer and wives were often left behind with the small children. They had to tend to the young and old left at home. Many soldiers were very homesick and letter writing took a long time to reach its destination. Some soldiers from the same family were fighting on opposite sides in the war. The war tore families apart and brought much sadness—just as it does today.)

Where were the battles held in the war? (The majority of the fighting took place in the South. Western Kentucky was in the thick of the fighting, but Washington, DC, also had battles very close to the capitol. At first the citizens thought it was entertaining to go to the battlefront and watch the fighting. They soon learned this was a "serious" undertaking and it wasn't so entertaining.)

How was the food supply during the Civil War? (Food was difficult to come by. Farmers grew the food to try to feed the troops, but they couldn't keep up with the demand and many soldiers died of malnutrition. The shortages also affected the families at home who had to sacrifice for the soldiers. Young boys in both the north and south did as much fishing and hunting as they could to try to put some meat on the table.)

Who won the war? (The North.)

What was the name of the Generals of the opposite sides during the Civil War? (General Lee was from the South and General Grant was from the North at the time of the final surrender and the end of the war.)

You might want to talk about the Gettysburg Address, or part of it. Probably some of your residents had to memorize the Address when they attended school. Can anyone still remember it?

Fifty thousand people were killed, wounded, or reported missing on the fields of Gettysburg and the surrounding area. Gettysburg became a common ground for a cemetery for the dead soldiers. President Lincoln spoke to the crowd for only a few brief moments. He spoke about words being more important than weapons, and the country being reborn from all those that died on that battlefield. He was right—his vision came true.

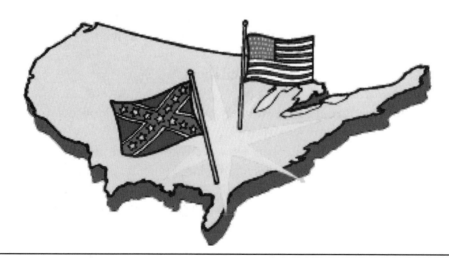

You can read the Gettysburg Address to the men and even show pictures of the battlefield.

The Gettysburg Address

Four score and seven years ago our fathers brought forth on this continent a new nation, conceived in liberty and dedicated to the proposition that all men are created equal.

Now we are engaged in a great civil war, testing whether that nation, or any nation so conceived and so dedicated, can long endure.

We are met on a great battlefield of that war.

We have come to dedicate a portion of that field as a final resting place for those who here gave their lives that that nation might live.

It is altogether fitting and proper that we should do this.

But in a larger sense, we cannot dedicate—we cannot consecrate—we cannot hallow this ground.

The brave men, living and dead, who struggled here have consecrated it far above our poor power to add or detract.

The world will little note, nor long remember what we say here, but it can never forget what they did here.

It is for us the living, rather, to be dedicated here to the unfinished work, which they who fought here have thus far so nobly advanced.

It is rather for us to be here dedicated to the great task remaining before us—that from these honored dead we take increased devotion to that cause for which they gave the last full measure of devotion—that we here highly resolve that these dead shall not have died in vain. That this nation, under God, shall have a new birth of freedom and that government of the people, by the people, for the people, shall not perish from the earth.

References:

The American Civil War by Earl Schenck Miers. This book illustrates the history of the years 1861-1865. The pictures are great to share with the men at the luncheon and will help get the conversation going.

Behind the Blue and Gray by Delia Ray. It is about the soldier's life in the Civil War.

The Gettysburg Address by Abraham Lincoln and illustrated by Michael McCurdy with Foreword by Gary Wills. The pictures paint a thousand words. It is very interesting.

Life in the North During the Civil War by Timothy Levi Biel.

American Civil War Biographies Volume I A-K by Kevin Hillstorm and Laurie Collier Hillstorm.

```
B U G L E Y B C I V I L W A R H I W M O O M G
R E E D O Y R H N M N M V I N E V I S T N H E
A A A G T V B A T T L E U H N E S I T N V C T
R B A E N V I T A J E E P G H T R O O P S O T
C R M N N N S O L D I E R S O D T U M M P N Y
O A L E A I E I O T Q I C E W Q B T G P N F S
N H A R E C C Í T O C M M U N I F O R M S E B
F A I A A Y A A A N S A T P B N G O W M I D U
E M G L P S O P K K C A R N I A C O P G R E R
D L E G I J M F N O E A N G E P F B L I C R G
E I N R M A E M O N I N W E O I U P A I V A A
R N E A I T O F T R L A T A U B O D N U A C D
A C R N T H I O F A T A T U A M U I T A K Y D
T O A T I O Y T E E C S W U C F A B A N B H R
E L L I H I A E I H R A U W E K D T T U U L E
F N L I H H V E I A A S E M E G Y E I E L A S
L O E L Q X U H S O M E O I T A E Q O R L G S
A I E O L J N G F D S A Z N Y E E U N T R R U
G D P K I U U N I O N P A R D X R Z I N U R S
C U N V E W Q A S E S W R Y D A Y E Y H N E O
T R N O R T H Q S S U L M T E A V V E R T K U
M A B A I P V I C T O R Y R A T D I I K G U T
T P H L D E F E A T T V I R G I N I S I D L H
```

Civil War Word Search

CIVIL WAR	VICTORY	SOUTH
BUGLE	TROOPS	KENTUCKY
ABRAHAM LINCOLN	BATTLE	CONFEDERATE FLAG
GENERAL LEE	CONFEDERACY	NORTH
GENERAL GRANT	SOLDIERS	UNION
GETTYSBURG ADDRESS	UNIFORMS	ARMY
JEFFERSON DAVIS	FORT SUMTER	BULL RUN
DEFEAT	PLANTATION	

B U G L E Y B C I V I L W A R H I W M O O M G
R E E D O Y R H N M N M V I N E V I S T N H E
A A A G T V B A T T L E U H N E S I T N V C T
R B A E N V I T A J E E P G H T R O O P S O T
R R M N N S O L D I E R S O D T U M M P N Y
C A N E A I E I O T Q I C E W Q B T G P N S
O A R A E C C Í T O C M M U N I F O R M S E B
N H R A A Y A A A N S A T P B N G O W M I U
F M A L P S O P K K C A R N I A C O P G R R
E L G G I J M F N O E A N G E P F B L I C G
D I R E J E O N I N W E O I U P L I V A A
E N A N I T O F T R L A T A U B O D N U A D
R C N E T H I O F A T A T U A M U I T A K D
A O T R I O Y T E F F C S W U C F A B N B R
T L A I H I A E E I H R A U W E K D T U L E
E N L L I H H V E I A A S E M E G Y E E R S
F O L E L Q X U H S O M E O I T A E Q O R S
L I E O L J N G F D S A Z N Y E E U N T U
A G D P K I U U N I O N P A R D X R Z I N S
G C U N V E W Q A S E S W R Y D A Y E Y H T O
T R N O R T H Q S S U L M T E A V V E R T K U
M A B A I P V I C T O R Y R A T D I I K G U T
T P H L D E F E A T T V I R G I N I S I D L H

Civil War Word Search

CIVIL WAR	VICTORY	SOUTH
BUGLE	TROOPS	KENTUCKY
ABRAHAM LINCOLN	BATTLE	CONFEDERATE FLAG
GENERAL LEE	CONFEDERACY	NORTH
GENERAL GRANT	SOLDIERS	UNION
GETTYSBURG ADDRESS	UNIFORMS	ARMY
JEFFERSON DAVIS	FORT SUMTER	BULL RUN
DEFEAT	PLANTATION	

August Activities

Picnics

The purpose of this section is to get people to reminisce and talk about picnics they have attended. The picnic exercise will keep their mind sharp and also get them to relax and have fun. Set up a simple picnic setting with a checked tablecloth and some sunflowers or cattails in the centerpiece on the table.

Music

Play background music, or get the residents involved in a sing-along, or "Name that Tune" to start the activity. Here are some song suggestions:

"In the Good Old Summertime"

"Sweet Adeline"

"Little Brown Jug"
I tell the story of how Uncle Herman came to every picnic. He always brought his little brown jug, but he never shared any of that liquid! I scratch my head and shrug my shoul-ders and say "I wonder why?" That gets s few snickers and laughs from the residents!

"Ida, Sweet as Apple Cider"

"Sweet Rosie O'Grady"

"My Wild Irish Rose"

"Edelweiss"

"My Merry Oldsmobile"

"Let Me Call You Sweetheart"

"She'll Be Comin' 'Round the Mountain"
I'm sure you know favorites of your residents—be sure to include those favorite tunes whenever you can.

Picnics Game

Using the letters in the word "Picnics" identify picnic foods and ingredients for the word blanks using the letter indicated as the first letter of the word.

Use the letter "P"

Name three snacks served at a picnic. P _ _ _ _ _ _ , P _ _ _ _ _ _ , and P _ _ _ _ _ _ _ .
    (Peanuts, Popcorn, Pretzels)

Three kinds of pie that could be served at a picnic. P _ _ _ _ , P _ _ _ _ _ _ , and P _ _ _ _ .
    (Peach, Pumpkin, and Pecan)

Two vegetables served on a relish tray. P _ _ _ _ _ _ and P _ _ _ _ _ _ B _ _ _ _ .
    (Pickles and Pickled Beets)

The name of a sandwich starting with a P. Most kids love a P _ _ _ _ _ B _ _ _ _ _ sandwich.
    (Peanut butter)

A fresh fruit served at a picnic. P _ _ _ _ _ _ _ _ . (Pineapple)

The animal you get ham from also served at a spanferkel. P _ _ . (Pig)

A red stuffing found in a green olive. P _ _ _ _ _ _ _ . (Pimiento)

A flavor of pudding. P _ _ _ _ _ _ _ _ . (Pistachio)

Something found in a black olive that shouldn't be eaten. P _ _ . (Pit)

A garnish used on a vegetable tray. P _ _ _ _ _ _ . (Parsley)

A cheese found on top of a seven-layer salad. P _ _ _ _ _ _ _ . (Parmesan)

A salad generally served at picnics. P _ _ _ _ _ S _ _ _ _ . (Potato Salad)

P _ _ _ _ _ _ is red and is used to garnish salads or deviled eggs. (Paprika)

A seasoning used on meats and vegetables is P _ _ _ _ _ . (Pepper)

A green vegetable used in cabbage salad. P _ _ _ _ _ (Pepper)

Meats such as turkey and chicken are called P _ _ _ _ _ _ . (Poultry)

Sliced P _ _ _ _ C _ _ _ is sometimes substituted for the biscuit in strawberry shortcake.
    (Pound Cake)

Use the letter "I"

Frosting used on cakes and cookies is called I _ _ _ _ . (Icing)

Frozen water used in beverages and to keep foods cold is an I _ _ C _ _ _. (Ice Cube)

Name of a popular frozen dessert or snack. I _ _ C _ _ _ _. (Ice Cream)

A brewed herbal beverage served cold with a lemon wedge. I _ _ T _ _. (Ice Tea)

A type of sausage served at a picnic. I _ _ _ _ _ _. (Italian)

Use the letter "C"

A type of salad with poultry as a main ingredient. C _ _ _ _ _ _ . (Chicken)

A popular dessert at the Wisconsin State Fair. C _ _ _ _ P _ _ _. (Cream Puff)

A dessert served with frosting. C _ _ _. (Cake)

A finger dessert or snack. C _ _ _ _ _ _ _ _ C _ _ _ C _ _ _ _. (Chocolate Chip Cookie)

Names two pies that start with "C". C _ _ _ _ _ and C _ _ _ _ _ _. (Cherry and Custard)

A large nut that has white, flaky meat and grows on palm trees. Used often in desserts.
       C _ _ _ _ _ _. (Coconut)

A melon. C _ _ _ _ _ _ _ _. (Cantaloupe)

A hot beverage served with cream and sugar. C _ _ _ _ _. (Coffee)

A grilled or boiled vegetable eaten with butter and seasonings and eaten with your fingers.
       C _ _ _ O _ T _ _ C _ _. (Corn On The Cob)

Three vegetables served on a relish tray. C _ _ _ _ _ _, C _ _ _ _ _, and C _ _ _ _ _ _ _ _ _ _ .
       (Carrots, Celery, and Cauliflower)

The vegetable that ends up in a pickle jar. C _ _ _ _ _ _ _ (Cucumber)

A child's favorite sweet tooth snack. C _ _ _ _. (Candy)

Two snacks served as appetizers at a picnic or party. C _ _ _ _ _ and C _ _ _ _ _ _ _.
       (Cheese and Crackers)

A dessert made in a muffin pan and frosted. C _ _ C _ _ _. (Cup Cake)

A product used in a grill to cook meats. C _ _ _ _ _ _ _. (Charcoal)

A type of bread served at a southern-style picnic. C _ _ _ Bread. (Corn Bread)

Some folks prefer soda or coffee without C _ _ _ _ _ _ _ . (Caffeine)

Apple C _ _ _ _ can be served at fall picnics. (Apple Cider)

A type of baked bean dish served at 4th of July picnics. C _ _ _ _ _. (Calico)

A condiment served on hamburgers and hot dogs. C _ _ _ _ _. (Catsup)

A New England picnic served at the beach is called a C _ _ _ _ _ _ _. (Clambake)

A favorite picnic dessert is a C _ _ _ _ _ _ _ _ brownie. (Chocolate)

C _ _ _ _ _ _ beverages hit the spot on a hot day. (Chilled)

Use the letter "N"

A garnish on top of frosted cake is N _ _ _ . (Nuts)

Tuna, vegetables, and seasonings mixed with pasta can make a large N _ _ _ _ _ salad. (Noodle)

A type of pie crust used to make a variety of pies. N _ F _ _ _. (No Fail)

Cinnamon and N _ _ _ _ _ are used in apple pie. (Nutmeg)

N _ _ potatoes are sometimes used to make potato dishes. (New)

Use the letter "S"

Chicken is often roasted on a S _ _ _ at a picnic. (Spit)

Barbecue S _ _ _ _ can be used on grilled meats such as chicken and pork. (Sauce)

A fresh fruit used as a garnish at a 4th of July picnic. S _ _ _ F _ _ _ _. (Star Fruit)

Bratwurst is served with S _ _ _ _ _ _ _ _ _ . (Sauerkraut)

In Wisconsin picnicers eat a lot of hamburgers, hot dogs, and B_ _ _ _ . (Brats)

A hamburger served on a bun is a hot S _ _ _ _ _ _ _ . (Sandwich)

A seasoning found on most tables is S _ _ _. (Salt)

A sweet staple used in baked goods is S _ _ _ _. (Sugar)

A grilled fish served at an Alaskan picnic is S _ _ _ _ _ . (Salmon)

A grilled meat used in shish kabob is tenderloin S _ _ _ _ . (Steak)

A favorite red fruit used on fresh fruit platters and in desserts is S _ _ _ _ _ _ _ _ _ _ _ .
   (Strawberries)

Most picnics consist of S _ _ _ _ _ , S _ _ _ _ _ , grilled meats, cold vegetables, dessert, and beverages.
   (Snacks, Salads)

A carbonated beverage is S _ _ _ (some regions call this pop). (Soda)

S _ _ _ _ _ _ _ _ and S _ _ _ _ _ make picnic foods tasty. (Seasonings and Spices)

S _ _ _ _ _ of butter can be melted in a pan on top of the grill for the corn on the cob.
   (Sticks)

Miscellaneous letters

Name five places where a picnic can be held:

P _ _ _   (Park)

B _ _ _ Y _ _ _   (Back Yard)

F _ _ _   (Farm)

L _ _ _   (Lake)

B _ _ _ _   (Beach)

Name four reasons for having a picnic:

F _ _ _ _ _ R _ _ _ _ _ _   (Family Reunion)

F _ _   (Fun)

A B_ _ _ _ _ _ _ D _ _   (Beautiful Day)

S _ _ _ _ _ _ _ C _ _ _ _ _ _ _ _ _ _   (Seasonal Celebration)

B	I	N	G	O
SUMMER-TIME	CALIFORNIA DREAMIN'	OH! SUSANNA	DOWN BY THE OLD MILL STREAM	BY THE LIGHT OF THE SILVERY MOON
IN THE GOOD OLD SUMMERTIME	IN THE SHADE OF THE OLD APPLE TREE	BICYCLE BUILT FOR TWO	TAKE ME OUT TO THE BALL GAME	PUT ON YOUR OLD GREY BONNET
IN MY MERRY OLDSMOBILE	HAPPY DAYS ARE HERE AGAIN	FREE	IT'S A MOST UNUSUAL DAY	IDA, SWEET AS APPLE CIDER
CAMPTOWN RACES	I'M LOOKING OVER A FOUR-LEAF CLOVER	MICHAEL ROW THE BOAT ASHORE	ON A SUNDAY AFTERNOON	RED RIVER VALLEY
DOWN BY THE RIVERSIDE	SWEET ADELINE	YANKEE DOODLE	HOME ON THE RANGE	SHE'LL BE COMIN' 'ROUND THE MOUNTAIN

Community Project for the Womens' Shelter

Our care facility learned there was a need for a rocking chair at our local Women's Shelter, as the Mothers didn't have any way to rock the babies. The women residents at the facility baked apple pies and other goodies with donated ingredients and we hosted three bake sales. They managed to make enough money to purchase a rocking chair for the shelter. They were so proud of their accomplishment!

Our local newspaper heard what we were doing and came in and took pictures. They did a very nice job to promote the bake sales and it was good PR for our facility.

The ladies enjoyed the bake sales so much that we continued them and they raised enough money to purchase twenty turkey dinners at Thanksgiving time for the shelter.

This kind of interaction with the community makes the residents feel needed and very important. They want to help and the projects boost their morale. They see themselves as a vital part of the community.

This improved the emotional health and self-respect of the residents. I would suggest this activity to any care facility. It makes a world of difference in the disposition of your residents, and the charities also benefit—it's a win-win situation. My experience makes me believe that "busy hands make happy campers".

I also gained from the project. I had never given much thought to abused women being homeless. I've never been hungry a day in my life, and it made me think how fortunate I am to have a good husband that takes care of me and loves me. It must be dreadful to be afraid to go home at night, never know - ing how you will be treated, or if your children will be abused—not to mention the emotional trau - ma. This eye-opening experience made me appreciate what I have in my life and spurred me on to help others.

Brain-Teaser Game

This brain-teaser game shows you the many uses of the letter "A". Following are questions in a variety of categories and the answers all have the letter "A" in them. Of course, you can make up additional categories as you need them—this is to get you started. This is a great exercise for coffee hour or an afternoon social. I hope you have as much fun with this brain-teaser as my residents did.

Holiday Category:

Think of the holidays and celebrations throughout the year that answer the questions and contain an "A" in their name.

Christians celebrate the day Christ was born in Bethlehem. (Christmas)

Christ died on the cross and arose from the dead on this day in the months of either March or April. (Easter)

We exchange sweetheart or friendship cards on this day in February. (Valentine's Day)

The birthday of a patron saint in March. Everything is green on this day. (St. Patrick's Day)

June 14 is set aside each year to celebrate this day. (Flag Day)

We give thanks and eat turkey on this day in November. (Thanksgiving)

The first day of a new year. (New Year's Day)

In the last weekend in May is a day of remembrance for the men and women who have served our country. (Memorial Day)

The first Monday in September, honoring working men and women. (Labor Day)

This holiday is celebrated by children and adults on October 31st. (Halloween)

November 1st is noted as a day of obligation by people of the Catholic faith. (All Saint's Day)

Every person all over the world celebrates this special personal day once a year, when they become a year older. (Birthday)

A special day when a newborn baby or person is brought into the church family. (Baptism)

A special family gathering when relatives come from all over the country to gather and reunite. (Family Reunion)

A celebration to honor the completion of schooling and receiving a diploma. (Graduation Party)

Classmates reunite for remembering and rekindling friendships after they've been out of school for 5, 10, 15, etc. years. (Class Reunion)

A special Jewish celebration when a boy becomes a man. (Barmitzvah)

A special celebration recognizing fifty years of marriage. (A Golden Wedding Anniversary)

A special party for a couple deciding to become man and wife. (Engagement Party)

A wedding celebration. (Marriage)

A special day celebrated in Mexico held in May. (Cinco de Mayo)

A special day celebrated in May in Norway. (Syttende Mai)

A special day in May when we honor our Mothers. (Mother's Day)

A special day in June when we honor our Fathers. (Father's Day)

President's Category:

We celebrate the first President's birthday in February. (George Washington)

The President in office when the Civil War broke out. He is known for the Gettysburg Address. (Abraham Lincoln)

His nickname was the "Sir Veto President". (Andrew Jackson)

The President known as "Old Zach". (Zachary Taylor)

This President was a General for the North during the Civil War. He fought against Robert E. Lee. (Ulysses S. Grant)

This President was known as the "Bachelor President" because he never married. (James Buchanan)

This President served four terms from 1933-1945 and was know for his "New Deal". (Franklin D. Roosevelt)

This man became President upon the death of Franklin D. Roosevelt. (Harry S. Truman)

This man was appointed President when Richard Nixon resigned over the Watergate scandal. (Gerald R. Ford)

This President served from 1977-1981 and was highly criticized for being too "Imperial". (James Carter Jr.)

This President served from 1981-1989. He started his career in radio and as a movie actor and became afflicted with Alzheimer's Disease late in his life. (Ronald Reagan)

Months of the Year Category:

Name the six months of the year that have an "A" in their name.
(January, February, March, April, May, August)

States in the U.S. Category (Use the map on page 58):

Name the states in the U.S. that have an "A" in their name.

Name the state in the far northwestern corner of the United States—the name starts with "W".
(Washington)

Name a large state in the far west that borders the Pacific Ocean—the name starts with "C".
(California)

This state's name starts with "N" and it is the state where there is a lot of gambling and nightly stage shows. (Nevada)

The Mormans settled this area and the state's name starts with "U". (Utah)

Many senior citizens and "snowbirds" travel to this state for the winter. Its name starts with "A".
(Arizona)

A western state that raises lots of potatoes. Its name starts with "I". (Idaho)

This state's name starts with "M" and it has a lot of cattle ranches. (Montana)

A very large state in the south that neighbors Mexico. The name starts with "T". (Texas)

This state is directly north of Texas. Rogers and Hammerstein wrote a popular musical using this state's name. (Oklahoma)

The Mardi Gras is held in New Orleans in this state. The name starts with an "L". (Louisiana)

This state's name starts with "A". It is know for being cold and dog sled races. (Alaska)

They grow pineapples in this state. It is surrounded by the Pacific Ocean and the residents greet you with "Aloha". (Hawaii)

This state is in the northeast and borders the Atlantic Ocean. Its name starts with "M". (Maine)

This state is a neighbor of Maine. Its initials are N.H. (New Hampshire)

The Kennedys live in this state. It is also known for the Boston Pops and the Boston Tea Party.
(Massachusetts)

This state is known for the Quakers and the home of the Declaration of Independence. Its name starts with a "P". (Pennsylvania)

This state has two parts and borders Lake Michigan. (Michigan)

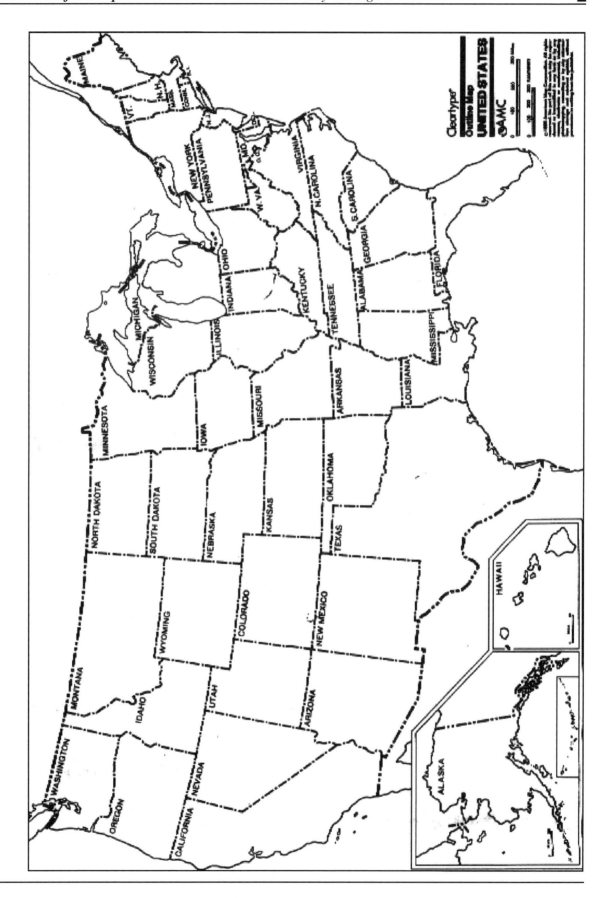

This is the Hoosier State. It is in the Midwest and the name starts with an "I". (Indiana)

This small state is the center of the Midwest and is known as the "Tall Corn State". Its name starts with an "I". (Iowa)

This tiny state is south of New Jersey. It is the only state name that starts with a "D". (Delaware).

This state is south of Pennsylvania and the name starts with an "M". (Maryland)

The first settlers lived at Jamestown in this state. The name starts with a "V". (Virginia)

The capital of the United States. Its name starts with a "W". (Washington, D.C.)

There is a lot of coal mining in this state and some areas are very poor. The name starts with "W.V." (West Virginia)

This state's name starts with "A". It is in the south and I think of this state when I hear the song "Oh! Suzanna". (Alabama)

This southern state is known for peaches. Its name starts with "G". (Georgia)

This warm weather state in the south is the destination of senior citizens and "snow birds" in the winter. Its name starts with "F". (Florida)

President Clinton was from this state. Its name starts with "A". (Arkansas)

This state neighbors Georgia on the east. Its initials are "S.C." (South Carolina)

This state borders South Carolina on the North and is its brother. (North Carolina)

This upper Midwestern state is known as the "Land of Lakes". The Mall of America is in Bloomington in this state. (Minnesota)

This state is another corn growing state. But they also have sugar beets and cattle ranches. Omaha is a large city in this state. (Nebraska)

This state is north of Oklahoma. Its name starts with a "K". (Kansas)

Tourists enjoy the mountains in this state and come to visit in both summer and winter. It has great skiing. Its name starts with "C". (Colorado)

Winters in this state are bitter cold. It is located between Minnesota and Montana. The initials of its name are "N.D." (North Dakota)

This state is located between Nebraska and North Dakota and is home to the Black Hills. (South Dakota)

Just think—over half of the states have an "A" in their name. That's very amazing to me!

Animals Category:

This animal is believed to be an ancestor of humans. It has dark brown hair and eats bananas. (Ape)

This large animal has a trunk and a very good memory. (Elephant)

This animal is found in Europe and America. It has long ears and a short fluffy tail. It is often thought of as a hare or Easter bunny. Its Walt Disney character is called Bugs Bunny. The Volkswagen car is also called by this name. (Rabbit)

This grayish-brown furry animal lives in North America. It has black rings around its eyes and a fluffy tail. (Raccoon)

I would like to stop here and tell you a story about Raccoons.

When I was young I worked at a golf course as a short order cook. One night I closed down as usual and thought everything was in order. When I came to work the next day I found raccoons had gotten into the building and opened the ice cream freezer. They ate all the ice cream.

We set live traps to catch the raccoons, and released them in a faraway field. Raccoons are pretty smart—they don't worry about the damage they do—they just enjoy the ice cream!!

This animal is white, black, or brown, and quite large with furry hair. They live in Alaska and the mountainous parts of the U.S. They enjoy salmon, or any fish—but they don't mind eating your garbage, too! (Bear)

This animal is found in Africa. It looks like a horse, but has black and white stripes. (Zebra)

This animal is one of our favorite pets, but can also live in the wild. It loves to rub against your legs and purrs. It is a very clean animal and uses a liter box. There are about thirty different breeds of this animal. Farmers keep these animals in their outbuildings to keep down the rodents. (Cat)

An African animal with a very long neck! (Giraffe)

An Australian animal that carries its young in its pouch. (Kangaroo)

A brown aquatic rodent in North America. It has webbed hind feet and a hairless tail. Part of its name is known to us as an odor. (Muskrat)

This animal lives in the northern hemisphere and is related to weasels and skunks. It has sort legs and stiff bristly hair. Wisconsin is known as this animal's state. (Badger)

A type of bird that lives in Africa and resembles a finch. (Weaverbird)

Here's a gopher story for you to use after your activity. Even though it doesn't have an "A" in its name!

My husband and I built a home in the country three years after we were married. We had a one-acre parcel with thistles and weeds. We planted grass and trees.

Once the yard began to take shape, the gophers frequented our yard and vegetable garden. Those visits made my husband a very unhappy camper! So, whenever he would see a gopher coming he would grab his shovel and swing at the gopher, trying to hit it. He always missed. I tried to explain that the gophers were too fast for him to catch.

One day he swung at the gopher, missed, and broke his shovel. He returned his broken shovel to Sears (at that time Sears had a no-questions policy and replaced broken tools). The gentleman at the store did ask him how he broke the shovel, and he answered that he was chasing a gopher. The clerk broke into a smile and asked my husband to wait there while he went to talk to the manager. We overheard the clerk's conversation with his manager.

The clerk said, " Now I've heard it all. This customer says he broke his shovel chasing a gopher."

"I'll come over and see if he will tell me the truth," the manager answered.

My husband repeated his story to the manager, and both the clerk and manager were having a hard time keeping a straight face.

"Well, Mister," the manager said, "now I've heard it all. Since you have told such a great story we will give you another shovel. I hope you will not come back again with such a story. Good luck!"

I still kid my husband about the shovel incident, and you know—it was the last time he chased a gopher with a shovel! He just put up a big fence around the vegetable garden to keep the gophers and rabbits out, and the problem was eliminated.

Foods Category:

In my experience, food is a big deal to residents. People really like to talk about food. I have had much success with cooking classes—especially if they know they get to eat the food when we have finished!

Name foods that begin with the following letters:

Name a fruit that starts with "A". It makes wonderful pies. (Apple)

Name a berry that starts with "R". (Raspberry)

Name a berry that starts with "S". (Strawberry)

This vegetable's name starts with "K". It is unusual and is eaten raw. (Kohlrabi)

This vegetable is white and looks like a flower. It is often served with cheese sauce, and the name starts with a "C". (Cauliflower)

Name that food:

Name a vegetable you use when making cole slaw. (Cabbage)

Name a vegetable that is good for your eyes. (Carrot)

This vegetable makes French fries. It was the staple food of the Irish before the famine. (Potato)

This potato is orange colored and is usually topped with marshmallows. (Sweet Potato)

This citrus fruit is grown in Florida. It has a lot of Vitamin C and the name starts with "O". (Orange)

This citrus fruit is also grown in Florida, and also in the southwest. Its name starts with "G" and it is sometimes sour. (Grapefruit)

This fruit grows on a vine and is made into wine, jams, and jellies. Its name starts with a "G". (Grape)

A meat that is often served in Jamaica. (Goat)

A beverage served in the summer and at picnics. (Lemonade)

The southern states serve this beverage all year-round and make it from scratch—sometimes in it is made in the sun. (Iced Tea)

An expensive cut of beef. (Steak)

A layered noodle dish with ground meat, ricotta cheese, Parmesan cheese, and mozzarella cheese. (Lasagna)

A common dish served at church suppers. It contains pasta, tomato sauce, and meatballs, and is accompanied with salad and garlic bread. (Spaghetti)

A meat dish made with ground chuck, sausage, veal, eggs, and bread crumbs. (Meatloaf)

A food served at every meal. It can be leavened—or unleavened. But it usually has yeast. (Bread)

This finger-food is two slices of bread with a filling of your choice. (Sandwich)

A type of fruit found in Jamaica that looks like a banana. (Plantain)

A very soft yellow fruit that is often mashed and fed to babies, or when very ripe it is baked into a sweet bread. (Banana)

A red vegetable that is eaten raw with salt, or served in salads. (Radish)

A meat usually served at Easter or Christmas. (Ham)

A dried grape that is usually served with oatmeal and brown sugar, or used in baked goodies like cookies or cake. (Raisin)

A breakfast bread that is placed in a toaster and served with butter and jam. (Toast)

The name of a sweet roll with frosting served at breakfast or coffee time. (Cinnamon Roll)

A dessert often served at a birthday party. (Cake)

A type of meat found on pizza. (Sausage)

A type of sausage that is very popular in Wisconsin and is served with beer. (Brat)

A type of German cabbage. (Sauerkraut)

A type of German cookie. (Springerle)

A type of Greek pastry. (Baklava)

A type of Italian pastry filled with cream. (Canoli)

A French pastry with cream and powdered sugar. (Cream Puff)

A French pastry that is long, filled with pudding, and frosted with chocolate. (Éclair)

A type of cut-out cookie usually made at Christmas time. (Sugar Cookie)

A fruit that is very tart and is often combined with strawberries in a pie. (Rhubarb)

A red vegetable eaten both raw and cooked. Most homemakers can them for winter. They are harvested in July and August. (Tomato)

An Italian or Greek spice used in Italian foods and grown in a herb garden. (Basil)

A type of breakfast food served with butter and syrup. In a restaurant you would order a "stack". (Pancake)

A breakfast food served with butter and syrup and made in a special hot iron. (Waffles)

A meat usually served at breakfast with eggs and toast. (Bacon)

A type of pancake that puffs up and is usually served with apples. (German Pancake)

A yellow or brown condiment served on hot dogs that isn't catsup. (Mustard)

Dog Days Party

How did Dog Days become a familiar term for the hot days of August? It all started back in 735. The hot weather in August would last from four to six weeks and some people in ancient times believed it was caused by the dog star, Sirius, in connection with the sun that caused such hot, sultry weather.

In Queen Elizabeth's time in the 1560s it was believed that Dog Days started on July 6 and ended on September 5. In the *British Almanac* it was stated that dog days started on July 30 and ended on September 11.

The *American Almanac* from 1890 to the present states that Dog Days start on July 25 and end on September 5. At any rate, Dog Days pertains to the hot weather and I find it quite amazing that it dates back so many centuries!

Following is a quiz and story. Let the residents talk about their dog and tell stories about their pets. The Dog Bone Picture Project is an easy activity and will give the residents a chance to show their dog pictures. The day before the party bake the dog bone cake and frost and decorate it on party day. Serve Dog Days' Floats with the cake, and of course, coffee and drinks.

Dog Quiz and Discussion

What is the sign of an angry dog? (The dog will show its teeth)

What does the term "Dog Days" mean? (Very hot weather)

Name three sounds a dog makes. (Bark, Growl, Whine)

What is the sign of a happy dog? (Wagging tail)

A newborn dog is called? (A puppy)

Dogs are descendants of what animal? (Wolves)

How many teeth does a dog have? (42)

Where are the four canine teeth found in a dog's mouth? (Front)

Do dogs sweat? (No)

Dogs have great hearing. How much better is it than human hearing? (Four times better)

What favorite game do dogs like to play with their master? (Fetch)

What is one of the oldest dog sports in America? (Dog Show)

Can dogs see better at night than humans? (Yes)

How many coats of fur does a dog have? (Two)

What are the coats called? (Outer Fur and Inner Fur)

What is the purpose of the two coats? (Inner Fur keeps the dog warm and the Outer Fur protects the dog from cold, snow, and rain.)

What are a dog's feet called? (Paws)

St. Bernards are large dogs. How much do they weigh? (300 pounds)

Name three famous movie star dogs. (Lassie, Rin-Tin-Tin, and Beethoven)

If a dog has its tail between its legs what is wrong? (It is scared.)

How many breeds of dogs are there in the world? (400)

How many of the dog breeds are in the U.S.? (100)

What was the name of the famous dog that traveled to space in 1957 in Sputnik II? (Laika)

What type of dog does a blind person have? (Seeing-Eye Dog)

Man's best friend is? (A Dog)

What type of dog does a hunter take hunting? (A Hunting Dog)

Dogs come in all sizes and _____? (Shapes)

How do dogs age in comparison with humans? (Each year of a dog's life equals 7 human years)

The cushion found on the bottom of a dog's foot is called a _____? (Pad)

One of a dog's favorite treats. (Dog Bone Biscuit)

Dog Stories

We had a dog named Sandy. She was a beautiful collie. She was very friendly and loved to eat "people food" with her master.

We had a cherry tree in our backyard and I used to pick the tart cherries and make homemade cherry pies. One day, I decided to make cherry pie for supper—but Sandy had a different idea. When the pie was baked and cooling on the kitchen table Sandy jumped up on the chair and ate the whole pie! Needless to say I was not too pleased, but she sure did enjoy the pie. I discovered what had happened when I went to check on her and she was licking her chops!

Our cocker spaniel neighbor dog was named Frikke. He liked frozen hot dogs. I really don't know how Frikke knew that Tuesday was "hot dog day".

Mom would come home with bags of groceries and it was up to us kids to put the groceries away. Frikke would come across the street and sit on our stoop waiting for Mom to come home. He would jump up as soon as he saw her. Mom was soft-hearted, so she would go into the house and come back out with a frozen hot dog for Frikke. He sat on our stoop and ate that frozen hot dog very slowly—enjoying every bite!

My parents ran a restaurant when I was younger, and we seemed to have a problem with robberies after closing time. Dad thought it would be a good idea to get a dog that would bark and sound ferocious, and one of our customers offered his Alaskan husky for the job.

Dad brought the dog home, but forgot to ask his name so he just called him Mutt. But Dad didn't think that was a very fair name so he had a contest to "Name the Dog". (Mind you my Dad's name was Howard Evans.) Everyone was talking about what to name the dog. The name that won the contest was HERO—which stood for Howard Evans' Roving Officer! Dad was pleased and Hero did his job—as we never had anymore night robberies!

In reality Hero was Mom's pal. One time when I was at the restaurant helping I was kidding Mom and going toward her to give her a hug—but Hero thought I had threatened Mom and he came jumping over the gate and protected her. Mom calmed Hero down and told him it was OK, which greatly relieved me!

Now, it is your turn to tell your dog stories! Have fun!

Easy Dog Bone Picture Art Project

This project will help bring back memories of an elderly person's pet.

Supplies needed:
Cardboard 5 x 5 1/2 inches
Construction paper 5 x 5 1/2 inches
4 Dog bones per picture
Shellac
Glue
Picture of the person with their pet

Shellac the dog bones and let dry overnight. Glue the construction paper onto the cardboard and glue the finished dog bones on each corner diagonally to make a frame for the picture. Now glue the photo in the center of the construction paper. The residents can place their pictures in their rooms, or give as gifts to a friend or family member.

Music for the Dog Days Party

"How Much is That Doggie in the Window?"

"B-I-N-G-O"

"It's the Talk of the Town"

"Blue Skies"

"Tiny Bubbles"

"Heat Wave"

"She Wore a Itsy-Bitsy, Teeny-Weenie, Yellow Polka-Dot Bikini"

"Oh! What a Beautiful Morning!"

"Shine On Harvest Moon"

"Side-by-Side"

"September Song"

"On the Sunny Side of the Street"

"In the Mood"

"Fly Me to the Moon"

"Cotton Fields"

"The Things We Did Last Summer"

"Try to Remember"

```
G E S A M O Y E D H E T V H A R R I E R I G U
O E E D O Y B N R O T T W E I L E R M O S D O
L J P M T S T A N D A R D P O O D L E T I M J
D K A E N V A Q C O L L I E C E A I T N B H O
E L M W K V I I A B E A G G H V C O O V E F C
N M L D E I G U N V T E W O O D S U M M R O G
G S A R X L N I O T Q I C E W Q H T W P I X O
L C I G A L S G T O B M M A C N U V H M A T L
I O C R P Y C H E N S E T P H N N A I M N E D
S T R E I S O D T S C A R N O A D K P P H R E
H T A Y K O C I A E E A N N W P U I P O U R N
S I D H M A K M I N R O I E A I O T E I S I R
H S A O I T E R T O P R B R U R U A T N K E E
E H L U T H R O W A C S I C I M D I C T Y R T
E D M N I O S T E Q H A B E U S K B A E K E R
P E A D H I P U G H P D E O R B H T Y R G U I
D E T L H H A E I A M E N I T G A S D E I H E
O R I O M O N G R E L L L B Y A E Q E R D A V
G H O K L J I G F D O B E A G L E U I T T G E
N O N V G R E A T D A N E R E X A Z I N T R R
T U B V E W L A S E S W T Y B O X E R H E E E
T N B A U O B A S S E T H O U N D V E R I E R
T D H D O B E R M A N P I N S C H E R K T K A
```

Dog Word Search

ROTTWEILER	SIBERIAN HUSKY	BEAGLE
PEKINGESE	GREYHOUND	WHIPPET
WELSH TERRIER	DALMATION	POINTER
STANDARD POODLE	DACHSHUND	BASSET HOUND
GOLDEN RETRIEVER	FOX TERRIER	HARRIER
IRISH SETTER	SAINT BERNARD	COLLIE
CHOW CHOW	OLD ENGLISH SHEEP DOG	BOXER
COCKER SPANIEL	SCOTTISH DEERHOUND	AKITA
GREAT DANE	SAMOYED	MONGREL
DOBERMAN PINSCHER	PUG	

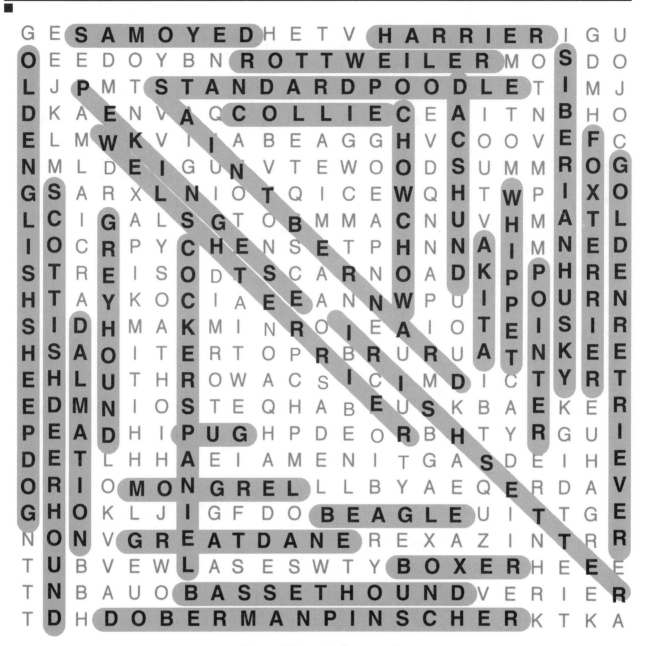

Dog Word Search

ROTTWEILER	SIBERIAN HUSKY	BEAGLE
PEKINGESE	GREYHOUND	WHIPPET
WELSH TERRIER	DALMATION	POINTER
STANDARD POODLE	DACHSHUND	BASSET HOUND
GOLDEN RETRIEVER	FOX TERRIER	HARRIER
IRISH SETTER	SAINT BERNARD	COLLIE
CHOW CHOW	OLD ENGLISH SHEEP DOG	BOXER
COCKER SPANIEL	SCOTTISH DEERHOUND	AKITA
GREAT DANE	SAMOYED	MONGREL
DOBERMAN PINSCHER	PUG	

About Guide Dogs

Did you know there is a Seeing-Eye Guide Dog Foundation for the blind? It is located in Smithtown, New York.

One of the best gifts to the blind is a guide dog. While traveling to work one day I spotted a guide dog walk with his master across the street at the stop light.

Labrador Retrievers make good guide dogs. When puppies are ready to leave their mother they are placed in a foster home until they are ready for training. When they are old enough the Guide Dog Foundation will train them and place them with a person in need of a guide dog.

The blind person comes to the training school to work with their dog. They usually will need two to four weeks to bond and learn with their dog. The guide dog has a harness with a tall handle the person uses to guide the animal. Part of the training includes going to the mall or on the street for practical experience before the person and dog are finished with their training.

When the pair is ready to leave a graduation ceremony completes the training.

There are many training centers around the U.S. The website address is: www.seeingeye.org/.

Recipes:

Dog Bone Cake

See page 1 in color section for color picture.

Yield: Depending on the size of the pieces you cut you should get 40-50 servings.

  3 cake mixes of your choice prepared
         according to box directions
  1 pound whipped topping
  1 can (20 ounces) crushed pineapple,
         drained well

4 six-inch cakes yield 32 pieces
1 six-inch cake yields 8 pieces
2 six-inch cakes in the shape of a dog bone
      yield 20 pieces

It takes three cake mixes to make this cake. The cake mixes will make two 8-inch square pans and four six-inch round pans. When the cake is formed you will have scraps of baked cake left over—do not throw these pieces away—instead cube the scraps and stir into a whipped topping and use as topping for cake pieces with fresh sliced strawberries on top. It is delicious! I just hate to waste anything and I always find some - one to eat the goodies!

Bake in two 8 x 8-inch cake pans and four 6-inch cake pans (be sure to grease the baking pans).

Cool the cakes.

Cut a cardboard 17 x 24 inches and cover the cardboard with foil and tape the foil to the back so it stays secure. (This is about the same size as a full sheet cake.)

Turn two of the 8-inch cakes out onto the cardboard so they are side-by-side in the middle of the cardboard and cut off each corner of the cake diagonally so round cakes will fit on the corners to form the dog bone.

Place one 6-inch cake on each corner of the two cakes you already have on the cardboard where you cut off the diagonal corners, so you have a circle at each corner of the rectangle. This will form the dog bone shape.

Mix the pineapple into the whipped topping and frost the cake with this mixture.

Use dog stickers placed at random on the foil around the edge of the decorated cake.

You might ask the residents if they can identify what breed of dogs the stickers represent— you'll be surprised how many they know!

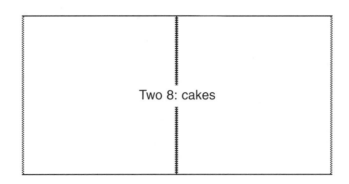

Two 8: cakes

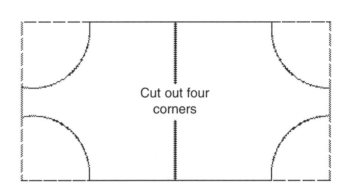

Cut out four corners

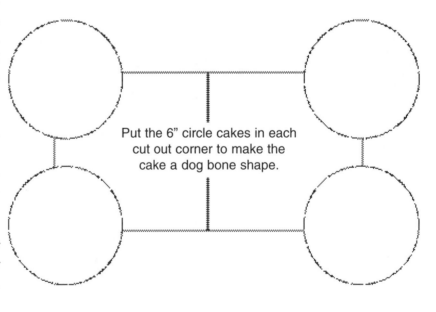

Put the 6" circle cakes in each cut out corner to make the cake a dog bone shape.

Dog Days Celebration Shakes

Yield: 6 servings.

3	cups skim milk
1	banana, sliced
1/2	cup raspberries
1/2	cup strawberries, sliced
5	scoops low-fat vanilla ice cream
2	tablespoons sugar

Supplies needed:

16-ounce slender fluted plastic glasses for serving
Tall straws

Place the milk into a blender add banana slices, raspberries, and strawberries and blend on low adding one scoop of ice cream at a time until mixture is smooth. Add sugar and blend again.

Place a dog sticker on each glass and a label with the dog's name, and encourage the residents to give their "sticker dog" a name!

Fill glasses half full, serve with a tall straw and enjoy!

Yarn Dog Art Project

See page 2 in the color section for finished project.

I enlisted a group of ladies to tie yarn. We made the dogs out of black and white yarn, and my husband bent the hangers into a dog shape. I have a friend who works at a dry cleaning establishment, so I got the hangers from her—if you go to your local dry cleaner they may be able to help you with the hang-ers.

Supplies needed:

2 eyes per dog
1 hanger per dog
2 skeins yarn per dog
3 ready-made gift ribbon bows per dog
Felt for the tongue
Fuzzy round ball for the nose
Cardboard to wrap the yarn on

Yarn for dog's ears

Yarn for dog's beard

Bent wire frame with yarn started

Yarn for dog's body

Yarn for dog's whiskers

Bend a hanger into the shape of a dog. The hook part of the hanger becomes the head of the dog. Shape four legs and the back from the hanger.

Cut the yarn into 12-foot lengths. Cut cardboard

strips 3 x 3-inches, and wrap yarn around the 3-inch side of the cardboard eight to ten times. Leave a 3-inch piece of yarn hanging out of both ends of the cardboard. Wrap the 3-inch loose ends around the center of each side of the wound yarn and tie into a knot—making a yarn bow. Tie the yarn bow onto the hanger around the head, across the back, and on the legs until the hanger is totally covered and full. After the face is completed hot glue the eyes, nose, and tongue on.

To make the ears wrap yard around the 8-inch piece of cardboard 60 times for each ear. (You need 28 yards of yarn for one ear.) Take yarn off cardboard and fold in half so each bunch of yarn is 4 1/2 inches. Tie the yarn ear where it is folded (in the middle) leaving 1/1 2 inches loose for the ear. Cut through the loops of yarn to make ear hairs (you need to do this twice, so you have two pieces for each ear). Tie the ear pieces to the wire on each side of the head. Place bows, for decoration, on each side of the ear at the top and one in the center of the head.

To make the tail wrap yarn around a 3-inch cardboard 90 to 100 times. Remove yarn from cardboard and tie in the center, cut yarn loops to form 1 1/2-inch pieces to form the tail and tie tail onto wire back.

Coffee Klatsch

The day before the coffee klatsch we made the coffeecake, I used a Bundt pan. This recipe is so easy.

It will serve 12-15 people depending on the thickness of the slices. You can use peach or apple pie filling instead of the blueberry. If you have a large crowd you may want to make cakes with different fillings and give the residents and guests a choice.

You can also use fresh blueberries, adding them at the end of the mixing process, and omit the pie filling.

Blueberry Coffeecake
Yield: 1 Bundt cake.

1	cup solid vegetable shortening
1 1/2	cups sugar
1	teaspoon vanilla
1	teaspoon almond extract
6	eggs
2	cups flour
1	teaspoon baking powder
1	can (21 ounces) blueberry pie filling

Preheat oven to 350 degrees.

Grease and flour the Bundt pan.

Cream shortening, sugar, vanilla, and almond extract until fluffy. Add eggs and beat well. Add flour and baking powder and mix well.

Pour half of the batter into the prepared pan and place pie filling on top of batter. Place remaining batter over the pie filling.

Bake for 1 hour, or until wooden toothpick in center of cake comes out clean.

Cool for 10 minutes, loosen edges with a spatula or knife and turn cake out onto a serving plate.

Glaze:

1	cup powdered sugar
1/2	teaspoon almond extract
1/2	teaspoon salt
3	tablespoons water

Mix powdered sugar, almond extract, salt, and water in a small bowl to form the glaze. Drizzle glaze over the top of the coffeecake while it is still warm.

Homonyms Game

Explain the meaning of each of the following homonyms.

Stake	A wooden post.
Steak	A tender cut of beef.
Meat	A food coming from an animal.
Meet	A get together with friends or family.
Beat	Win at a game or race.
Beet	A deep red-colored vegetable.
To	A preposition.
Too	Meaning also.
Two	A number.
Flower	Grown in your garden.
Flour	Used in baked goods.
Sail	You sail your boat on Lake Michigan.
Sale	Buy something at a bargain price.
Male	Men's gender.
Mail	Letters and catalogs that come to you from the post office.
Tale	A story.
Tail	An animal's tail. A dog wags its tail.
Bale	A package of hay or cotton.
Bail	A security deposit paid by suspects to get out of jail.
Hair	Fibrous substance that grows on our heads, and on animal's bodies.
Hare	A rabbit.

Bear	A large furry animal living in wooded areas.
Bare	As in naked—no clothing or covering.
Stair	A step to get to another level.
Stare	To look intently.
Dear	A pet name for a favorite person. Greeting in a letter.
Deer	A wild animal.
Deere	Name of farm implements.
Steal	To take away.
Steel	A hard substance used for machinery and tools.
There	At a certain place.
Their	More than one person's things.
Hale	Sound or robust.
Hail	Ice pellets usually coming with a thunderstorm.
Tow	To pull a large object, such as a car or truck
Toe	You have five on them on your foot.
Heir	A family member or friend that is given a person's worldly goods in a will.
Air	The atmosphere we breath.
Son	A male child.
Sun	Heavenly body that rises in the east in the morning and sets in the west in the evening.
Carrot	An orange-colored vegetable.
Karat	Weight of gold and diamonds.
Earn	Working for remuneration at a job.
Urn	A large vessel holding water, or other substance.
Tern	A slender gull-like bird.
Turn	To change direction.
Fare	A price charged for riding public transportation.
Fair	A condition of well-being.
Fair	An outside entertainment where people take animals and produce for judging. There are usually games, amusement rides, and snack foods.

| I | A first person designation. |
| Eye | A part of the body, used for seeing. |

| Here | Where you are. |
| Hear | Noises you decipher with your ears. |

| Waist | The center of a person's body between the rib cage and hips. |
| Waste | To spoil or throw away. |

Rhyming Words

Think of words that rhyme with the following.

Snake   (Bake, Take, Cake, Stake, Steak, Make, Sake, Lake, Rake)

Rat   (Cat, Bat, Mat, Gnat, Slat, Scat)

Treat   (Heat, Meat, Meet, Beat, Beet, Eat, Feet)

Arm   (Charm, Harm, Alarm)

Leg   (Beg, Keg, Meg, Peg)

Flag   (Lag, Bag, Rag, Gag, Tag)

Book   (Look, Cook, Shook, Hook, Nook, Took)

Bike   (Mike, Hike, Spike)

Berry   (Cherry, Larry, Carry, Sherry, Mary, Tarry, Harry, Marry, Merry, Fairy)

Mad   (Glad, Lad, Bad, Sad, Had)

Male   (Ale, Bale, Bail, Sale, Sail, Tale, Tail, Rail, Fail)

Mare   (Hair, Hare, Care, Share, Bare, Bear, Stare, Fair, Fare)

Spelling Bee
Animals with the letter "A".

Easy Words:

Shark	Eagle	Snake	Dragon
Panther	Bat	Buffalo	Polar Bear
Zebra	Cat	Camel	Beaver
Cougar	Weasel	Rat	Muskrat
Badger	Raccoon	Rabbit	Lizard
Crane	Ram	Whale	

Challenging Words:

Saint Bernard	Dinosaur	Flamingo	Hyena
Hippopotamus	Alligator	Cocker Spaniel	Iguana
Elephant	Baboon	Caribou	Chimpanzee
Antelope	Alaskan Husky	Kangaroo	Doberman Pinscher
Giraffe	Chihuahua	Orangutan	

Flower Project

There are many books on flowers. I used a book entitled *The Big Book of Flower Gardening.* It is a Time Life book and I found it at my local library. If you can't find this book I'm sure there are others that will serve the same purpose. My book had many color pictures of the annual, perennial, and biennial flowers. It was very complete in explanations of planting and garden design.

I showed the various flower pictures during the Spelling Bee. If someone said they didn't know what a flower looked like I was able to show them a picture. Since I have a large flower garden I also brought in fresh-cut flowers for this project.

When I did the Spelling Bee I ran off extra copies of the words, and when we were finished I handed out the lists and had people mark which flowers were annuals and perennials. I used a portable board and wrote the names on it after we spelled them. This gave the residents a chance to familiarize themselves with some of the difficult spellings.

I am always amazed at how many people had gardens. It is a very easy topic to get the conversation going with the elderly. Most men and women had both flowers and vegetable gardens. The elderly may have gardened by the *Old Farmer's Almanac* and signs of the moon—ask them about it!

I also bring roses into the conversation. Ask them about rose bouquets they may have given or received—it will get their memories going. My mother had a beautiful rose garden. She took great pride in the large roses and enjoyed watching the flowers grow.

I also do some flower arranging, and since I have a friend that owns a flower shop she is a good resource for supplies and also for demonstrating to the residents how to arrange different bouquets.

Most care facilities receive flowers brought by funeral homes after their services. Lots of times the families will request that the flowers be sent for the residents to enjoy. I had a group of ladies that would take these bouquets apart and place them in vases donated to our facility—that way small bouquets could be placed all around the facility for all to enjoy.

Know Your Flowers

Here is a list of flowers. **Circle** the flowers that are **Perennials** and **underline** the flowers that are **Annuals**.

Hibiscus	(P)	Daisy	(P)	Lavender	(P)
Gladiola	(A)	Zinnia	(A)	Marigold	(A)
Daffodil	(P)	Rose	(P)	Pansy	(A)
Geranium	(A)	Sweet William	(A)	Aster	(P)
Poinsettia	(P)	Corn Poppy	(P)	Peony	(P)
Magnolia	(P)	Rhododendron	(P)	Orchid	(P)
Begonias	(A)	Delphinium	(P)	Hyacinth	(P)
Lily of the Valley	(P)	Chrysanthemum	(P)	Narcissus	(A)
Violet	(P)	Snapdragon	(A)	Petunia	(A)
Bleeding Heart	(P)	Phlox	(P)	Dahlia	(P)
Purple Coneflower	(P)	Yarrow or Achillea	(P)		
Black-eyed Susan	(P)	Hollyhock	(P)		

Spelling Bee
Flowers

Easy Words:

Rose	Poppy	Zinnia	Violet
Tulip	Lily	Sunflower	Russian Sage
Orchid	Aster	Daisy	Iris
Sweet Pea	Pansy	Marigold	Lavender
Baby's Breath	Yarrow	Gay Feather	Sundrop

Challenging Words:

Hibiscus	Magnolia	Chrysanthemum	Begonia
Gladiolia	Peony	Delphinium	Campanula
Daffodil	Petunia	Rhododendron	Purple Coneflower
Geranium	Dahlia	Snapdragon	Bleeding Heart
Poinsettia	Cymbidium	Phlox	Camellia

```
G E O R G I A L G H E T R I L L I U M D I D Y
R E E D O Y B N O M A R I G O L D W M O O M A
A J A C O L U M B I N E V I N E V I S T C H R
R W A T N V B Q A D A Y L I L Y S I T N O I R
I Y M M N A S T E R E E P G H V S O O V R W O
N S L A A N G U N V T E W O O D T U M M A D W
O T A G E I E I O T Q I D A F F O D I L L E C
D E I N A C C I T O C M M A I N Y V N M B L T
A R C O P Y A A C N S A T P E O N Y W M E P Q
P I R L I S O S Y H C A R N I A C O P G L H K
O A A I K O M W M O R A N G E P F B L I L I I
S P M A M L S E B N I Y W E O I U P Q I V N G
W T Q O I I O E I O R O S E U P O D A U A I E
E S S H T L I T D A M A T A A M E I C A K U R
E V Y H I Y Y P I Q C A W U N F A T A N G M A
T Q I T H I A E U H H A R W E T D T U U I E N
P O P P Y H V A M A A D E I E G H E D N D A I
E I P O Q X U H F O D E N I C A E E D R I G U
A D U K L J N G P D A A Z X Y T E U M T G A M
N U N V I U M A U I I P G R E X A Z I U E R E
T R B V E W Q A S E S W T Y D P H L O X M E E
T U L I P O P Q S S Y L Z T E A A V E R T K D
T P H L I R I S N L S E W R A T D T I K G U A
```

Flower Word Search

IRIS	GERANIUM	ROSE
TULIP	DELPHINIUM	DAY LILY
PHLOX	POPPY	MARIGOLD
DAFFODIL	ASTER	CYMBIDIUM
CORAL BELL	YARROW	SWEET PEA
PEONY	PETUNIA	WYSTERIA
LILY	CHRYSANTHEMUM	TRILLIUM
MAGNOLIA	DAISY	COLUMBINE

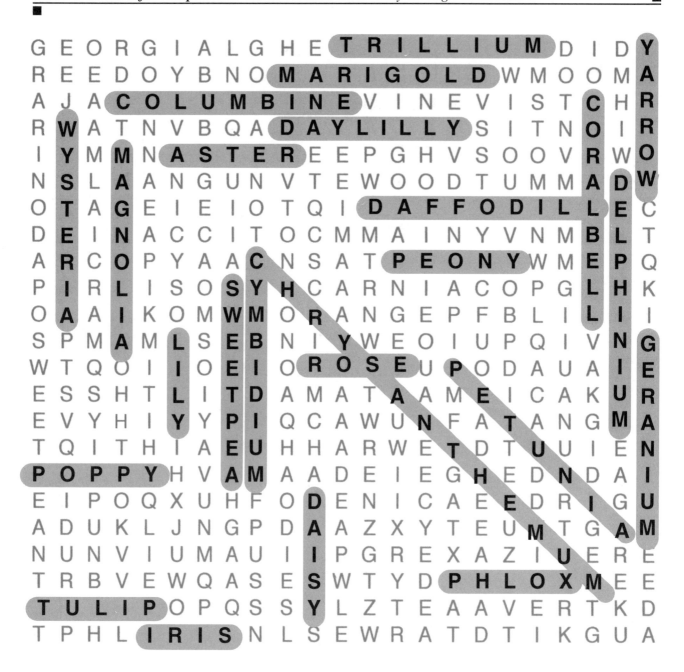

Flower Word Search

IRIS	GERANIUM	ROSE
TULIP	DELPHINIUM	DAY LILY
PHLOX	POPPY	MARIGOLD
DAFFODIL	ASTER	CYMBIDIUM
CORAL BELL	YARROW	SWEET PEA
PEONY	PETUNIA	WYSTERIA
LILY	CHRYSANTHEMUM	TRILLIUM
MAGNOLIA	DAISY	COLUMBINE

Men's Social

We held this activity at 2:30 in the afternoon and served popcorn. The wonderful smell permeated the entire building! The kitchen also prepared a cheese platter and I arranged baskets of crackers, and pretzels. We offered non-alcoholic beer and wine with the snacks.

A gentleman from our community collects fire truck models and he brought them in for display and conversation. If you don't have anyone available for this you might ask one of your local fireman to come and talk about the Fire Department and what their training involves. They can also tell the men about the history of the fire department and some of their fire trucks. The residents will be interested in the cost of new equipment, etc.

We included a talk of the firemen involved in 9-11.

The men really enjoyed this topic and had a nice afternoon.

Aviation Day for Men

I always reserve a room at the facility for the men's lunch and work with the kitchen staff to have the men's meals sent to this room. We always offer non-alcoholic beer and wine if the men want it with their lunch.

At one of the men's lunches I invited my friend's husband to come and show his model airplanes. After lunch a couple of the men were willing to go outside and watch the airplanes fly. It was a pleasant day and perfect for flying the models.

I began the program by saying, "Well, today is August 19. Do you know what is special about today? It is National Aviation Day, so we want to celebrate." I continued by asking questions about aviation.

Who were the first people to fly?   (The Wright Brothers)

Do you know their first names?   (Orville and Wilbur)

Do you know the date and year
when they flew their plane?   (December 17, 1903)

The brothers had to work with the wind and make many trial runs. Their plane weighed 600 pounds, and flew for 852 feet in less than one minute.

The Wright Brothers received many awards for their invention and there is a National Monument in North Carolina in their honor. Their original plane is in the National Air and Space Museum in Washington, D.C.

Left-Handed Recognition Dinner Party

My best friend is left-handed. She had to teach herself to crochet and knit because all the instruction books were for right-handed people. In earlier times the scissors were only right-handed, but now we have left-handed scissors.

Find out who is left-handed among your residents and make up certificates for each one saying "I am proud to be left-handed!" Make name tags with the same saying and present the certificates and name tags at dinner. Make a big deal of it!

Involve the kitchen staff to notice the "lefty" residents and find out if they would prepare a special dinner and dessert that would be favorites of the "lefties". Seat the left-handers among the other residents, but serve all the "lefties" first—recognizing them as special.

This is just one more "excuse" to create a little excitement among the residents. Find any "excuse" you can to recognize all of your residents at one time or another.

A Day at the Ballgame

Both men and women signed up for this enjoyable outing.

We are lucky in that we are close to professional ball team facilities. So I hired a bus and we went to a Brewer's home game. I got plenty of volunteer caregivers and family members to join us and help with the residents. The kitchen staff prepared sandwiches, chips, fruit dessert, and beverages. We ate our lunch in a "tail-gating" fashion in the parking lot and everyone enjoyed the whole event.

The stadium has a special setting for the elderly.

On the way home we sang old-time songs and had a great time!

If you can't attend a professional game how about a Little League hometown game, or arrange with your local high school to attend one of their games. Where there's a will—there's a way!

A Flamingo Party

See page 2 in color section.

On the day of the party decorate the buffet table with a shocking pink tablecloth or a paper one with flamingos. Use standing flamingos on the table and scatter smaller paper ones around the tabletop.

Use tropical plates, napkins, and cups that can be purchased at a party store.

Heat the chicken dish and rice that you prepared the day before. Display the cold food on the buffet table and have the staff help serve the residents.

You might hire someone to come in and play tropical music or tapes.

Flamingo Menu

Coconut Shrimp

Curried Chicken Served on Rice

❀

Flamingo Cole Slaw

❀

Rolls and Butter

❀

Pina Colada Cake

❀

Tropical Fruit Pie

❀

Ambrosia Punch

Recipes:

Coconut Shrimp
Yield: 8-10 servings.

1	13.4-ounce box breaded shrimp
6 oz.	honey
	coconut

I purchased pre-breaded shrimp in 13.4-ounce box at the grocery store. Bake the shrimp at 400 degrees for 10 minutes. When shrimp are almost heated through brush honey over the top and sprinkle with coconut. Broil only until the coconut is lightly browned.

Serve as an appetizer with the Ambrosia Punch.

Note: I purchased a 12-ounce bottle of honey. I only needed half of the honey to make 24 ready-to-bake fantail style shrimp 'n batter. Serve two or three shrimp per person. Coconut comes in a 14-ounce bag. You only need 1/4 of the bag for the shrimp.

Ambrosia Punch
Yield: 3 1/2 quarts.

2	cups apricot nectar, chilled
2	cups orange juice, chilled
2	cups unsweetened pineapple juice, chilled
2	cups Pina Colada mix
1	bottle (32 ounces) club soda or white soda, chilled

Mix apricot nectar, orange juice, pineapple juice, and Pina Colada mix in a large punch bowl. Add club soda at the last minute. Make up an ice ring in advance of soda or juice and freeze overnight. Add to punch just before serving.

Note: If you use water for the ice ring it will dilute the punch.

Curried Chicken
Yield: Serves 6.

2	teaspoons olive oil
1	cup chicken stock
2	pounds chicken breast, cubed
1	onion, chopped
1	green pepper, diced
1	red pepper, diced
1/4	cup minced fresh ginger

1	tablespoon minced garlic
2	teaspoons curry powder
1/2	teaspoon celery salt
1	teaspoon onion powder
1	teaspoon pepper
1/4	cup white wine
1/2	cup milk
2	tablespoons cornstarch

In a large wok or fry pan add the olive oil, chicken stock, and chicken breast. Stir until meat is cooked through. Remove the chicken and add the onion, green and red pepper, ginger, and garlic and cook until peppers are crisp tender. Add cooked chicken back to wok along with the curry powder, celery salt, onion powder, and pepper. Stir all ingredients together. Add the wine and simmer slightly.

Make a liquid paste with the cornstarch and milk. Bring chicken dish to a boil and slowly add the cornstarch mixture, stirring constantly until the dish is thickened.

Serve over cooked rice.

Flamingo Cole Slaw

Yield: 16 half-cup servings.

1	pound ready-to-eat cole slaw mix
1	mango, cored and chopped
1	can (15 ounces) tropical fruit, drained well
1	can (1 pound, 4 ounces) pineapple tidbits
1	cup halved red grapes
1/3	cup almond slices (optional)
1	cup fat-free sour cream
2	cartons (6-ounces each) fat-free orange cream yogurt

Garnish ideas:
Flamingo picks
Mango strip
Parsley
Strawberry
Grape (2 per individual)

Place cole slaw mix in a large bowl and add the mango, tropical fruit, pineapple tidbits, grapes, and nuts. In a separate bowl mix the sour cream and yogurt together and blend into the salad.

Using a half-cup measure place salad in plastic or glass champagne stemware. Place a mango strip across the top center of the salad and place two grapes, the strawberry and parsley on the flamingo pick. Stick the flamingo pick through the mango strip.

Pina Colada Cake

Yield: Serves 12.

1	package (18 1/2 ounces) yellow cake mix
3	eggs
1/3	cup oil
1	cup water
1	cup coconut
1/3	cup pina colada mix
2	teaspoons rum flavoring

Grease and flour Bundt pan.

Preheat oven to 350 degrees.

Mix the pina colada and rum flavoring together before adding to batter. Follow cake mix directions except substitute the 1/3 cup pina colada mix for 1/3 cup of water.

Place cake mix in large mixing bowl and add eggs, oil, water, coconut, pina colada mix, and rum flavoring. Beat until smooth.

Fold coconut into batter.

Place batter in prepared Bundt pan and bake for 50 minutes at 350 degrees. Cool slightly and remove from pan and place on serving tray.

Glaze:

1	cup powdered sugar
3	tablespoons pina colada mix
1/4	teaspoon salt

Stir pina colada mix into powdered sugar until smooth and drizzle over the cooled cake.

Tropical Fruit Pie

Yield: 1 pie or 8 pieces.

Note: You will not use all of the non-dairy whipped topping—only enough for the border. Although I make very tasty pie crusts, due to the lack of time I buy the frozen crusts and bake them. Be sure to remember to poke tiny fork holes in the crust to prevent it from blistering during baking. I bake my crust at 400 degrees, because sometimes 425 degrees will burn the crust. Follow the directions on your package.

Crust:

1	pie crust, baked and cooled

Filling:

- 2   packages (8-ounces each) softened cream cheese
- 1   cup powdered sugar
- 1   teaspoon coconut extract
- 1   can (8 ounces) crushed pineapple, drain well and reserve liquid
- 1   envelope unflavored gelatin
- 1/4   cup cold water
- 1/4   cup of the pineapple juice

Cream powdered sugar and cream cheese together in a large bowl. Blend in the coconut extract and pineapple.

Add the unflavored gelatin to the cold water and stir to dissolve. Let it set for 2 minutes, microwave for 40 seconds and cool slightly. When cooled add to cream cheese mixture and beat until smooth. Add the pineapple juice and mix again.

Pour into cooled pie shell and refrigerate one hour, or until filling is set.

Sour Cream Layer:

- 1/2   cup sour cream
- 1   tablespoon sugar
- 1   teaspoon pina colada mix
- 1/2   cup finely chopped macadamia nuts

In a small bowl blend the sour cream, sugar, and pina colada mix together and spread over the top of the cream cheese layer in the pie crust. Sprinkle macadamia nuts over the sour cream mixture.

Topping:

- 1/2   cup toasted coconut
- 1   tablespoon butter
- 1   teaspoon imitation rum flavoring
- 1   carton (12 ounces) non-dairy whipped topping
- 1   can (11 ounces) mandarin oranges, well drained
- 1/2   kiwi fruit peeled and cut into half slices

Melt butter in a small fry pan and add the coconut and stir constantly over medium heat until the coconut is toasted. Stir in rum flavoring. Set aside and cool slightly.

Using a number 849 tip pipe on a border with the non-dairy whipped topping. Sprinkle the coconut over the border and center of the pie. Alternate mandarin oranges pieces with kiwi making a circle around the edge of the border. Repeat the oranges and kiwi in a second circle in the middle of the pie.

Purchase whole wheat and white rolls and serve with the Curried Chicken.

Flamingo Pin Art Project

See page 2 in color section for finished project.

Note: Three 2-inch oval-shaped wooden pieces come in one package. Try to buy 60-inch wide fab -
ric—if possible in shocking pink. I found fabric that had various shades of pink and it made the pin
more interesting. You can purchase miniature gift-wrap bows in a package of 12 or 24 at a craft store.
I purchased flamingo picks and cut them down to fit on the pin.

Supplies needed:
1 2-inch oval-shaped wood piece for each pin
1/4 yard soft fabric (pink) 60-inches wide
1 leaf per pin
1 flamingo per pin
1 small gift-wrap bow per pin
1 pin for the back
Cloth glue
Hot glue gun and glue

Cut fabric to fit the size of the wooden piece. Using
cloth glue attach fabric to the wood piece. Hot glue leaf on
the front of the pin with the point of the leaf sticking up about
one inch above the edge of the pin. Cut the flamingo pick so it
measures 3 1/2 inches including the flamingo. Hot glue the
flamingo to the cloth and leaf, hot glue the bow to the pick about one
inch from the bottom of the pin. Hot glue the pin to the back of the
wooden piece and let it all dry overnight.

Note: I used the same material for the hats as I did for the pins so they would match. Purchase party
hats that have a brim that is at least 3 1/2 inches to 4 inches wide. The height of the hat should be
about 4 inches.

```
G E O M T V B P A L M T R E E S S I S T N H O
R E E T N V I T A J E E P G H V E O F N V I O
A J A M P N G U N V T E W O O D X U R V Q W C
R M S Q I I F R U I T P U N C H O T E F P V E
I M H R N C C I T O C M M A I N T V S A N B A
N A R P E Y A A A N S A T P B N I O H M I E N
O U I P A S O M K J C A R N I A C O A I I I Q
D P M V P O M E N O C A N G E P B B I L R L K
A A P K P A S M I F I P W E O I I P R Y C H I
P R A O L T O O T L L I B A U B R D Q G V I M
O T P H E H I R W A M N T C A M D I A A A N U
S Y P I S O Y I E M C K W U U F S B C T K E S
S D E I H I T E I I H C O C O N U T A H G U I
E E T T H H R S I N A O E W E G A E Y E I H C
K C I L Q X O H S G M L N I C A E Q D R D A D
I O Z O L J P G F O S O Z X F T E R D I T G U
P R E K W U I A U S O R G R U X A O I N G R S
C A R V A W C A S E S S T Y N G Y M I G E R E
O T S V R O A Q S S U L Z T E A A A Y H I E D
N I B A M P L O N L S E W R A T D N E R T K A
T O H L I A L G H E T V I R G I N T I K G U S
T N R G Y B B U F F E T E R H I W I A I D O U
T S D O Y P I N A C O L A D A V I C O O M J N
```

Flamingo Party Word Search

TROPICAL	FAMILY GATHERING	FRUIT PUNCH
WARM	MEMORIES	PALM TREES
FUN	SUN	EXOTIC BIRDS
FRESH AIR	MUSIC	PINK COLORS
ROMANTIC	OCEAN	PARTY DECORATIONS
FLAMINGOS	COCONUT	SHRIMP APPETIZERS
BUFFET	PINA COLADA	PINEAPPLES

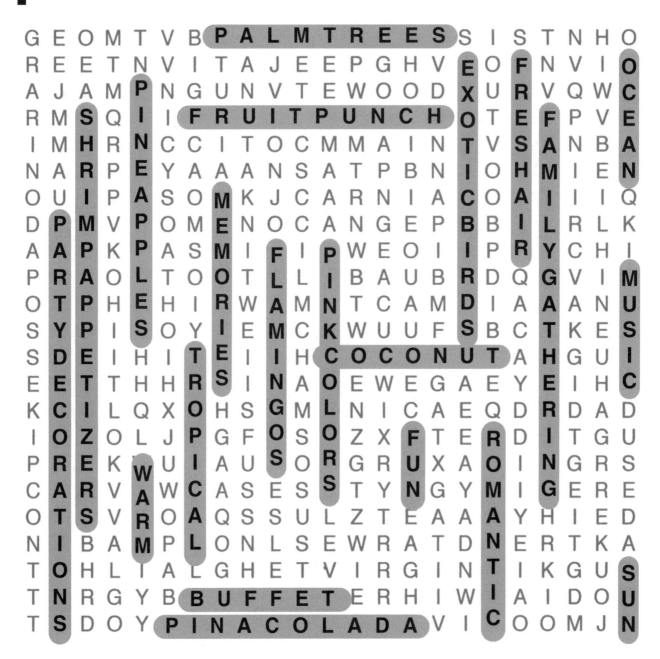

Flamingo Party Word Search

TROPICAL	FAMILY GATHERING	FRUIT PUNCH
WARM	MEMORIES	PALM TREES
FUN	SUN	EXOTIC BIRDS
FRESH AIR	MUSIC	PINK COLORS
ROMANTIC	OCEAN	PARTY DECORATIONS
FLAMINGOS	COCONUT	SHRIMP APPETIZERS
BUFFET	PINA COLADA	PINEAPPLES

Flamingo Hats

Supplies needed:
Same shocking pink material as used for the flamingo pin
3 flamingo picks per hat
Hot glue

Measure band around crown of hat. Cut a 3-inch (in height) strip to fit around the crown of the hat, making sure you have one-inch extra to overlap. Hot glue the hatband to the hat. Cut three flamingo picks at different heights. Center the tallest flamingo in the center of the hat with the two shorter ones on either side.

A Day at the State Fair

Since our residents live so close to the State Fairgrounds, we took some of them to the fair. We had many helpers. Each resident could pick where they wanted to go and what they wanted to see. We divided up into small groups with each group having a cell phone to contact the others. We had a two-hour block of time and then we would all meet for a group lunch before returning home. Our residents enjoyed this very much.

Even if you aren't near a State Fair maybe you can plan to take in your local fair with some of your residents.

Before we went to the Fair we talked about 4-H. Did you know there are 5.4 million young Americans taking part in 4-H programs? Everyone is welcome to participate, even if they live in the city or suburbs.

The four-leaf clover is the national symbol of 4-H and was adopted in 1911. The clover helps people to remember that the four "Hs" stand for Head, Heart, Hands, and Health. 4-H helps young people to explore their interests and become better community leaders. 4-H members do many good community services such as planting trees, gathering clothing and food for the disadvantaged, cleaning parks and roadsides, etc.

Many young people learn how to care for their animals. They learn to be responsible for the animals and show them off at the fair—being judged on showmanship as well as the best animal. Fair judges have many years of experience in working with animals and young people.

4-H members also enter foods, garden products, sewing, artwork, craft projects, writings, etc. in the fair competitions. 4-H is a very well-rounded activity for any young person.

Have fun at the Fair!

Harvest Cooking Gathering

I took several cucumbers and zucchinis into the care facility. The ladies usually gather for coffee at 10 a.m. a couple of days a week and I brought the vegetables in and asked the ladies how many would like a cucumber or zucchini. They made their choice.

I presented a little cooking demonstration, making a zucchini pasta dish and oriental cucumbers. After the demonstration one of the ladies said that her son was coming to visit the following weekend and she was going to make the zucchini dish for him!

Harvest Lunch Menu

August Harvest Soup

Pickled Beets

Dilly Cucumbers

Summer Leaf Lettuce Salad with French Dressing

Garden Kohlrabi Slices

Cantaloupe Slices with Blueberry Garnish

Assorted Cheeses and Crackers

Zucchini and French Bread and Butter

Coffee and Milk

Granny's Soup Kitchen

Two days before the Granny's Soup Kitchen project I picked all the fresh vegetables from my garden.

We had taken a vote a week earlier on what type of meat the residents would like in their soup. Most felt they ate a lot of chicken so they would prefer to have beef in the soup. Our supermarket had a sale on rump roast so I purchased the meat and cut it up for the soup.

The residents prepared all of the vegetables and I helped them assemble the soup. The good smells of our cooking had residents asking what was going on.

The day of the lunch we set the table with jars of fresh flowers and I set up the buffet table. We used a vegetable patterned tablecloth on the buffet table and set out the soup bowls.

The residents were allowed to go through the buffet with an aide or activity person available to offer help where needed. We carried the food for them and helped them get seated at their places. The folks relaxed and enjoyed the meal, and I had fun helping them prepare the soup.

Note: I used 100 percent fat-free beef broth with reduced sodium for the soup base. I used all my fresh garden vegetables. Blanch the fresh garden tomatoes to make the skin come off easily. To do this bring a medium pot of water to a boil and drop the tomatoes into the hot water for about two min- utes. Dip the tomatoes out and the skin will come right off. Cut the fresh corn off the cob in the raw state. I grow garlic and basil in my garden.

I use one cup of the beef broth to cook the beef. If you don't have fresh garlic you can substitute 2 tea- spoons of dehydrated garlic. You can substitute Italian seasoning for the pasta seasoning. You can also substitute chicken for the beef (use one 3-pound chicken).

The soup in the smaller crockpot will take about 4 hours, while the larger crockpot will take about 6 hours.

This soup freezes very well—even with the pasta. When I freeze soup I like to freeze it in one-cup butter or margarine containers—it is just the right amount for one serving.

August Harvest Soup

Yield: 30-35 servings.

2 1/2	pounds turnips, peeled and cubed
1	medium onion, diced
2	cups sliced carrots
1	pound green beans, bite-size pieces
1	pound tomatoes, peeled and diced
1/3	cup chopped fresh basil
2	tablespoons pasta seasoning
1	medium zucchini, diced
1	cup diced celery
2	green peppers, diced
4	ears sweet corn (cut off the cob raw)
1	small, fresh garlic clove, minced
2	teaspoons granulated onion powder
1	quart plus one can (11.5 ounces) V-8 juice
4	cans (14-ounces each) beef broth
1	pound mini Penne pasta, cooked
2 1/2	pounds round steak cubed
1	leek, chopped
2	teaspoons Worcestershire sauce
1	teaspoon olive oil
1	cup water
1	cup beef broth

Fill a large-size pan half-full with water. Add one tablespoon olive oil, bring to boil, add the mini Penne pasta, cook until tender. Drain and rinse the pasta in cold water. Set aside in the refrigerator.

Peel and cube the turnips and place all the vegetables, onion powder, and garlic into the large pot.

In a large skillet or wok add the 1 cup of beef broth, water, olive oil, Worcestershire sauce, leek, and beef and cook on medium heat until the meat is brown. Add this mixture to the vegetable mixture in the large pot. Add the V-8 juice and 4 cans of beef broth to the vegetables.

Divide the mixture into the large and small crockpots and cook on medium heat for 4 to 6 hours.

On the day of the soup party add the pasta to the soup and heat all in a large stock pot. When heated through serve in bowls or mugs.

❧

Pickled Beets

Yield: 15-20 servings.

3	pounds beets
1/2	cup sugar
1	cup cider vinegar
1/2	cup cold water
1	teaspoon salt
1	teaspoon pepper

Peel and slice the beets. Add enough water to cover and boil and simmer for 10-12 minutes or until the beets are fork tender. Drain the water and rinse. Place in a large bowl and cool in the refrigerator.

Stir sugar into the chilled beets and toss. In a separate medium-sized bowl mix the vinegar, water, salt, and pepper and wire whip to mix. Pour dressing over the beets and mix well.

Note: Not everyone will like the beet pickles, but they look nice on the relish tray and some folks will enjoy tasting them.

Dilly Cucumbers

Yield: 4 pounds or 18 to 20 servings.

4	pounds cucumbers, sliced
6	sprigs fresh dill tops
1	teaspoon black pepper
1	pint Ranch dressing (light style)

Wash the garden cucumbers. You don't need to peel garden cucumbers, as they are very tender.

Chop the dill tops medium fine, add dill to the cucumbers. Add pepper and pour ranch dressing over mixture. Stir together well and serve as a side dish.

Summer Leaf Lettuce Salad

Yield: Serves 20.

4	pounds garden leaf lettuce
7 or 8	fresh garden tomatoes, sliced

Clean and dry lettuce with a paper towel. Chop lettuce into a large bowl. Slice the tomatoes and serve on a separate large platter.

Note: You can serve salad toppers for the lettuce such as almond toppers seasoned with Parmesan cheese. They come in 3-ounce packages, but they go quite a ways and you don't need very many. Not everyone likes almonds so that is why I suggest serving them on the side. I also like seasoned crou - tons—again serve them on the side. If you have residents on a restricted salt diet don't serve them the croutons as they are salty.

We used to make wilted lettuce from fresh garden lettuce. You do this by frying and crumbling bacon and making a sauce similar to German Potato salad sauce, but this dish is very high in salt and is not good for anyone dealing with cholesterol.

Granny's Old-Fashioned French Dressing

Yield: 2 3/4 cups.

2	cans (10 2/3-ounces each) tomato soup
1	cup cider vinegar
1/2	cup oil
1/2	cup sugar
1	teaspoon pepper
2	teaspoons paprika
1	teaspoon granulated white onion powder
1	teaspoon dehydrated garlic, minced (optional)

Note: You can substitute artificial sweetener for the sugar in the recipe. Just add a couple of drops instead of the sugar.

Place ingredients into a wide mouth bottle or jar with a lid and shake until well blended. Or wire whip ingredients in a large bowl until well blended and the oil doesn't separate. Chill. Serve with salad.

Kohlrabi Slices

Yield: 1 vegetable serves 5.

1	Kohlrabi

Peel and slice kohlrabi. Place on a tray and garnish with red pepper strips.

Cantaloupe with Blueberry Garnish

Yield: 10 servings.

1   cantaloupe
1   pint blueberries
1/2 bunch parsley

Clean and cut cantaloupe into thin pieces. Clean one pint blueberries for each 10 people. Arrange cantaloupe on a serving tray. Clean parsley and blueberries. Garnish melon with blueberries and parsley. Serve chilled.

Assorted Cheese and Crackers

Yield: Serves 20.

1   pound Colby cheese
1   pound Swiss cheese
1   pound medium sharp Cheddar
1   pound red grapes
1/2 bunch green grapes
     fresh parsley sprigs

Slice the cheese and arrange on a platter. Clean parsley and grapes and dry thoroughly. Garnish cheese slices with parsley and grapes.

Zucchini Pasta Dish

Yield: Serves 8-10.

1   pound Italian sausage
1   pound rigatoni pasta, cooked
3   teaspoons olive oil (divided)
1   large zucchini, julienne
2   carrots, sliced
1   red onion, cut into half slices
1   pound mushrooms, sliced
1   green pepper, chopped
1   red pepper, chopped
1   can (16 ounces) diced tomatoes with juice
2   tablespoons fresh basil, finely chopped
1   teaspoon Italian seasoning
1   teaspoon black pepper
1   jar (16 ounces) prepared spaghetti sauce
     fresh Parmesan cheese

In a large pan bring water and 2 teaspoons olive oil to a boil. Add the rigatoni pasta and cook until tender. Drain and rinse with cold water. Set aside.

In large skillet break apart the bulk sausage, add a little water, and sauté until cooked through. Drain and press any extra grease out of the sausage with a paper towel. Set aside.

Add 1 teaspoon olive oil and 1 cup water to the skillet and stir fry zucchini, carrots, red onion, mushrooms, and green and red pepper until barely tender. Add the tomatoes and fresh basil, Italian seasoning, and black pepper. Stir in the spaghetti sauce and simmer on low for 5 to 10 minutes. Add the sausage back to the skillet and add the precooked pasta. Mix thoroughly and turn the ingredients into a casserole dish for serving. Have Parmesan cheese available for garnishing.

Chinese Cucumbers

Yield: 4-6 servings.

2	medium cucumbers, sliced
1/2	cup cider vinegar
2	teaspoons sesame oil
1	tablespoon soy sauce
2 or 3	drops Tabasco sauce
1/2	teaspoon black pepper
2	tablespoons sugar
1	teaspoon sesame seeds

Note: When I use fresh-picked cucumbers from my garden I never peel them. However, if I purchase cucumbers at the store I do peel them because the cucumbers may have wax on them to preserve them. There is nothing like fresh garden cucumber salad! You may use raspberry vinegar instead of cider vinegar—it is a little more tart, but very tasty!

I always dress up as a chef when I do my cooking demonstrations. I was a chef for 18 years, so I have the uniform. The people enjoy me playing the part. I always let the people sample the food and ask questions.

Place cucmbers in a bowl.
Wire whip together the vinegar, sesame oil, soy sauce, Tabasco sauce, and black pepper.
Pour over the cucmbers.
Garnish with sesame seeds.
Chill and serve as a side dish with your favorite oriental pork or chicken dish.

Make Zucchini Bread one or two days ahead of the party. You will find the recipe on page 52 in *Elder Activities for People Who Care: Volume One-January through June.*

Slice French Bread. One loaf will serve 10 people. Serve breads with butter and/or margarine.

Spud Day

Gather the residents together and review the history of the potato. There are many books on potato history, plus books on potato recipes.

Make up some of the potato dishes for tasting. If you can manage it ahead of time, let the residents peel and help prepare the dishes. It is a fun project for them and gives them something to look forward to the next day.

History

The potato is the leading vegetable in the world. Most kids favorite dish is French fries (many adults, too). There is a 700-page book entitled *History and Social Influence of the Potato* written by Dr. Redcliffe.

Taking all restaurants into account, there are millions of potatoes eaten every year. Of course, the fast food chains serve a big percentage of the total, but every restaurant in the country serves some style of potato. So the potato brings in revenue of $100 billion a year. How many years would it take to count $100 billion dollars? The answer is 1,000 years. That is more time than anyone has on this earth!

This is how I came to that answer: If 10 people live to be 100 and they could count 24 hours a day for 7 days a week they might just be able to count the money. I think I would rather use my time in a different way by sharing it with you. It is more fun and productive. Do you agree? One man said, "Well, it would be fun to have the money!" I asked him what he would do with it, did he really think he could spend that much in a lifetime? Someone else said they would give it to charity, or help their surrounding communities.

While visiting in Santa Fe, New Mexico, I became acquainted with garlic mashed potatoes. They are so yummy and are always made from "scratch".

The potato is one of the most versatile vegetables in the world. It's an almost perfect vegetable, nutrition wise. If I am hungry for a potato I will bake or microwave an Idaho baking potato. Did you know the potato is relatively low in calories? It is the condiments such as sour cream and butter that add up the calories. Salsa is low in calories and I've learned to put it on my baked potato. It is very good.

Once when I was in the catering business I had an order for 300 one-pound potatoes with the works. These potatoes were served to cross-country runners after their race. It was interesting to see what they selected for their toppings (I called these potatoes "loaded potatoes").

The potato has been very important to kings and queens, presidents, and peasants.

Way back in the 1500s Spaniards noticed this strange vegetable growing in the Inca villages. Some of them had red skins while others were light brown. This food was the main food of the villagers. They also used raw potato slices in their medicine, believing the potato could cure skin diseases and headaches.

Many of the people in Peru were vegetarians and the potato was their main vegetable along with maize, which grew in the lowlands. Maize did not grow in the higher levels so the people ate potatoes. Did you know people were growing and eating potatoes 2,000 years before Christopher Columbus? That would have been around 1242.

Do you know that China produces 80 percent of all the sweet potatoes? Yams and sweet potatoes are often confused. Yams are both yellow and white in color.

My husband and I have had a large garden for 30 years. In the first year we planted potatoes. Potatoes grow underground. You cut an eye out of the potato (called a seed potato) and when you plant it, it will sprout and grow. (See picture of potato plant on the following page.) I became very excited to dig our first potatoes and see what we had. They were beautiful!

There are all kinds of rumors about how the first potato was grown in the U.S. It is believed to have been around the 1500s. The Irish did carry potatoes to Virginia when the first colonies were established.

In the 1600s potatoes were one of the vegetables sold at a marketplace in the Netherlands. Some believed at that time that the potato would help cure diarrhea. Others believed if you ate too many you might get leprosy. Some peasants thought the potato could cause great harm and bring disease. Do you know, the potato is never mentioned in the Bible? So why eat a vegetable that may be evil and not God-like?

In the 1700s Queen Marie Antoinette wore white potato blossoms in her hair. She set the style and fashion in Paris at that time. In 1764 a Swedish king demanded that every person be required to grow potatoes.

Ireland was first introduced to the potato in 1588. The Irish had captured a Spanish ship and took everything on board including the potatoes. They planted the potatoes and very soon the people were eating many potatoes, but the potato crop failed in 1845 and many Irish people died.

The Irish farmers had been very excited about their potato crop in 1845, it looked like it was going to be their best crop. But terrible rainstorms and wind came and in the following days the farmers noticed brown spots on the potato leaves. Then the stalks became black and fell over and the air smelled of decaying potatoes. The disease spread all over the country. The Irish had known famine before, but none was as devastating as the potato crop of 1845. They were totally unprepared for the disease and didn't have any extra food.

The problem was not in the potato itself, but with a fungus. It took over 40 years before the farmers figured out and corrected this problem. Everywhere in Ireland there was a spirit of hopelessness, but they weren't the only country to suffer. Others were Egypt from 1064-1072; Europe 1315-1317; China and Russia in the 1300s, and Sudan and Ethiopia in Africa in 1784-1785.

Do you realize that hunger strikes here in the U.S. even today? Many poor people go to bed hungry every night. There are 500 million people all over the world that are not fed and go to sleep hungry.

I can remember my folks saying to me—do not waste any food. Eat everything on your plate. It is a sin to waste because many people are starving to death. If we did not clean up our plates we would get a big tongue-lashing. Mom and Dad grew up in the Depression. They had to be the breadwinners for each of their families. They knew what tough times were like. Many people of their age experienced that same thing.

Question: Why is a person called a potato pile?
Answer: He loves his potatoes.

If you want to learn more about potatoes, here is a list of references.

What's For Lunch? Potatoes by Clair Llewellyn.
Potato by Barrie Watts.
Potatoes by Sylvia Johnson.
Potatoes and People by Bertha S. Dodge
The Irish Potato Famine by Don Nardo
The International Spud by Mara Reed Rogers. (This is a great recipe book!)
For the Love of Potatoes by Darlene Kronschnable. (Describes varieties of potatoes and general cooking terms.)
Skinny Potatoes by Barbara Grimes. (There are over 100 great low-fat recipes in this book.)
The Irish Famine by Tony Allan
Feed the Children First edited by Mary E. Lyons. (Irish memories of the great hunger. This book made an impression on me about hunger. The pictures show how sad the children and families were during the Irish Famine. It describes that potatoes were boiled in jackets and delivered to doorsteps. People would use their thumbnail to peel the potatoes. It also talks about the plagues, black fever, and the poorhouses and soup kitchens. I found this book to be very enlightening and it made me appreciate what I have in life.)
One Potato, Two Potato by Roy Finamore with Molly Stevens. (This book contains 300 potato recipes and is just fun to read.)

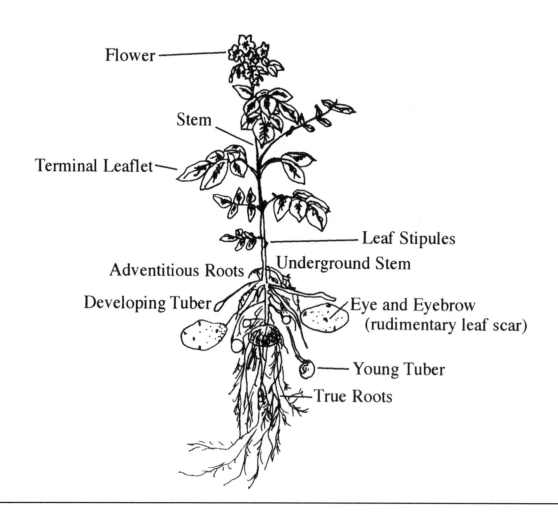

```
G E O R G D O G G I E S P U D S I N C A I D O
R I R I S H L N T W I C E B A K E D R O O P J
A J A M T F R O N M N M V I N E V I A T N I O
R D A T N V A P A E R I U H B E P I B N V E O
I O M M N V I R A D E E P G A V A O C V Q R G
N N L G A N G U M V E E W O K D R U A M P O A
S U A B R E A D O E Q D C E E Q S T K P N G R
I T L P A E C I U O R M P A D N L V E M I I L
N S Y P P Y E A A M S O T O B N E O S M I I I
F E O V I T O K K J P A M N T A Y O P G O F C
U P N K H A M I P O C L N E E A F B L I V R M
L T N O A T S A I O I Q I E L I T P Q I E E A
P T A H S E O U T O T A B N U E O O A U N N S
O S I I H R I G W R M A T C G M T I E A B C H
T V S I B T Y R E U C S T U U F A T A S R H E
A Q E T R O A A I S R I U O E B D T E U O F D
T O K L O T V T I S A D E W S O U P D E W R W
O I P O W S U I S E M E N I C A E Q D R N I D
E D U K N J N N F T S A Z X Y T L U I T E E I
S U N V S U M A U I O P G R E X A A I N D S D
T R B V E W S O U F F L E Y D G Y E D H T R A
K P A N C A K E S S U L Z T E A A V E R G E H
T P H L I P M O N L C R O Q U E T T E S L U O
```

Potato Word Search

IRISH	CROQUETTES	PANCAKES
RUSSET	SOUFFLE	PIEROGI
IDAHO	OVEN BROWNED	GARLIC MASHED
HASH BROWNS	SINFUL POTATOES	SOUP
FRENCH FRIES	LYONNAISE	FARMER OMELETTE
LOADED POTATOES	PARSLEY	DUMPLING
CRAB CAKES	DOGGIE SPUDS	BREAD
BAKED	TATER TOTS	DONUTS
TWICE BAKED	AU GRATIN	GREEK POTATO SALAD

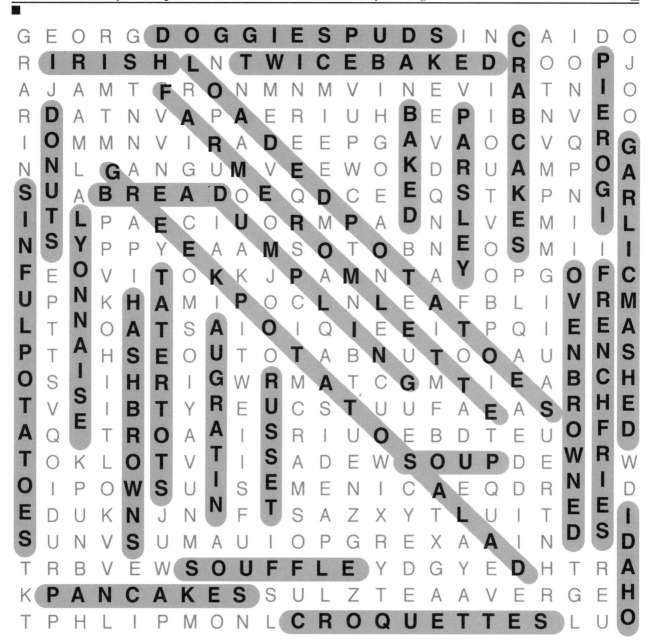

Potato Word Search

IRISH	CROQUETTES	PANCAKES
RUSSET	SOUFFLE	PIEROGI
IDAHO	OVEN BROWNED	GARLIC MASHED
HASH BROWNS	SINFUL POTATOES	SOUP
FRENCH FRIES	LYONNAISE	FARMER OMELETTE
LOADED POTATOES	PARSLEY	DUMPLING
CRAB CAKES	DOGGIE SPUDS	BREAD
BAKED	TATER TOTS	DONUTS
TWICE BAKED	AU GRATIN	GREEK POTATO SALAD

Spelling Bee
Potatoes

Easy Words:

Potato	Hash Browns	Parsley	Fried
Mashed	Russet	Pancakes	
Bread	Idaho	Donuts	

Challenging Words:

Au Gratin	Scalloped	Vichyssoise	Farmer Omelet
Lyonnaise	Crab Cakes	Souffle	Dilly Salmon Potatoes
Pierogi	Tator Tots	Crouquettes	

Potato Talk Game

Connect the lines to the right definition to describe the word or words pertaining to a potato, or potato dish.

1. Idaho	a. A good baking potato.	
2. Pierogie	b. A Polish potato dumpling.	
3. Vichyssoise	c. Made with raw potatoes, grated onion, eggs, flour, salt, and pepper.	
4. Potato Pancake	d. Cold Potato Soup.	

5. Scalloped a. A boiled potato with parsley and butter.
6. Dilly Salmon Potatoes b. A dish made with fish and potatoes.
7. Cream of Potato Soup c. A potato dish made with bacon and milk and thickened with flour.
8. Parsley Potatoes d. A baked, layered, sliced potato dish with flour, salt, pepper, onion, and milk.

9. Lyonnaise a. Crab, onions, mashed potatoes, fish seasoning, egg, and flour. It is shaped into a log, rolled in cracker crumbs and fried.
10. Crab Cakes b. Sliced boiled potatoes, fried in bacon drippings.
11. Potato Soufflé c. A potato dish served cold with salad dressing, celery, and eggs.
12. French Potato Salad d. Baked dish made with egg whites and mashed potatoes.

13. Croquettes a. Mashed potatoes, eggs, margarine, salt, pepper, and shaped into a log.
14. Sinful Potatoes b. A baked potato cut in half lengthwise, with the potato scooped out and mashed. The filling is placed back into the potato skin and baked a second time.
15. Potato Garden Mix c. Hash browns with cream of mushroom soup, sour cream, and cheese.
16. Twice Baked d. A dish with potatoes, carrots, zucchini, tomatoes, onions, and beef broth.

17. Doggie Spuds a. Deep-fried potatoes sold at fast-food restaurants.
18. Oven Browned b. A dish with onions, green pepper, hot dogs, and potatoes.
19. French Fries c. A type of dough cooked with a broth base and served with roasted chicken on Sunday for company in the "good ole days".
20. Dumplings d. A potato chunk deep-fat fried, drained, and baked.

Answer Key to Potato Talk

1. a.	4. c.	7. c.	10. a.	13. a.	16. b.	19. a.
2. b.	5. d.	8. a.	11. d.	14. c.	17. b.	20. c.
3. d.	6. b.	9. b.	12. c.	15. d.	18. d.	

Recipes:

Let the residents select four or five recipes they may like to try, or encourage them to give you their favorite potato recipe. It makes them very happy to make choices.

Spanish Potatoes
Yield: 6 to 8 servings.

6	large potatoes, peeled
1	pound bulk pork sausage
1/2	cup diced green pepper
1/2	cup diced celery
1	jar (12 ounces) salsa
1	teaspoon pepper
1	teaspoon cumin
1	package (8 ounces) shredded taco cheese

Boil potatoes. Fry and drain the sausage. Mix cooked sausage, green pepper, celery, salsa, pepper, cumin together, blending well. Simmer sausage and vegetable mixture for about 8 minutes, stirring every 2 minutes to make sure the mixture doesn't stick to the pan. Turn mixture into a casserole dish and top with the cheese. Bake at 375 degrees for 15 to 20 minutes, or until the cheese melts.

ॐ

Doggie Spuds
Yield: Serves 8.

8	medium potatoes
8	hot dogs
1	green pepper, diced
1	onion, diced
1/2	cup diced celery
1	bottle (12 ounces) barbecue sauce

Cook the potatoes in their jackets, cool, and peel. Cut hot dogs into circles by slicing crosswise. Combine potatoes, hot dogs, green pepper, onion, celery, and barbecue sauce. Place mixture in a baking dish or pan and cover with foil. Bake at 375 degrees for 30 minutes or until bubbly.

ॐ

Greek Potato Salad
Yield: Serves 8.

2	pounds potatoes
1/2	cup chopped onion
3/4	cup diced celery
2	carrots, grated
1	tablespoon chopped parsley
1/2	cup sliced Greek and green olives
1/4	cup oil
1/4	cup vinegar
2	teaspoons Greek oregano
	salt and pepper
	tomato wedges
	feta cheese

Peel and cook the potatoes until tender, when cooled cube the potatoes. Add the onion, celery, carrots, parsley, and olives to the potatoes. Mix the vinegar, Greek oregano, and oil together and pour over the potato salad, tossing lightly. Garnish with feta cheese, tomato wedges, and Greek and green olives.

ॐ

Garden Vegetable Mix
Yield: Serves 8.

3	large potatoes sliced with peeling left on
3	carrots, chunked
2	tablespoons crushed garlic
1	onion, diced
1	green pepper, chopped
1	yellow pepper, chopped
2	medium zucchini, sliced with peeling left on
2	large fresh garden tomatoes, skinned and chunked
1	teaspoon pepper
1	teaspoon herb seasoning, or Italian seasoning
1	can (14 ounces) 100% fat free, low sodium beef broth
1	package (8 ounces) shredded Mozzarella cheese

Mix together in a casserole: potatoes, carrots, garlic, onions, green and yellow peppers, zucchini, tomatoes, pepper, and herb or Italian seasoning. Pour broth over the vegetables and sprinkle the cheese over the top of the vegetables. Cover with foil and bake at 375 degrees for one hour, or until the vegetables are tender.

ॐ

Potato Pancakes

Yield: 8 servings.

8	potatoes, peeled
1/3	cup grated onion
4	eggs, slightly beaten
1/4	cup flour
3/4	teaspoon salt
	dash of pepper
	oil for frying

Using a medium grater, grate the potatoes. Drain well and measure 6 cups of potatoes.

In large bowl, combine the potatoes, onion, eggs, flour, salt, and pepper, mixing gently.

Add oil to a large, heavy skillet until you have 1/8 inch in the bottom of the skillet. Heat oil slowly until a bread cube dropped into the skillet becomes golden brown. For one pancake place 2 tablespoons of the potato mixture into the hot oil. With a spatula, flatten potatoes into a 4-inch pancake. Fry 2 or 3 minutes on each side, or until golden brown. Drain well on paper towel and serve hot with butter and applesauce.

Potato Dumplings

Yield: 18 dumplings.

3	pounds medium potatoes
1	teaspoon salt
	dash of pepper
1/2	(15-ounce package) breadcrumbs
1	teaspoon nutmeg
1/2	cup chopped parsley
2	eggs
1	cup flour
2	quarts 100% fat free chicken broth

Cook potatoes until just tender, remove from heat and drain and rinse to cool slightly. Peel and place potatoes in a large bowl, mash, and add the salt and pepper. Make a well in the center of the potatoes and place the breadcrumbs, nutmeg, and parsley in the well. Add eggs and flour. Work the mixture until smooth and it will hold its shape. Shape into 18 balls.

In a large stockpot bring 2 quarts of the chicken stock to a boil. Reduce the heat and add the dumplings. Boil gently, uncovered, for about 2 minutes or until the dumplings rise to the surface.

Use a slotted spoon to transfer the dumplings to a paper towel to drain. Serve hot with chicken, beef, or sauerbraten.

Potato Donuts

Yield: 12 donuts.

3	cups sifted all-purpose flour
4	teaspoons baking powder
1	teaspoon salt
1	teaspoon nutmeg
3	eggs (3/4 cup)
1	cup sugar
1	cup soft butter
1	cup cold unseasoned mashed potatoes (you may use instant)
1	cup milk
	oil
	cinnamon sugar and/or powdered sugar

I use a small brown paper lunch bag to sugar the donuts. I place the cinnamon sugar or powder and the donuts in the bag and give them a shake. It works very slick! Place the sugared donuts on cooling racks.

You can have a donut sale. Make the donuts in the morning just before lunch time and you will get the staff and residents to buy them.

Mix the baking powder, salt, and nutmeg with the flour and set aside. Beat the eggs, sugar, and butter in a large bowl until fluffy (about 2 minutes). At low speed on the mixer, beat in the potatoes and milk and then the rest of the dry ingredients. The dough will be soft so refrigerate it covered with Saran wrap or waxed paper until it is well chilled (about 1 hour).

Remove half of the chilled dough and roll out on a well-floured board. The remaining dough should be kept in the refrigerator to stay chilled. Roll the dough out to 1/2-inch thickness. Cut the donuts out with a floured 3-inch donut cutter. Transfer the cut doughnuts with a spatula to another board to let them rest for 10 minutes—uncovered.

Heat an electric skillet or a heavy pan on the cook top, place the oil in the skillet and heat until 375 degrees (using a thermometer to check heat). Place the donuts into the hot oil. As they rise to the top, turn them over with a slotted spoon. Fry until golden brown on both sides (about 3 minutes). Lift donuts from oil with the slotted spoon holding them over the skillet to drip excess oil off. Place donuts on paper towel to drain slightly and then sugar them.

ॐ

Pierogi

Yield: 16 servings.
Note: I like Pierogis in chicken soup.

Pastry:
4	cups flour
4	egg whites, slightly beaten
1	cup water

Filling:
1	tablespoon plus 1 teaspoon butter
1/2	cup finely chopped green onions
3	cups cooked mashed potatoes, hot
1	cup frozen spinach, drained well and dried
6 1/2	ounces skim ricotta cheese
1/2	teaspoon nutmeg

Pastry:

In a mixing bowl, combine the flour, egg whites, and water. Knead until a soft dough is formed. Shape into a dough ball and cover the bowl with plastic wrap to keep the dough moist.

Filling:

Melt butter in a frying pan over medium heat. Saute onions for 3 minutes, stirring occasionally.

In a separate bowl, mix the mashed potatoes and cheese, add the spinach and stir. Place the mixture in the frying pan with the onions and stir, sprinkle with nutmeg and blend together.

Assembly:

Roll out dough on a lightly floured board to a thickness of 1/2 inch. Cut out 1 1/2 -inch squares with a cookie cutter. Mound 1 teaspoon of filling in the center of each cutout. Place a second square over the top and using a fork, press the edges shut. Continue in the fashion until all the dough and filling is used up.

Bring a large pot of water to a boil over medium-high heat. Add the pierogies, cover and cook until the pierogies float to the top (about 5 minutes). Using a slotted spoon, remove the pierogies to a greased plate. Continue in this manner until all the dough is used.

Serve hot.

Pierogi Appetizers

Yield: 16 servings.

Pastry:

1   box (1 pound) filo dough
1   stick (1/2 cup) butter

Filling:

4   cups mashed potatoes
8   ounces cream cheese
6   scallions, including part of the tops
1   cup grated Parmesan cheese
1/2   teaspoon pepper
2   large egg yolks, lightly beaten
1   teaspoon salt

Refer to *Picnics, Catering on the Move* cookbook (page 173) to explain how to use filo dough. You can purchase filo dough in the frozen foods section at the supermarket in a 1-pound box (contains twenty 14 x 18-inch sheets). The sheets are paper thin and very fragile. Keep the unused dough in a sealed, plastic bag while working to keep it from drying out.

Beat the cream cheese until smooth and add to the mashed potatoes. Add the scallions, Parmesan cheese, pepper, egg yolks, and salt, and mix all together thoroughly.

Melt the butter in the microwave and brush some in the bottom of the pan. Lay 1 piece of filo dough in the bottom of the pan and brush with butter, lay a second sheet of filo and brush with butter again, lay the third sheet of filo and spread the filling on the third sheet. Place another sheet of filo on top of the filling and brush with butter.

Bake at 400 degrees for about 10 to 15 minutes, or until golden brown. Cut into 16 squares and serve as an appetizer—or serve as a side dish with beef or chicken.

Note: You can add 1 cup of diced ham, cooked chicken or bacon to the filling.

ॐ

Pat's Sinful Potato Dish

Yield: 6 to 8 servings.

8	medium potatoes, peeled and sliced
1	teaspoon dehydrated garlic
2	tablespoons diced celery
1	tablespoon chopped fresh chives
1/3	cup chopped green onions
1	cup sour cream
1	can (10 3/4 ounces) cream of mushroom soup
1	teaspoon pasta seasoning
1	teaspoon California pepper

I took this potato dish to my friend's birthday party—I came home with an empty bowl! We had a huge table of assorted of dishes, but mine was all gone. Many of the elderly at the party raved about this dish.

Grease a large casserole dish.

In a separate bowl mix the potatoes, garlic, celery, chives, and onions. Stir in the soup and sour cream, add seasonings and mix well.

Place the mixture in casserole dish, cover with foil, and bake at 350 degrees for 1 hour, or until potatoes are fork tender.

If you want to make Sinful Potatoes your main entrée, add 2 cups diced ham and 2 cups frozen broccoli spears (thaw and squeeze out the liquid in the broccoli). Add one additional can of mushroom soup and an extra 1/2 cup of sour cream.

ॐ

Dill Potato Biscuits

Yield: 14 biscuits.

2	cups flour
2	teaspoons baking powder
1/2	teaspoon baking soda
3	tablespoons sugar
2	teaspoons dill weed
1	cup cooked instant mashed potatoes, warm
1	cup buttermilk
1 1/2	tablespoons butter

Preheat oven to 400 degrees.

Combine flour, baking powder, baking soda, sugar, and dill weed in a large mixing bowl. Mix in buttermilk, butter, and potatoes.

Drop batter onto a non-stick cookie sheet.

Bake biscuits 15 minutes, or until light brown. Test with a toothpick for doneness.

Serve warm.

ॐ

Blue Ribbon Pickle Day

A day before the making pickles day show the audio tape called "Pure and Simple, An Introduction to the Joys of Canning," featuring Alice Waters of Chez Panisse. Alice lives in Northern California. This wonderful tape leads a person through a step-by-step canning process. There are simple procedures to help a person have good results in their home canning project. There is a website sponsored by the Ball Corporation that you might like to investigate: www.homecanning.com. You can also call the Home Canner's Hotline at 1-800-240-3340 for information and recipes. The turn-around time to receive recipes is five days, so plan accordingly.

Many residents know how to can because that was the method of preserving vegetables and fruits in their lifetime. But if you have never canned before it is wise to study up on canning and also to practice at home before you present this material.

Supplies needed:
Quart and pint jars
Lids
Lid Wand
Canning Funnel
Jar Lifter
Bubble Freer
Canning Pan
1 round rack for the bottom of the pan to set jars on
Canning Labeling Pen
Labels

Background of the Cucumber

The cucumber is a gourd and is related to the pumpkin and zucchini family. There are cucumbers for slicing and for pickling. The gherkin and the French cornichon pickle are very small. The American dill pickle can be small or large. Polish dill pickles are very popular, especially in the Midwest. Japanese cucumbers have very few seeds and are a narrow, thin-skinned variety. You can make pickle relish, or crisp pickles from pickling cucumbers. While cucumbers are available all year long, it is best to use the pickles from the August and September harvest. Most people like their pickles to be crunchy.

You can store fresh-picked cucumbers in your crisper for up to five days. If the cucumbers are grown in a greenhouse, peel the cucumber. These cucumbers usually have wax on the outside to preserve them. If you want to seed the cucumber, peel and cut it lengthwise, then scoop out the seeds with a spoon.

It is interesting to me that cooks in Japan use cucumbers in sushi and cold salads. While the English would not have tea without cucumber sandwiches.

The Pickle Scene

Pickles are very simple to can. After the audio tape get the ladies to talk about how they canned their pickles.

Assign residents to two teams to can pickles. Choose the judges to decide which team will get the blue ribbon for making the best pickles. (Be sure you have a blue ribbon for each person on the team.) Each team will make a batch of dill pickle spears and bread and butter pickles. (Men are welcome to participate, too. Most men just like tasting the pickles though!)

Be sure each person has a chance to sample both types of pickles after they are canned.

Use quart jars for the dill pickles. I grow cucumbers and dill so I donated those for this project. Ask family members and staff to bring vinegar and sugar to help defray the cost of the project.

Start by assembling the equipment and explaining its use—then explain the recipes.

Sterilize the jars. I usually place my jars in the dishwasher. Although in your residents' days they probably boiled the jars and lids and then air dried the jars. So follow the boiling water method to sterilize the jars and bottles before use. Place the clean, washed jars in a bath of water, covering them completely. Bring water to boiling and boil for 10 minutes. Drain the jars upside down on paper towels. Be sure to sterilize the rubber seals and lids, also.

Vinegar is the acid in canning that prevents bacteria from growing. Vinegar also flavors the pickles and other canned vegetables. Distilled vinegar is usually used for most canning recipes. Salt is another ingredient used in canning. In ancient times people discovered that salt had a great preserving quality. They also learned that excluding air would help preserve food.

Before canning—or any cooking project—be sure to wash your hands. Good hygiene and proper temperature, timing, and the acid and sugar levels all affect the shelf life of canned foods.

There are jars that are boil-type jars. They have a hinge on the jar. The rubber seal should always be new. Another type of jar is a vacuum one-piece lidded canning jar. There is also the lid and screw band jar. Have samples of the style of jars to show the residents.

The lid wand is a great tool! It has a magnet in the center and you just place the wand onto a lid and lift it onto the top of the jar.

When the canning jars are filled and sealed, place them into the canning pan. Pour hot water over the jars, covering them completely. Bring canning pan to a boil, making sure the water level stays over the jars. When the boiling time is completed remove the jars from the hot water bath with the jar lifter.

Bread and Butter Pickles

Yield: 8 pints.

3	pounds pickling cucumbers
2 1/2	pounds onions
1 1/2	pounds diced red peppers
2	tablespoons salt
8	cups cider or white distilled vinegar
4	cups white sugar
4	teaspoons tumeric
2	tablespoons mustard seed
4	teaspoons dill seed

This is a fairly easy recipe. There is no doubt about it, canning just takes time. But the residents enjoy the canning. They will reminisce about their gardens and canning days.

Place sliced cucumbers and onions in a large stainless steel or glass bowl. Pour boiling water over cucumbers, then drain. Place cold running water over cucumbers. Cut the cucumbers into 1/2-inch thick chunks. Place onions, sliced cucumbers, and red peppers in a large glass or stainless steel bowl. Sprinkle salt over mixture and mix well. Cover bowl with clean cloth and let set overnight in a cool place.

The next day drain off the liquid in the bowl. Rinse the cucumbers, onions, and peppers under cold running water and drain well. Make sure the cucumbers are not too salty. Cover mixture with cold water and let stand for about 10 minutes. Drain, rinse, and drain again.

Place the vinegar, sugar, and spices in a saucepan and bring to a boil, boiling for 10 minutes. Add the drained vegetables and boil again. Remove from heat. Pack the hot pickles and vegetables and juice into the sterilized jars and seal.

These pickles can be eaten immediately, and the shelf life is about one year in the refrigerator.

Refrigerator Polish Dill Pickles
Yield: 4 quarts.

4	pounds fresh, firm, pickling cucumbers (4-5 inch size)
1	piece fresh dill per jar (optional)
2 1/2	cups distilled white vinegar
3 1/2	cups water
2	pouches (1.94 ounces each) refrigerator Polish dill pickle mix

These Polish pickles are very easy to make. You can even get the Polish dill pickle mix at your super market in the canning department during canning season.

Cut the ends off the cucumbers. Cut cucumbers into spear shapes. Pack the cucumbers tightly in quart jars. Add dill sprig.

Combine the vinegar, water, and pickle mix in a 4-quart stainless steel container. Bring mixture to a boil, stirring until the mixture is dissolved. Evenly divide the liquid among the four jars, leaving 1/2-inch space at the top. Seal each jar. Cool the jars at room temperature and then refrigerate. Within 24 hours the pickles are ready to serve.

Blue Ribbon Pickle Contest

With several teams making pickles you can encourage them to change or add to the ingredients to make your contest interesting!

Label pickles with the labeling pen and place the date and recipe name on the label. Also mark the jars with the team name to help identify the winners!

Ask the judges to take pickles from the jars, being sure to only take small samples. Have plenty of drinking water to help the judges cleanse the pallet before tasting the next recipe. When finished with the tasting, the judges should confer among themselves and pick a winner, which they should announce when the decision is made.

Pass out blue ribbons to each team member on the winning team and make a big deal of the tasting and winner announcement.

September Activities

Labor Day Party

How did Labor Day come about?

Due to the industrial revolution many sweat shops were created where workers worked for little pay in dangerous conditions. The hours were long and tedious.

Peter J. McGuire was a union leader in New York. In 1882 he got the idea to set aside a day in honor of the workers. The idea caught on quickly and Labor Day became a holiday. Labor Day is celebrated on the first Monday in September.

In New York they celebrated with fireworks and picnics. This holiday usually denotes the end of summer vacation and the beginning of the school year.

Our facility Labor Day Celebration included inviting residents' families to a potluck picnic with the facility providing the meat course, buns, and condiments for the meal. We received a great variety of salads, baked beans, and desserts. We invited an accordion player and a magician to entertain the people attending. It makes for a great social and creates a relaxing atmosphere for the day.

Use American tunes music bingo on page 12 for the party.

Flag Centerpiece

Supplies needed:
See page 2 in the color section for completed project.

1 small aluminum bucket
6 stars, 2 each in red, white, and blue for decoration on
   each bucket
Sand to fill the bucket
5 or 6 small American flags

Directions:

Decorate the bucket by pasting or taping the three colors of stars to the outside of the bucket. Fill the bucket with sand until a little over half-full. Place the flags in the sand randomly.

Of course, you can make as many bucket decorations as you have tables, or other places to display them.

Watch how the residents will help themselves to the flags to take back to their rooms. So—you might want to have extra flags!

Granny's Soup Kitchen

Note: You can cut this soup recipe in half and it will still be just as tasty and easy to do. I have the residents peel the vegetables and I cook the turkey bacon. It becomes a social event for the residents involved in the project.

I grow most of the vegetables and the basil, which really adds a lot to the flavor of the soup, in my garden. The basil and other seasonings will help neutralized the strong flavor of a turnip. I add the turnip last. Be sure to reserve 1 cup of the chicken stock to cook the turkey bacon. I usually use California pepper, but black pepper is good, too. California pepper is a blend of various peppers—it is a wonderful seasoning for soups and casseroles.

Garden Turnip Soup

Yield: 24 one-cup servings.

3	quarts 99% fat-free chicken broth
2	pounds turnips, peeled and cubed
2	pounds turkey bacon, diced
3/4	ounce fresh basil, rinsed and chopped
1	red pepper, diced
1	yellow pepper, diced
1	leek, sliced in ringlets
2	bunches bunching onions, chopped with the tops
1	pound portabello mushrooms, chopped
1	tablespoon minced garlic
1	teaspoon pepper

Cook turnips separately in boiling water until tender.

Combine 1 cup of the chicken stock with the diced turkey bacon and cook until done.

In a large stockpot place the remaining chicken stock, cooked bacon, basil, red and yellow pepper, leek, onions, mushrooms, garlic, and pepper. Bring to a hardy boil and then reduce heat to medium low and simmer for 2 hours.

Add the turnips last and cook for 15 minutes more.

Serve with Kohlrabi Vegetable Salad (recipe on page 124) and Potato Dill Bread (page 115).

National Grandparents' Day

National Grandparents' Day takes place the first Sunday after Labor Day. Marian McQuade from West Virginia was responsible for West Virginia Governor Arch Moore designating a special day for honoring grandparents. She worked with senior citizens for many years, and had 15 children and 40 grandchildren of her own.

Grandparents' Day is a big deal to the elderly.

To start the day, the facility served special pancakes with blueberries for breakfast. I entertained in the afternoon and had the privilege of having 50 grandparents at our program. They brought pictures of their grandchildren and great-grandchildren. It gave them an opportunity to show off their pictures and talk about their family. I presented prizes for the grandchildren living the farthest away, the most grandchildren and great-grandchildren. I brought a map of the United States and Europe and we marked the locations where the residents' grandchildren lived.

We ended the gathering with music and a sing-a-long.

Scrapbooking for Grandparents' Day

See color section page 3 for a scrapbook example.

Scrapbooking brings back many memories. It can include: cards, photographs, recipes, programs, letters, postcards, buttons, or coins. You can also include items from family holidays and other gatherings. If your residents are sports fans include some sports memorabilia.

My Alzheimer's-afflicted mother collected buttons and recipes. Memories were triggered with her favorite recipes and button collections. Remember, any items your residents bring for the scrapbook can help spark their memories. Sometimes, it's even an item someone else has brought for his or her scrapbook!

Carefully place the keepsakes throughout the book so you have proper space for the items. By doing this before you "fix" the items in the book you will be able to see negative spaces and move items to compensate. Placing a picture horizontal on a horizontal page, or vertical on a vertical page, makes the item more interesting and the space will be more evenly distributed around the item. Use a glue stick for pasting items on the pages. Contact paper is great for affixing flowers, and sew buttons on the page if they are very heavy. Also, always consider the paper you are using for the book as you want it to last and remain attractive. Also, consider photo collages for a different effect on some pages. You can use paper punches to make various designs and stencils are great for borders on some pages.

It is important to understand color when scrapbooking. The warm colors are: red, orange, and yellow. These colors jump out at you. Cool colors such as blue, purple, and green are also called the "soft" colors. Complementary colors will be opposite each other on the color wheel. Analogous colors are beside each other. Use the color wheel on page 3 in the color section to help you balance the colors to catch the eye of anyone looking through the scrapbook.

Here are some suggestions for the cover of your scrapbook:

a .felt.

b. cotton calico fabric.

c. cardboard.

d. brown grocery bag paper. (Use your own design on the bag and finish by covering with contact paper.

e. wallpaper.

When your scrapbook is completed wrap in tissue paper and store in a flat box away from the sunlight.

References:

Quick and Easy Scrapbook Pages. Check at your local library or write to: Memory Makers Magazine, F&W Publications, Inc., 12365 Huron Street, Suite 500, Denver, CO 80234. Phone: 303-452-0048. Other books by this same company include: *Scrapbook Borders, Corners and Titles, Scrapbook Lettering, and Punch Art 2.*

Kohlrabi Vegetable Salad
Yield: 20 servings.

1 red onion, sliced in half-rings
5 medium kohlrabi, peeled and julienne
1 cup julienne carrots
3 fresh Italian tomatoes, sliced in half-circles
3 cups broccoli flowerets
1 cup diced celery
1 bottle (16 ounces) low-fat country Italian dressing with herbs

Clean and cut vegetables. Stir together and add dressing, mixing well. Marinate for at least two hours to let the flavors blend.

Serve on a bed of romaine lettuce and garnish with a tomato slice.

Bread-Making Day

Bread is one of the most common foods in every nation. Bread is so common it is called the "staff of life". Most breads fall into three types: yeast breads, quick breads, and flat breads. The most common yeast breads eaten in the United States are white, whole wheat, and French. Yeast is the leavening agent in these breads.

Calzone is a bread that is popular in Italy. Calzone is the Italian word for trousers, and the original calzone bread was long like a tube or trousers. Focaccia bread is an Italian flat bread that is round in shape. It is sliced the long way and filled with meats, cheese, condiments, tomatoes, onions, and other vegetables then it is cut in half to eat.

Flat breads are enjoyed by other cultures. In India people eat flat bread called chapatty. It is made of coarsely-ground wheat. Matzo bread is enjoyed by the Jewish people. The tortilla is a main dish used in Latin America. Pita bread has no yeast. It is a Greek flat bread that is filled with meats, tomato, and onions. A special Greek sauce is placed on this sandwich.

Bread dates back to pre-historic times. The flat bread was made by mixing ground meal and water. Heated rocks were used to bake the bread. The Egyptians taught the ancient Greeks how to make bread. In earlier times most people ate wheat bread because white flour was too expensive. However, in today's market in the U.S. white bread is the least expensive.

I live near a bakery. They make the best Greek Olive and sour dough bread. On my travels I encountered a wonderful Dutch bakery in Boone, Iowa. I always look for bakeries with different breads.

Commercial bakeries began around 1640. Although, most people baked their own bread at home through 1899.

Beginning in the 1940s commercial bakeries began adding B vitamins and iron to their breads at the request of the U.S. Health Department. They felt it would help cut down on cases of pellagra and beriberi. Because of this action those diseases are almost eliminated. Breads with added vitamins and minerals are now called enriched bread.

Most yeast breads consist of flour, water or milk, salt, and yeast. Commercial bakeries add a substance called mono-glycerides to improve shelf life. Chlorine dioxide and potassium bromate are also added to commercially baked breads to make the bread dough smooth.

In my opinion there is nothing like the good smell of bread baking in a home. My mom baked bread every week—it was one of her favorite pastimes in her elder years before she became afflicted with Alzheimer's Disease.

Some Bread Terms and Activities:

- Always butter the pan with some type of oil or shortening.
- Proofing means letting the bread dough rise.
- All-purpose or unbleached white flour is the most common type available. They contain sifted and hard wheat composed of endosperm (the starch part of the wheat grains). Unbleached flour is high in protein.
- Whole-wheat flour has an outer coating of bran.
- Gluten flour is made mostly from starch.
- Ancient flours were made from rye, oats, and barley.

How Wheat is Grown

The majority of bread is made from wheat flour. As you travel you may see wheat growing in almost all parts of the world.

The wheat plant grows from tiny, thin sprouts into tall stems. Farmers try to protect the wheat seed and plants from insects and disease. Each stem has an ear at the top. With time the ear will become grains. When the grain is mature it is harvested by cutting the stems and then the grain is separated from the stem and placed in storage for drying. When dry the grain is sold to a flour company, which crushes the grain and mixes it into various kinds of flour. Vitamins and minerals are added to the flour before it is marketed.

Since white bread is so common I thought it would be good to stick to this recipe. Gather the residents together to help make the bread. Encourage them to share their favorite bread recipes and stories. My mom loved to share her bread recipe, it was great for her self-esteem and that made me feel good for her.

Mary's White Bread

Yield: 3 loaves.

1 1/2	cups scalded milk
2	teaspoons salt
1/2	cup plus 1 teaspoon sugar, divided
1/2	cup cold water
2	packages active dry yeast
1	cup warm water
1/2	cup melted butter
6	cups unbleached white flour

Combine warm milk, salt, and 1/2 cup sugar in a large mixing bowl. Add the cold water and cool to lukewarm.

In a small bowl mix the yeast and 1 cup warm water, add the teaspoon of sugar and stir until dissolved. Add the yeast mixture to the milk mixture. Blend in the butter and beat in 3 cups of the flour to make a smooth mixture.

Continue adding the flour to make a workable dough that pulls away from the sides of the bowl. Place the dough on a floured board and knead for 8 to 10 minutes. Form into a ball and place in a warm buttered bowl, cover with plastic wrap and a towel, and let rise until doubled in bulk, about 1 hour. Punch down and divide into three balls. Knead each ball, cover, and let rest for 10 to 15 minutes. Butter or grease three 8 1/2-inch loaf pans. Form each ball into a loaf and place in baking pan. Cover with a damp cloth and let the dough rise to almost the top of the pan. Bake for 30 minutes at 400 degrees. Cool on a wire rack, brushing the tops of the loaves with melted butter.

You can serve the bread for dinner or lunch, or sell the bread by the slice to help raise funds for the residents.

Enjoy the wonderful smell of the bread baking—and of course, enjoy the eating!!

References:
Traditional American Recipes by Frances Towner Gredt. Reader's Digest.
The Bread Bible by Beth Henspiger. This book is especially good. There are 300 favorite bread recipes for every kind of bread imaginable.

```
G R Y E L I P M T N L S E W R A T D T I K G U
R Z U C C H I N I H E T F R U I T B R E A D O
A E E D O Y B N O O N S T E R H I W M O O M J
C J A M T Y R H N M N M V I N E V I S T N H O
I M A T O V B Q A B R I W H I T E I T C V I K
N M M E M V I T A A E E P G H V S O O V O W C
N A L N A N S U N N B E C O O L I V E M P N I
A U A G T I O I O A I I R E W Q B T G P N B E
M A I L O C U I T N S M A A I N Y V A M I E T
O P C I P Y R A A A C A N P B N G O W L I I Q
N U R S E S D P F J U A B N I A C O P G I L K
R M A H S O O I L O I A E G E P F B L I C A I
A P M M T A U T A N T Q R E O I U P Q I V I N
I E Q U O T G A T O S A R A U B O D A U A N T
S R S F T H H B B A M A Y C F M U I C A K E E
I N Y F I O Y R R Q C S N U U L A B A N G U I
N I I I H I A E E H H A U W E B A T R U I H W
P C K N H H V A A A A D T W E G A T D E D A U
C K P S Q X U D D O M E N I C A E Q B R T G P
O E U O L J N G F D S F R E N C H U I R G R S
N L N V U U M A U I O P G R E X A Z I N E R E
T R B V E W H O L E W H E A T G Y E Y H I A D
J A L A P E N O C H E E S E E A A V E R T K D
```

Bread Word Search

ZUCCHINI	OLIVE	PITA BREAD	CINNAMON
BANANA	ITALIAN	SCONE	RAISIN
RYE	FRENCH	BISCUITS	PUMPERNICKEL
WHITE	FRUIT BREAD	ENGLISH MUFFINS	
WHOLE WHEAT	TOMATO PESTO	CRANBERRY NUT	
JALAPENO CHEESE	FLAT BREAD	SOURDOUGH	

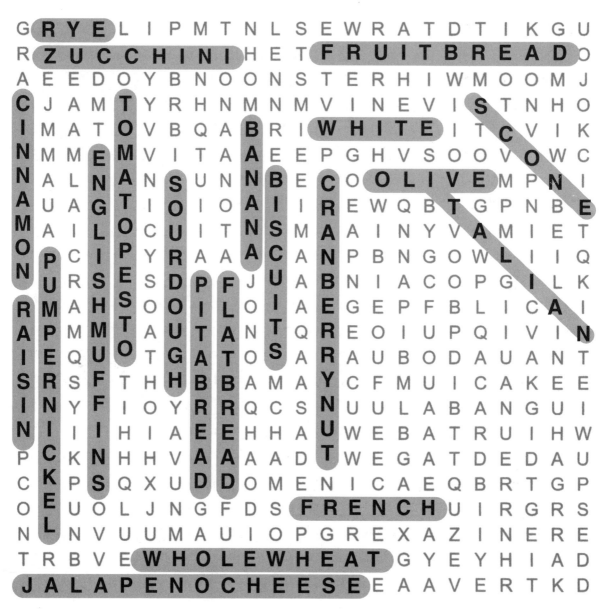

Bread Word Search

ZUCCHINI	OLIVE	PITA BREAD	CINNAMON
BANANA	ITALIAN	SCONE	RAISIN
RYE	FRENCH	BISCUITS	PUMPERNICKEL
WHITE	FRUIT BREAD	ENGLISH MUFFINS	
WHOLE WHEAT	TOMATO PESTO	CRANBERRY NUT	
JALAPENO CHEESE	FLAT BREAD	SOURDOUGH	

The "Z" Word Game

1. Z _ _ _ e _   A closure on ladies and mens trousers.
2. Z _ _ n   A hill in Jerusalem where the palace of King David was built.
3. Z _ _ _ a   A striped animal living in Africa.
4. Z e _ _   A lot of enthusiasm for life.
5. Z _ _ c   A metal.
6. Z _ _ Z _ _   Stitch back and forth.
7. Z _ _ _ e   The democratic republic of the Congo in central Africa.
8. Z _ _   A place to visit animals kept in captivity within a community.
9. Z e _ _   Pertains to cold temperature.
10. Z _ t _ _ _ _   A county in Scotland.
11. Z _ _ _   A supreme God identified with the Latin Jupiter.
12. Z _ _ _   The sixth letter of the Greek alphabet.
13. Z o _ _ _ _   An imaginary band on the celestial sphere of 16 inches width bounded by two circles equidistant from the ecliptic. It is also a figure showing 12 parts with their symbols and emblems. Chinese believe in these symbols.
14. Z _ _   A sudden hit.
15. Z _ _   To close a baggie.
16. Z u _ _ _ _ _ _   A green vegetable used for making a sweet bread.
17. Z _ _ _   A type of camera lens.
18. Z _ _ _   Pertains to time, or a parcel, or a city district or postal delivery, or the north or south between latitudes.
19. Z _ _ _   The product of a single egg.
20. Z _ _ _   A thronged Japanese sandal.
21. Z _ _ _ _ _ _   A branch of biology dealing with animal life.
22. Z _ g g _ _ _ _   A lofty pyramidal tower of ancient Babylonia.
23. Z _ _ g   With much energy.
24. Z _ _ c _ _ _ _ p _ y   The art of engraving on zinc.

"Z" Word Game Answer Key:

1.Zipper	6.Zigzag	11.Zeus	16.Zucchini	21.Zoology
2.Zion	7.Zaire	12.Zeta	17.Zoom	22.Ziggurat
3.Zebra	8.Zoo	13.Zodiac	18.Zone	23.Zing
4.Zest	9.Zero	14.Zap	19.Zoon	24.Zincography
5.Zinc	10.Zetland	15.Zip	20.Zori	

You Are Our Stars Dinner Dance

This is a great activity for independent living residents.

Help the residents dress up for the evening. This will take some work and many staff and family members may have to get involved in this project. People will volunteer to help—don't be afraid to ask them.

Select a sit-down dinner menu that is fairly simple and easy to eat. I would avoid meat with bones and anything that is sloppy—after all they will be all dressed up! A chicken breast and potato is a nice choice. Add a vegetable, salad, and a simple dessert. Let the residents get involved in the choices.

Cover the tables with white tablecloths and place star confetti in the middle of the table with a vase with a simple rose and fern. Roses signify love and go well with a formal dance activity.

Hire a dance band to come in and play old-time dance tunes that remind the residents of the ballroom dancing days.

A two-hour block is long enough for this activity. Serve the dinner first with the dance to follow.

Ceiling Star Decorations

See page 2 of the color section for completed project.

Supplies needed:
Lightweight construction paper
Multi-purpose glue
Glitter
Newspaper
Yarn
Large paper clips
Paper punch

Note: If you wish, you can buy 12-inch stars ready to hang. Just string them on royal blue yarn and cut yarn to whatever length you wish.

Spread newspaper on the worktable. Trace the star onto the construction paper and cut out. Swirl glue around on the star and sprinkle with glitter. Let glue/glitter dry and then repeat the glue/glitter technique on the backside of the star. Let dry again. Punch a hole in the tip of the star. Cut various lengths of yarn and string through the hole in the star. Tie the yarn to a paper clip and hang from the ceiling.

Clean up the excess glitter by placing on a small dish and pour into the glitter container by using a funnel.

Apple Pie and Poetry

The apple pie recipe is from Picnics Catering on the Move *page 163, or you can select a resident's favorite recipe. Gather the residents to make enough pie for all the residents participating in the activity. Make a couple extra pies because most often residents come to the event when they say, "No, I'm not attending." When they smell the apple pie they change their mind. Food is a great drawing card!*

Select your favorite poems and have various residents practice reading the poem they choose. Let the residents have input into the type of poem they would like to read. You may need a microphone so residents can hear them. You can also get staff involved in reading the poetry.

The Alzheimer's Guide, Activities and Issues for People Who Care has "Haddie's Apple Story" on page 227-228. There is also apple information and songs on page 225, recipes on page 226 and 229.

Poetry

The Apple
by Pat Nekola

Many people across the nation
Say apples, apples, apples please.
Apples have many purposes and give the cook
time to travel and explore
Apples, apples, apples, and more.
As orchards have bushels of apples to store.

Apple desserts and apple meatloaf, too.
Time is limited—but so many apple dishes to do.
Communities have apple fests
And pie-eating contests
With blue- ribbon prizes
For the winner.
The judges may say, "This pie tastes the best."

Orchards sort varieties of apples
To sell to the grocery stores.
As the customers come to the door
Clamoring for apples
To make their favorite apple dishes.
Big smiles and praises
Come from family and guests,
Because every bite is so delicious.

My Apple Story
Author unknown

Bob for apples,
Halloween was fun
With Grandma around.
She enjoyed making apple dishes
Like caramel apples.
She washed and shined
The apples for bobbing.
She had a big shiny silver-looking tub
She filled with water
And all flavors of apples
From her orchard.

Sharing an Apple
Author unknown

Apples are fun to share
Especially with people who care.
Give an apple to your teacher,
Or to a favorite friend.
Hotels shine apples and
Place them in baskets.
This expresses a sign of welcome.
So today share an apple
With someone special.

An Apple
Author unknown

Take an apple round and red
Don't slice it down
Slice through instead.
Right inside it you will see
A star as pretty as can be.

The Apple Tree
Author unknown

Way up high in the apple tree
All the little apples smiled at me.
I shook that tree hard as I could.
Down came the apples,
Mmmm, were they good!

Applesauce
Author unknown

Peel an apple
Sugar it fine.
Cook it in a pot!
When you taste it,
You will find
It's applesauce
You've got!

The Apple Pie
Author unknown

This apple is happy,
This apple is sad.
This apple is sleepy,
This apple is mad.
Cut this apple into pieces
That are small
To make an apple pie—
Tastes best of all!

Apples Plus
Author unknown

There are a variety of apples.
What a treat,
They are so good to eat.
Apples come in colors
Of yellow, green, and red.
I see the hanging branches overhead.
I watch the apples drop from my bed.
I think of all the yummy apple dishes
From the apple so red.

The Apple
Author unknown

Pick apples,
Peel apples,
Eat apples,
Share an apple,
On all the early fall days.

Climbing up the Apple Tree
by Pat Nekola

As a child the apple tree I climbed,
For my mother—I did not mind.
With arms stretched out and hands
Clinging to the branch of the tree.
The red applies I could see.
My mother would call me with a plea,
"Oh, come down Missy Bee,
And peel some apples for me."

I am an Apple Lover,
I am a Naughty Worm
by Pat Nekola

I wiggle through the apple with all my might
As I taste the juicy apple with delight.
I enjoy every bite.
Tommy's grandfather says,
"I'll get that worm tonight."

I wiggled back out of the apple
With a big smile.
I said, "Just hide out for awhile."
I see the wind blow the apples to the ground,
I am the naughty worm that cannot be found.

I Am an Apple Lover
Author unknown

Big apples,
Medium apples,
Red apples,
Green apples,
Yellow apples,
Sweet apples,
Tart apples,
Apples that are small,
I will eat them all!

Johnny Appleseed
Author unknown

You are famous
For planting apple seeds
You walked the frontier
Helping people to plant
Their land.
Thus apple trees grew.
You are great John Appleseed,
Thank you for the trees and apples.

Eating Apples
Author unknown

It is hard to eat apples
With braces on my teeth.
It is hard to eat apples with my false teeth.
So pick the apples,
Place them in a basket.
Give the apples to others
With strong front teeth
Or make applesauce
For the person with only two front teeth.

The Worm and the Apple
Author unknown

The worm wiggled through the apple.
The bird found the worm.
The child asked mom,
"Why did the worm wiggle,
through the apple?"
"Why did the bird eat the worm?"
Mom said,
"It is Nature's way.
Just thank God for
The good apple treats."

Apples are Wonderful
Author unknown

Apples are nutritious.
Apples are delicious.
They say
An apple a day
Keeps the doctor away.
However, an onion a day
Keeps everyone away!

```
S R Y E A P E N O C H E E S E C A K E Y H I A
R T U C L I P M T N L S E T R A P K E E R T P
A E E D C H I N A P P T F R U I P D T I K G P
B J A M O Y B N O K N S T U R H L B R E A D L
A P P L E P I E N R N M V D N E E W M O O M E
K M M E O V B Q A I R I W E I T B I S T N J S
E G L N S V I T A N E E P L H V E I T C V E A
D E A G T N S U N G T E C L O L T O O V O L U
A R I L E F O I O L Q I R E W Q T V E M P L C
P M C I W R U I T E C M A A I N Y T G P N Y E
P A R S E I R A A F S A N P B N Y V A M J E Q
L N A H D E D P F R C D B N I A G O W L U I K
E P M M S D O I L I C A U G E P C O P G I L I
S A Q U T A U T A T I Q P M O I F B L I C A N
I N S F O T G A T T L A R P P B U P Q I E I T
S C Y F T H H B B E M A Y C L L O D S U A N E
N A I I I O Y R R R C S C U U E I I C A K E I
P K K N H I A E E S H A U O E B C N A N L U W
C E P S H H D O N U T S T W O G A R G U I A U
O S U O Q X U D D O M E N I C K A T I S D A D
N L N K L J N W A F F L E S N C I Q B S T G E
T R B V I U M A U I O K G R E X H E I R P R D
J A L V E C O F F E E C A K E G A Z S N E R D
```

Apple Dish Word Search

APPLE PIE	DONUTS	FRITTERS	COOKIES
STRUDEL	APPLESAUCE	SALAD	GERMAN PANCAKES
APPLE BETTY	JELLY	WAFFLES	
COFFEECAKE	JUICE	STEWED	
DUMPLINGS	KRINGLE	FRIED	
APPLE CRISP	BAKED APPLES	CHEESECAKE	

```
S R Y E A P E N O C H E E S E C A K E Y H I A
R T U C L I P M T N L S E T R A P K E E R T P
A E E D C H I N A P P T F R U I P D T I K G P
B J A M O Y B N O K N S T U R H L B R E A D L
A P P L E P I E N R N M V D N E E W M O O M E
K M M E O V B Q A R I W E I T B I S T N J S
E G L N S V I T A E E P L H V E I T C V E A
D E A G T N S U N G T E C L O L T O O V O L U
A R I L C I I E F O I O Q I R E W Q T V E M P L C
P M R S A H R U I T C M A A I N Y T G P N Y E
P A C I N U I T R A A S A N P B N Y V A M J Q
L N A H M M S O I L D P F C D B N I A G O W L U I K
E P Q U T A U T A T I Q P M O I F B L I C I A N
S A N S F O T G A T L A R P P B U P Q I C E I T
I Y F T H H B B E M A Y C L L O D S U A N E
S C I I I O Y R R R C S C U U E I C A K E I
N A K N H I A E E S H A U O E B C N A N L U W
P K E P S H H D O N U T S T W O G A R G U I A U
C S U O Q X U D D O M E N I C K A T I S D A D
O S N L N K L J N W A F F L E S N C I Q B S T G E
N T R B V I U M A U I O K G R E X H E I R P R D
J A L V E C O F F E E C A K E G A Z S N E R D
```

Apple Dish Word Search

APPLE PIE	DONUTS	FRITTERS	COOKIES
STRUDEL	APPLESAUCE	SALAD	GERMAN PANCAKES
APPLE BETTY	JELLY	WAFFLES	
COFFEECAKE	JUICE	STEWED	
DUMPLINGS	KRINGLE	FRIED	
APPLE CRISP	BAKED APPLES	CHEESECAKE	

Apple-Tasting Party

Work with your residents to prepare the apple recipes on the following pages. When they are all completed set a time for lunch, or late afternoon, to taste the dishes they have prepared. Encourage them to express how they like each recipe—or how they would change it.

There are thousands of apple recipes. Perhaps some of the residents have their own favorites. Encourage them to bring these recipes to the apple gathering. You might even prepare some of their favorites. Being able to share their recipes and taking part in the preparation makes them feel important. It is great for their self-esteem!

When I made apple pies with the residents they had a wonderful time! It is a great social event.

Purchase a variety of apples for the tasting party and let the residents identify each variety. Peel and taste them for sweetness or tartness.

Your residents will enjoy the food—both the making and the tasting—as well as the fresh apple exercise. As you may have already guessed, just tasting the apples is a very simple activity and the preparation time is so quick and easy.

Recipes:

Apple Meatloaf
Yield: 12 servings.

          2   pounds ground beef
        1/2   pound unseasoned pork sausage
          2   medium apples, peeled and finely chopped
          2   medium potatoes, peeled and finely chopped
          1   medium onion, peeled and minced
          1   teaspoon salt
        1/2   teaspoon pepper
          2   eggs
          1   cup bread crumbs, finely ground

Mix ground beef, sausage, apples, potatoes, onions, salt and pepper, eggs, and bread crumbs until the meatloaf holds together. Divide into two 8-inch loaf pans. Bake at 375 degrees for about one hour.

You can use cracker crumbs instead of bread crumbs in this recipe. This is a deliciously different meatloaf.

Applesauce Meatballs

Yield: 32 one-ounce meatballs.

- 2 pounds ground beef
- 1 cup applesauce
- 1/2 cup soft bread crumbs
- 2 eggs
- 1 teaspoon salt
- 1/2 teaspoon pepper
- 2 tablespoons oil
- 1 stalk celery, thinly sliced
- 1 green pepper, minced
- 2 carrots, thinly sliced
- 1 small onion, peeled and thinly sliced
- 2 cups tomato juice

Combine ground beef, applesauce, bread crumbs, and eggs. Add salt and pepper and mix well. Shape into small balls, dredge them in flour, and brown in skillet with oil. Drain on paper towels and place in casserole dish.

Stir together celery, green pepper, carrot, onion, and tomato juice and pour over meatballs. Cover and bake in a 350-degree oven for 30 to 45 minutes. Serve at once with sauce spooned over the meatballs.

These meatballs are good! You can serve them over rice or pasta bows.

Molded Apple-Lime Salad

Yield: 8 servings.

- 2 1/2 cups boiling water
- 4 whole cloves
- 2 packages (3-ounces each) lime Jell-O
- 1 can (2 cups) very smooth applesauce
- 1 teaspoon vinegar

Simmer the cloves in water for 3 minutes. Remove water from heat and add Jell-O and stir until dissolved. Remove the cloves. Add the applesauce and vinegar. Pour into individual molds and chill until set. Unmold on lettuce and serve with a dab of sour cream or lite mayonnaise.

This salad is excellent with roast pork or lamb.

There are raisins especially designed for baking. I find these raisins are great in any baked goodies. You will find them in the baking section of your supermarket. You can use Granny Smith apples instead of McIntosh if you wish. However, Granny Smith apples are more tart. Or, use one of each variety of apple.

Apple Drop Cookies
Yield: 6 dozen.

2	cups firmly packed light brown sugar
1	cup softened shortening
2	eggs, beaten
4	cups sifted flour
1	teaspoon cinnamon
1	teaspoon salt
1/2	teaspoon ground cloves
1/2	teaspoon baking soda
2/3	cup boiling water
2	large McIntosh apples, peeled and diced
1	cup seedless raisins

Cream sugar and shortening and blend in beaten eggs. Add cinnamon, salt, and cloves to the flour. Add the flour mixture to the creamed shortening mixture. Add soda to the boiling water and stir into the flour mixture, mixing well. Stir in apples and raisins. Drop by tablespoonfuls onto greased cookie sheet and bake at 350 degrees for 12 to 15 minutes, or until a toothpick comes out clean.

Apple Slice Kuchen
Yield: 16 servings.

1	cup shortening
2 1/2	cups flour
3/4	cup plus 1 tablespoon sugar
1/2	teaspoon salt
1/2	cake yeast (1/2 ounce)
1/2	cup milk
8 to 10	McIntosh apples, peeled and diced
1/4 cup	butter

Topping for apples:

1	teaspoon cinnamon
1/4	cup cornstarch
3/4	cup sugar

Cut shortening into flour and then add the sugar and salt and mix well. Add the cake yeast to the scaled milk (cook milk slightly so as not to kill action of yeast), then add yeast mixture to dough and stir.

Roll out half of the dough to 1/4-inch thickness to fit in a 9 x 13-inch baking pan. Place bottom crust in pan and cover with diced apples. Dot the apples with butter and spread cornstarch mixture on top of apples.

Roll out remaining dough for the top crust. Seal edges well and bake at 350 degrees for 45 minutes, then reduce heat to 325 degrees and continue baking for an additional 15 minutes.

Frosting for Apple Slice Kuchen:
1   cup powdered sugar
1   tablespoon butter
3   tablespoons hot milk
1   teaspoon almond flavoring

Microwave milk and butter together, add to powdered sugar and blend well. Add the flavoring and blend again. Drizzle over baked kuchen while still warm.

Apple Salad
Yield: 8 to 10 servings.

4   red Delicious apples, peeled and diced
1   pound red grapes, washed and cut in half
1   package (6 ounces) baking raisins
1   cup chopped walnuts
2   yogurt cups (6-ounces each) fat-free lemon cream pie flavor

Mix apples, grapes, raisins, and nuts together and moisten with yogurt. Serve in custard cups garnished with parsley and a small clump of grapes.

Casino Night

This is a great event—especially for independent living seniors or assisted living facilities.

Prepare a buffet supper just like at the casino, but not as much variety, of course. Help the residents choose the menu with the assistance of the dietary department. Invite family members to be present for the meal and evening event. If you are on a limited budget you can ask the family members to pay for their meal.

Suggestions for the buffet menu:
Beef, Chicken, or Fish
Mashed Potatoes
Carrots
Broccoli or Green Beans
Corn
Salad Bar with Assorted Dressings
Assorted Breads
Ice Cream
Cookies or Cake

Be sure you include the dietary department in the planning, so they can prepare the meal and serve it.

We secured an entertainment company to come in and set up gaming tables. Prizes were won, but no money was involved in the gaming. Families could sit with their loved one at a gaming table and play black jack or poker. It was a fun evening. (Of course, you can play any card games your residents prefer.)

Decorations included tablecloths made from fabric with cards printed on it, and we included the residents in making of the following decorative centerpieces for the dining tables.

Centerpieces
See page 4 in the color section for completed project.

Supplies:
1 board 12 x 5 1/2 inches
2 casino design paper plates
10 dice
Green play money dollars
1 package green dollar confetti
7 or 8 playing cards with the Ace, King, Queen, Jack, and Joker
4 party picks (one each with a heart, spade, club, and diamond design)
Gold paint
Hot glue

Saw slits in the board ahead of time with a power saw. (My neighbor is very handy and he did this for me.) Paint the board with the gold spray paint and allow to dry. Hot glue the two paper plates back-to-back. Place paper plates in slit. Hot glue the party picks, cards, dice, and green dollars in place. Place your centerpiece on the table and sprinkle the dollar confetti around the base.

Penny Jackpot Game

This is a perfect game for a small-group social. There should be six to eight people per table for best results. Use chips instead of pennies. At the end have the players "cash in" their chips for the real pennies or a small prize if you don't play for pennies.

The idea of the game is to get people to socialize and to get them thinking and exercise their brain. One lady touched her toes illegally and others cheated during the game so Thelma got everyone's pennies—you should have heard the conversation during this particular game—it was too funny!

You can make up your own questions, which can then be very pertinent to your own residents. Here are some questions to get you started.

* Anyone that can touch your toes legally gets a penny.
* Give a penny to any person with blue eyes.
* Give a penny to any person with brown eyes.
* Give a penny to any person who has 5 great-grandchildren.
* Give a penny to any person who has 10 or more grandchildren.
* Give a penny to anyone who owns red tennis shoes.
* Give a penny to anyone that has been married 50 years or more.
* Give a penny to anyone who can play Euchre.
* Give a penny to anyone who likes pizza with "the works".
* Give a penny to anyone who likes a special variety of pie.
* Give a penny to anyone who doesn't like chocolate.
* Give a penny to anyone who was married in June.
* Give a penny to anyone who met their mate at a dance hall and got married.
* Give a penny to anyone who never had children.
* Give a penny to anyone who can cross their legs both ways—right over left, and left over right.
* Give a penny to a person who always smiles.
* Give a penny to any person who can wiggle their ears.
* Give a penny to the best storyteller.
* Give a penny to any person wearing a gold watch.
* Give a penny to any person wearing clip-on earrings.
* Give a penny to any person wearing black slacks.
* Give a penny to any person who doesn't wear glasses.
* Give a penny to anyone who can name the Governor of your state.
* Give a penny to any person who can name five flowers grown in your area.
* Give a penny to any person wearing navy blue socks.
* Give a penny to any person who can name your state bird.
* Give a penny to anyone who can count to 10 backwards.
* Give a penny to anyone who can recite the alphabet backwards.
* Give a penny to anyone who can name five musicals.
* Give a penny to anyone who raised a vegetable garden.
* Give a penny to anyone wearing a brown belt.
* Give a penny to any person who went out to lunch with their family within the last month.
* Give a penny to any person who had a dog or cat for a pet.

- Give a penny to any gentleman with a beard or mustache.
- Give a penny to anyone who remembers where they were when President Kennedy was shot.
- Give a penny to anyone who can name the movie star who became President in the '80s.
- Give a penny to anyone who can give the date of Pearl Harbor.
- Give a penny to anyone who can give the name of the President who served three terms during the Depression and died in office.

Lighthouse Gathering Mens' Lunch

Arrange for a special room for the mens' lunch. Work with the dietary department to bring the lunches to the room. Invite someone from your community who has a lighthouse collection, or background information on the subject, to present a lighthouse program.

The day before the lunch get the men together and discuss the following terms about lighthouses and share any other information they may have on the subject. This will create interest in attending the lunch program the following day. Take a poll of your residents to find out how many will be attending the lunch and make sure the dietary department knows how many to plan for.

Terms for discussion:

Watchroom:	An area where the lighthouse keepers watch the light to be sure it is burning.
Inspector:	A person who checks the lighthouse for cleanliness and working order.
Galley:	The kitchen area on a ship.
Beacon:	A light used as a warning or signal.
Tender:	A ship that carries supplies.
Prism lens:	A special lens that bends light beams and is designed to be seen from far away.
Kerosene:	A colorless fuel.
Fog Signal:	The signal warns ships in foggy weather.
Lantern:	A light with a glass lens in the case for emitting the light.
Gangway:	A pathway around the light tower of the lighthouse.
Tramcar:	A car on a tramway that transports people and supplies.
Steamer:	A boat powered by steam.

Story to Share about Lighthouses

The Split Rock Light Station

Many storms on Lake Superior destroyed ships in the early 1900s. Because of this dilemma the government built lighthouses around the Great Lakes, including Lake Superior, which helped the sailors navigate their ships through storms and foggy weather.

From 1910 to the late '30s families lived next to the Split Rock light station. Their homes were often cold, so the people would stay in the kitchen area around the stove on cold winter days to stay warm. The Split Rock light station was located at the edge of a massive rock formation on Lake Superior in northern Minnesota. This lighthouse was built in 1910.

A lighthouse is a tower with powerful lights. The beacon from the lighthouse alerted sailors of a dangerous shoreline. The fog was sometimes so thick the sailors couldn't see the light so the keepers used a loud horn to alert the sailors of the danger. In some instances the lighthouse keeper would climb down to the shore and blow the foghorn to alert the sailors. By doing this, the keeper saved many ships and lives from the danger.

Many times the keeper would need to stay up all night to make sure the light kept burning. In the early days before electricity the light was fueled with kerosene. After they got electricity in 1940 a 100-watt bulb was used in the beacon.

Lighthouse inspectors came on boats called tenders to conduct inspections. These inspections were always on a surprise basis, but sometimes sailors on ships would tip off the lighthouse keeper to the inspectors whereabouts by flying a white flag on their ship. When the keeper saw the white flag he and his family would scurry to make sure everything was in perfect order before the inspector arrived.

Sometimes bad storms would damage the keeper's residence and the lighthouse. It was not unusual to have a lightning strike during a storm.

Most lighthouse keeper's quarters were quite primitive and they felt lucky if they had running water and indoor plumbing. Because of the harsh winters on the coast many times the pipes would freeze when they finally did get running water.

The lighthouse keeper worked during the night and slept during the day, so it was a different way of life for their family.

What did a lighthouse look like inside? There were several steps to climb to the top of the tower. At the top was a big prism lens had to be cleaned and shined daily. Large machinery was needed to turn the light in the tower. The Split Rock lighthouse had a large clock with weights and the keeper was responsible for winding the clock and keeping all the equipment in working order. The light and foghorn signal needed to work constantly. If a lens did not work they needed to be able to repair it and not rely on someone else for help.

Split Rock lighthouse received supplies only twice a year, so the keeper and his family had to be very organized to make sure they had everything they needed until the next supply tender would arrive.

From 1910-1924 there was no road into Split Rock lighthouse. They did have a small boat they would use to go into Beaver Bay, Minnesota, to pick up mail and provisions. Eventually a tramway was built to bring in supplies in 1924.

By 1934 the keeper had a truck to travel into town for supplies.

Lighthouse keeper's families were very close knit. It was a simple life, but very meaningful.

To this day the grandchildren of the light keepers still hold deep memories of the light keeper's life and events passed down to them from their grandparents and parents.

Today automation has taken the place of the old lighthouses. Radio beacons give ships more accurate information and warning than the lighthouse beams could ever do. As a result many lighthouses on the Great Lakes have been abandoned or automated. We need to honor the dedication of the light keepers from an earlier time.

Here's a poem to read during lunch time.

The Lighthouse Keeper Speaking from His Heart
by Pat Nekola

I gave my life to the lighthouse.
I worried so about the sailors on their ships.
I felt responsible to stay up all night
Working on the beam,
To ensure the safety of the sailors.

The lightning storm took my house,
But I remained calm for I had a job to accomplish.
Now I am being replaced by automation.
I am not bitter, but amazed at how
Automation can change one's life.

I have given forty years of my life,
Which I would not trade.
For my family and I
Are richer in experiences
As we reminisce.

I will remember my children winding the clock,
Holding my hand as we climbed the stairs
To see the wonders of Lake Superior,
And laugh at how we scurried
To prepare for the inspector.

The gardens gave flowers of love to my wife,
The vegetables sustained life.
I will hold all of these memories,
In my heart
Forever.

References:

Eastern Great Lakes Lighthouses (Ontario, Erie, and Huron) by Bruce Roberts and Ray Jones.
The Northern Lights, Lighthouses of the Upper Great Lakes by Charles K. Hyde.

For more information on lighthouses here are some addresses:

Lighthouse Digest, P.O. Box 1690, Wells, ME 04090.
U.S. Lighthouse Society, 244 Kearny Street, 5th Floor, San Francisco, CA 94108.
Great Lakes Lighthouse Keepers Association, P.O. Box 580, Allen Park, MI 48101.
Lighthouse Preservation Society, P.O. Box 736, Rockport, MA 01966.

```
N O E R I E L A N D S A Q U T A U A Z P S T Q
M T N L C H E B O Y G A N C R I B Y E R P O U
N A P P B F R U I P S C Y F T H H K E I L L E
N O K N A T E R H L N A I I I O Y D T N I E E
F N R N R M U N E E P K K N H I A B R C T D N
O E I R C A D I T M I S S U S S A G I E R O S
R W N E E R E H V R O C K I S L A N D E O H W
T P G T L B L O L T N L N K L J N I T D C A H
Y R L Q O L E W Q T T R B V I U M O N W K R A
M E E C N E A I N Y J A L V E C O V I A L B R
I S B S A H P B N S R Y E A P E J T N R I O F
L Q R R D E N I A R T U C L O P Y V E D G R E
E U I C A A B E P A E E D C I I G O M P H I Q
P E C I Q D A O I B J A M O N B C O I O T L K
O I A L A R D S B A P P L E T I F B L I T A S
I S B M A Y C O H K M M E O C B U P E N T I E
N L O C S C U U C T G L N S L I O D P T E N L
T E T H A U O E B K A A G T A S I I O A C E K
O N H T S T W O G A P B L E R O C N I N A U U
D D E M E N I C K P M O U W K U A R N U M A K
W A A F P O E R E E F R I L Z R A T T S I A U
A U D O K G R E X L N A H N A D I Q B S N S D
O L D M A C K I N A C P O I N T A I G H T R L
```

Great Lakes Lighthouse Word Search

ERIE LAND	ASHTABULA	POINT CLARK	NINE MILE POINT
FORTY MILE POINT	BARCELONA	QUEENS WHARF	POE REEF
CHEBOYGAN CRIB	MARBLEHEAD	SELKUK	PRINCE EDWARD POINT
CABOT HEAD	NEW PRESQUE ISLE	TOLEDO HARBOR	ROCK ISLAND
BRADDOCK POINT	OLD MACKINAC POINT	MISSUSSAGI	SPLIT ROCK LIGHT

Great Lakes Lighthouse Word Search

ERIE LAND	ASHTABULA	POINT CLARK	NINE MILE POINT
FORTY MILE POINT	BARCELONA	QUEENS WHARF	POE REEF
CHEBOYGAN CRIB	MARBLEHEAD	SELKUK	PRINCE EDWARD POINT
CABOT HEAD	NEW PRESQUE ISLE	TOLEDO HARBOR	ROCK ISLAND
BRADDOCK POINT	OLD MACKINAC POINT	MISSUSSAGI	SPLIT ROCK LIGHT

Games with Kids

I contacted a 5ᵗʰ grade teacher and worked with her to bring her class to the care facility. The class brought 15 students to teach a game to our residents. They picked two or three residents to play the game with them.

The object of the exercise was for the students to teach the elders how to play the game. Of course, the real purpose was for the children to communicate with the elders and for both groups to have fun. The students also learned respect for the residents.

Before the students came for their game we trained them in methods of communication with the elderly. It is a definite skill needed in our country.

Everyone had a grand time! It was a learning experience for the students, and a memorable day for the elders.

I enjoy seeing this interaction between the two generations. It is a win/win situation for everyone!

You can use any reason or activity that suits your facility and school. I'm sure the teachers in your area will have lots of good ideas for this kind of activity.

Talent Show with Students

Contact a dance school in your area and work with the teacher and students to put together an hour talent show.

The residents in our facility really enjoyed the 3- to 5-year olds doing the ballet and tap dancing.

We were fortunate in that two of the students participating were grandchildren of one of our residents (you will probably also find this in your area). The Grandmother was so proud to see her grandchildren performing and, of course, had to brag a little (which is fine)!

It warms my heart (and will warm yours, too) to see the elderly feeling a part of the community and enjoying the children. It gives the residents something to look forward to and to talk about at dinnertime for days—it's a better topic than their aches and pains!

Use your imagination and use what resources are available in your area. Maybe it's a Tae Kwondo class, or Scouts, or a church group of children. They are out there and eager to perform—ask them!

Disney World Project for Ronald McDonald House

A gentleman came to our facility to speak to the residents about the Ronald McDonald House. His enthusiasm spilled over to our residents and they decided to make Disney World pictures of Mickey Mouse that came to us in a kit.

A dozen residents worked on the pictures of Disney characters (such as Mickey Mouse and Donald Duck) for about one month. When they were complete and framed we hired a bus and traveled to the Ronald McDonald House for a visit and to present the pictures to the staff there for gifts to children who might be staying in the house during their hospital visits. (You can paint or stitch the pictures—use any type of picture that your residents want to do.) This project gave our residents a great sense of accomplishment and pride to know they were helping young sick children.

For more information here's the website address: www.rmhc.com.

Inventor's Trivia Game

1. This man developed the cotton gin. His machine could produce 50 pounds of cotton a day.
   (Eli Whitney)
2. The inventor of the telephone. (Alexander Graham Bell)
3. This person developed the first practical steam pumping engine in 1712. (Thomas Newcome)
4. The inventor of the automatic loom to weave different patterns and fabrics in 1801. He had sold over 10,000 machines by 1812. (Joseph Marie Jacquad)
5. This person invented peanut butter. (George Washington Carver)
6. This man's reaper revolutionized farming. Many hours of manual labor were saved due to his invention in 1831. (Cyrus McCormick)
7. Who invented the first Model-T Ford? (Henry Ford)
8. This man invented the condensing steam engine in 1765, and the double-acting steam engine in 1782. (James Watt)
9. Who invented the light bulb? (Thomas Edison)
10. He invented the first telegraph system known as the Morse Code. The first city-to-city line was finished in 1844. (Samuel Morse)
11. He invented the first practical electric motor in 1829. (Joseph Henry)
12. He developed the electric battery in 1800. (Alessandro Volta)
13. This wealthy Italian sent the first radio signal across the English Channel in 1898.
    (Guglielmo Marconi)
14. He invented radar in 1935. (Robert Watson-Watt)
15. The English inventor of the picket calculator in 1972, and the home computer in 1979-88. He also invented the electric tricycle in 1985. (Clive Sinclair)
16. The inventor of the diesel engine in 1893. (Rudolf Diesel)
17. The inventor of the self-polishing cast steel plow. (John Deere)
18. The German physicist who invented a temperature scale in 1724. (Daniel Fahrenheit)
19. This popular carnival ride was invented by a bridge builder. (George Ferris)
20. He invented bi-focal glasses and also the stove. (Benjamin Franklin)
21. He is the Father of Baseball. (Alexander Cartwright)
22. The founder of a chemical company who invented the process of extracting bromine.
    (Henry Dow)
23. The man who started the first Farmer's Market. (Benjamin Bann)
24. He invented the "comfort zone" in connection with air conditioning. (Willis Carrier)
25. He invented the flexible photographic film. (George Eastman)
26. He developed the theories of relativity, which led to the invention of nuclear power 1905-1916.
    (Albert Einstein)
27. He built the first rocket in 1829. (George Stephenson)
28. The inventor of the first modern submarine in 1897. (John Holland)
29. He invented the first successful steam-powered boat in 1802. (William Symington)
30. He is responsible for the air-filled bicycle tire in 1888 and the car tire in 1906. (John Dunlop)
31. He invented the first successful jet engine in 1937. (Frank Whittle)
32. He invented the first liquid fueled rocket in 1926. (Robert Goddard)
33. The inventor of the transistor in 1947. (Walter Brattain)

34.He invented the first working television in 1926 and the first TV broadcasts in 1929.

(John Logie Baird)

35.These two brothers invented the first passenger carrying hot-air balloon in 1783.

(The Montgolfer Brothers)

36.He invented the first working submarine in 1620. (Cornelis Drebbel)

37.He invented the first printing press in 1450. (Johannes Guttenberg)

38.The inventor of the pendulum clock in 1856. (Christian Huygens)

39.He built the first rigid airship in 1900 and introduced the first commercial air service in 1910.

(Ferdinand Van Zeppelin)

40.He built the modern helicopter in 1939-41. (Igor Skiorsky)

41.He built the first accurate marine chronometer in 1763. (John Harrison)

42.He invented the first telescope in 1608. (Hans Leppershey)

43.He invented flash photography in 1851. (William Talbot)

44.He invented dynamite in 1867. He also wrote plays and poems. He left the majority of his wealth to establish the annual Nobel Prizes awarded in Sweden. (Alfred Nobel)

45.These two brothers invented the motion picture camera and projector in 1895.

(Auguste and Louis Lumiere)

46.The inventor of the first commercial frozen foods in 1929. (Clarence Birdseye)

47.The inventor of the first ballpoint pen in 1938. (Lazlo Biro)

48.He invented the first pocket transistor radio in 1957, the color video recorder in 1966, and the Walkman portable cassette player in 1979. (Akeo Morita)

49.The inventor of Velcro nylon fasteners in 1955. (George de Mestral)

50.He started the first U.S. Yo-Yo fad in 1929. (D. F. Duncan)

School Days Quiz Social

This is a good activity for a 10 a.m. morning coffee. People are usually alert and up to a challenge of word games. I suggest serving Blueberry or Peach Coffeecake and coffee.

Easy Coffeecake
Yield: 16 servings from one cake.

1	cup solid vegetable shortening
1 1/2	cups sugar
2	teaspoons lemon extract
1	teaspoon vanilla
6	eggs
2	cups flour
1	teaspoon baking powder
1	can (20 ounces) pie filling flavor of your choice

Glaze:

1	cup powdered sugar
1/2	teaspoon almond extract
1/4	teaspoon salt
3	tablespoons water

Use a Bundt pan to make the coffeecake. It will serve 16 people, or you can double it if you have a larger group. Any flavor pie filling that is a favorite of your residents can be used in the recipe—blueberry, peach, apple, etc. (Apple is my favorite!)

Preheat oven to 350 degrees. Grease and flour a Bundt pan.

In a mixing bowl, cream shortening, sugar, lemon extract, and vanilla together until fluffy. Add eggs and beat well. Add flour and baking powder and mix well.

Pour half of the dough into the bundt pan. Spoon the pie filling on top of the first layer of batter and pour remainder of batter over the filling.

Bake for 55 to 60 minutes. Cool for 5 minutes before loosening edges of cake and turning over onto the serving plate. Tap the top of the pan to be sure the coffeecake will come out of the pan smoothly. Glaze with the frosting and cool for another half-hour before serving.

October Activities

Trivia
What Do You Know About America's Past?

1. Which President was in office when the Betsy Ross flag was made?
2. What was prohibited during prohibition years?
3. Who was Harry Houdini?
4. Who was Tecumseh?
5. Where did Tecumseh live?
6. Who was General Henry Harrison?
7. In which state was Thomas Jefferson born?
8. What were some of Thomas Jefferson's accomplishments?
9. Which man rode his horse shouting, "The British are coming"?
10. What was the purpose of the Civil War?
11. Name the most prominent Confederate General in the South.
12. Who won the Civil War?
13. Name the famous youth who ran away from home to join the army and become the drummer boy.
14. What was the famous address Lincoln gave, and where was the program held where he gave the address?
15. How many minutes did it take President Lincoln to give the Gettysburg Address?
16. What was the purpose of Lincoln going to Gettysburg, Pennsylvania?
17. What was the date on which the Gettysburg Address was given?
18. Name the statesman who delivered the two and one-half hour speech at Gettysburg, Pennsylvania.
19. Who became President after President Lincoln was assassinated?
20. If the President of the U.S. commits a crime while in office what is the means of getting him out of office called?
21. What happens if a President is impeached by Congress?
22. Name an early President who Congress tried to impeach.
23. How many votes saved Andrew Jackson from being impeached?
24. What were the grounds for the impeachment proceedings against Jackson?
25. What was the name of the Secretary of War during Jackson's presidency?
26. What is the name of America's first professional baseball team?
27. What is the popular song that is connected with baseball?

28. Name two snacks associated with a baseball game.
29. What type of weather challenges did the pioneers encountered while living on the plains?
30. What type of carpets were used to cover the floors of homes of the pioneers on the plains in the late 1800s?
31. Name the large animal that roamed the prairies.
32. Name the man who killed large numbers of buffalo to feed the railroad workers.
33. What is the name of the greatest circus that toured the U.S.?
34. Name the soldier blamed for the murder of Crow men, women, and children at the Little Big Horn in 1890.
35. Name the businessman who built a steamship empire. He lived from 1794 - 1877.
36. Name the man who revolutionized the steel industry. He lived from 1835 - 1919.
37. Who founded the Standard Oil Company in 1870? He lived from 1839 - 1937.
38. Name the man who was a banker, and whose company controlled American shipping, electric power, and insurance. He owned half of the nation's railroads by 1900. He lived from 1837 1913.
39. Name the two men who invented cornflakes in 1894.
40. Name the bridge in New York state that was the longest and highest at the time it was built in 1883.
41. What is the name of the statue in New York Harbor near Ellis Island?
42. What color is the statue?
43. Name the lady most admired in her day for campaigning for peace.
44. What motto is President Teddy Roosevelt famous for?
45. Name the president in office during World War I.
46. Name the president in office during World War II.
47. What city in the U.S. is known as the city where Coca Cola was first produced?
48. Tell what happened when Coca Cola was first discovered.
49. Name two favorite gifts given to your sweetheart on Valentine's Day.
50. In the football world, what does the "Dust Bowl" mean?
51. Name the sport that developed from rugby.
52. The first football super bowl was in what year?
53. Who won the first super bowl?
54. What was the name of Franklin D. Roosevelt's plan that put people back to work?
55. In what year did television sets and fast-food restaurants come on the scene in the U.S.
56. Name the fast-food restaurant founded by two brothers in Bernardino, California. Their logo is two golden arches.
57. Name the salesman who purchased the fast-food idea from the two brothers in 1955. He opened his first franchise in Des Plaines, Illinois.
58. How many McDonald's restaurants are there in the world?
59. What American president was assassinated on November 22, 1963?
60. Where was he assassinated?

Answer Key America's Past Trivia:

1. George Washington.
2. Alcoholic beverages.
3. Greatest escape artist.
4. A young Shawnee Chief.
5. Ohio River Valley.
6. Governor of Indiana territory and President of the U.S.
7. Virginia.
8. Lawyer, politician, musician, self-taught architect, naturalist, spoke six languages, inventor, founder of the University of Virginia, President of the U.S., author of the Declaration of Independence.
9. Paul Revere.
10. To abolish slavery and bridge the gap of economic and life-style differences between the North and the South.
11. General Robert E. Lee.
12. North.
13. Johnny Clem.
14. The Gettysburg Address at Gettysburg, Pennsylvania.
15. Three.
16. To dedicate the National Cemetery at Gettysburg, Pennsylvania.
17. November 19, 1863.
18. Edward Everett.
19. Andrew Johnson.
20. Impeached.
21. He is fired from the presidency.
22. Andrew Jackson.
23. One.
24. Violation of the tenure of office. Jackson disagreed with Congress on the Secretary of War and removed him.
25. Edwin Stanton.
26. Cincinnati Red Stockings.
27. "Take Me Out to the Ballgame".
28. Peanuts and Cracker Jacks.
29. Blizzards, cold winters, drought, dust storms, prairie fires, and tornadoes.
30. Rag rugs.
31. Buffalo.
32. Buffalo Bill Cody.
33. Barnum's Greatest Show on Earth.
34. General George Custer.

35. Cornelius Vanderbilt.
36. Andrew Carnegie.
37. John D. Rockefeller.
38. John Piermont Morgan.
39. John Harvey and Will Keith Kellogg.
40. Brooklyn Bridge.
41. Statue of Liberty.
42. Green.
43. Jane Adams.
44. "Speak softly and carry a big stick."
45. Woodrow Wilson.
46. Franklin D. Roosevelt.
47. Atlanta, Georgia.
48. The cola syrup was mixed with carbonated water by accident.
49. Roses and chocolate.
50. If a team doesn't qualify for the Rose Bowl, it is said they are in the Dust Bowl.
51. Football.
52. 1967.
53. The Green Bay Packers.
54. The New Deal.
55. 1950.
56. McDonald's.
57. Ray Kroc.
58. 30,000.
59. John F. Kennedy.
60. Dallas, Texas.

The Bone Party

The Bone Party is a lot of fun for the higher functioning residents. Refer to the
August chapter page 71 to make a bone cake and serve coffee with the dessert.

I have thrown this party several times in different facilities. At one program I handed out the skeleton and we discussed the bones in our body. A resident piped up and said, "I'm wondering if we should count the ribs to learn if the skeleton is a male or female." At that point another person got into a big discussion about Adam and Eve.

There is enough information here for you to do a couple of programs if you so choose.

Have fun—it is an excellent program!

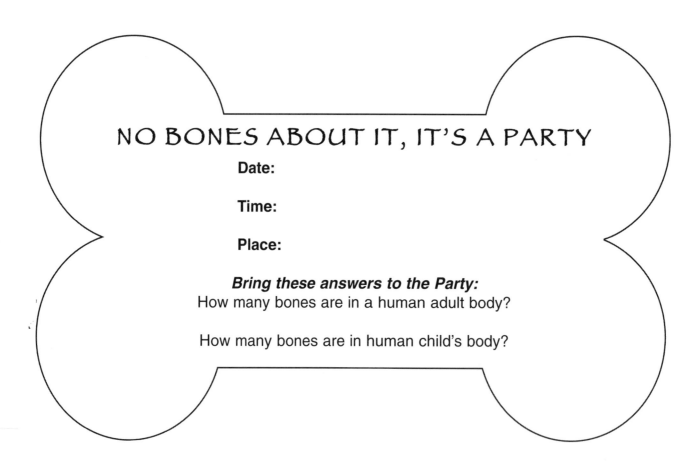

NO BONES ABOUT IT, IT'S A PARTY

Date:

Time:

Place:

Bring these answers to the Party:
How many bones are in a human adult body?

How many bones are in human child's body?

ANSWERS
How many bones are in a human adult body? *(206)*
How many bones are in human child's body? *(300)*

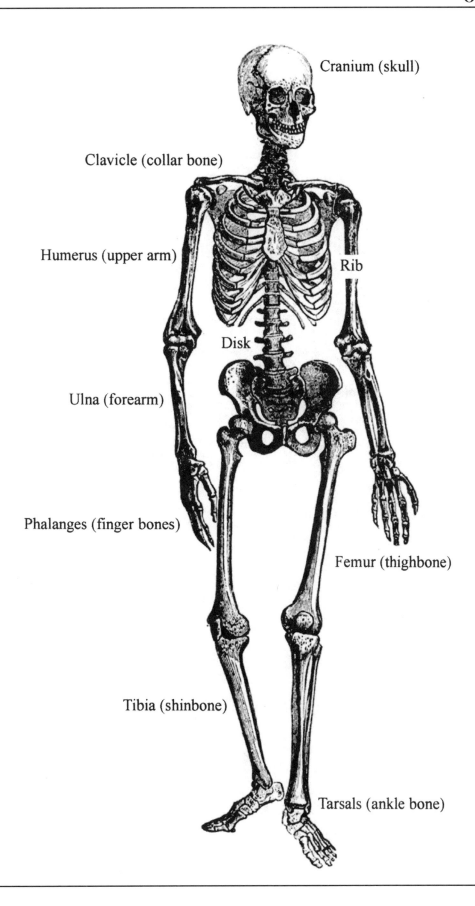

Cranium (skull)

Clavicle (collar bone)

Humerus (upper arm)

Rib

Disk

Ulna (forearm)

Phalanges (finger bones)

Femur (thighbone)

Tibia (shinbone)

Tarsals (ankle bone)

No Bones About It Trivia with Conversation and Coffee

1. If you don't use your head, you will use your _____.
2. The bone located in the elbow that makes your fingers tingle when it is hit is called the _____ bone, or the _____ bone.
3. _____ in the body helps bones and teeth to stay strong.
4. _____ is a disease found in elderly women in which bones become extremely porous.
5. The _____ is located in the head.
6. A person without character is said to have no _____ bone.
7. God created Adam, and then he used Adam's _____ to create Eve.
8. Someone who talks a lot is _____ boning.
9. A foot bone weakness named after an ancient Greek warrior in the Trojan War is called an _____ heel.
10. Milk keeps _____ healthy.
11. The spinal _____ is the backbone.
12. The _____ is the widest bone in the body.
13. The femur bone is located in the _____ and is the longest bone in the body.
14. Stapes are the innermost of _____ minute bones found in the inner ear. These bones are a little larger than rice grains.
15. _____ keeps human bones physically fit.
16. Each bone in the spinal chord is known as a _____.
17. There is _____ between bones.
18. The _____ bone is found in the skull.
19. To dance you move your feet and your _____. You hold the _____ of your partner and dance cheek to _____.
20. As children grow their bones _____ together.

No Bones About It Trivia Answer Key:

1. Feet.
2. Funny or crazy.
3. Calcium.
4. Osteoporosis.
5. Skull.
6. Back.
7. Rib.
8. Jaw.
9. Achilles'.
10. Bones.
11. Column.
12. Pelvic.
13. Leg.
14. Three.
15. Exercise.
16. Vertebra.
17. Cartilage.
18. Temporal.
19. Hips, Hands, Cheek.
20. Fuse.

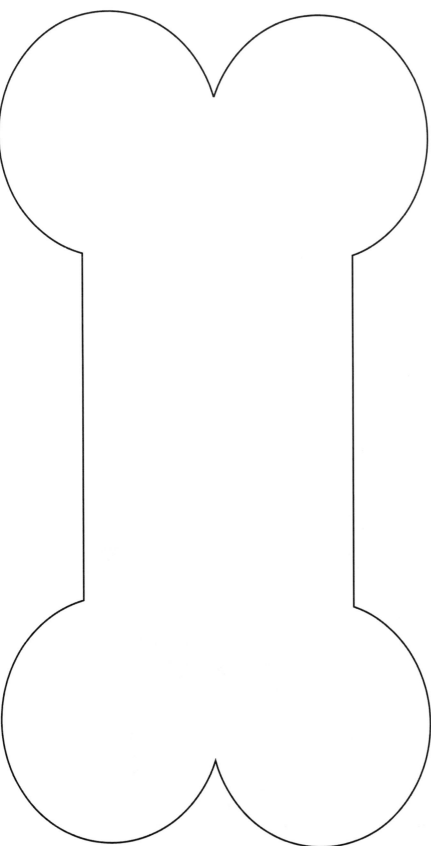

One-to-One Bone Keepsake

The purpose of this activity is to encourage your residents to use their hearing, vision, and hands while they learn new information on our bones.

Obtain the book entitled *The Glow in the Dark of the Human Skeleton* by Michael Novak, 1997. Have someone from the staff read the story aloud to the group while they work on their keepsake mementoes.

Use Crayola wet-set clay. Roll out and cut into shape of bone (left). Then let each resident make their handprint and name in the wet clay. (Or make any other design in the clay that is appropriate for your residents. You might even make a hole for small rope or raffia to go through that will act as a hanger for your keepsake.) Set "bones" aside to dry. When completed they can be given to a family member or friend as a memento from your resident.

Spelling Bee
Bones

Easy Words:

Disk	Heel	Toes	Knee
Skull	Ankle	Arm	Wrist
Forearm	Fingers	Neck	Rib
Elbow	Leg	Pelvic	
Jaw	Hip	Thigh	

Challenging Words:

Clavicle	Vertebra	Femur	Funny Bone
Ulna	Achilles' Heel	Knuckle	
Tibia	Temporal	Phalanges	
Cartilage	Hummers	Osteoporosis	
Tarsal	Cranium	Spinal Column	

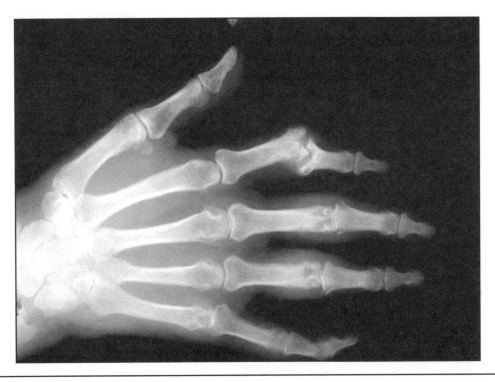

Songs that have parts of the body in the title or lyrics.

B	I	N	G	O
Peg of My Heart	Your Cheatin' Heart	Don't Let the Stars get in Your Eyes	When Your Hair has Turned to Silver	Anchors Away (Bones)
Baby Face	Five Foot Two Eyes of Blue	Ma, He's Making Eyes at Me	Chinatown (Heart and Eyes)	I Want a Girl (Just Like the Girl that Married Dear Old Dad)(Heart)
Smoke Gets in Your Eyes	When Irish Eyes are Smiling	**FREE**	Cuddle up a Little Closer, Lovey Mine (Cheek)	In the Shade of the Old Apple Tree (Eyes)
I Dream of Jeannie with the Light Brown Hair	Put Your Arms Around Me, Honey	Dancing Cheek to Cheek	Merry Widow Waltz (Feet and Heart)	Moonlight Bay (Heart)
Beautiful Brown Eyes	My Heart Belongs to Daddy	Dear Hearts and Gentle People	Pretty Baby (Dimples)	School Days (Foot)

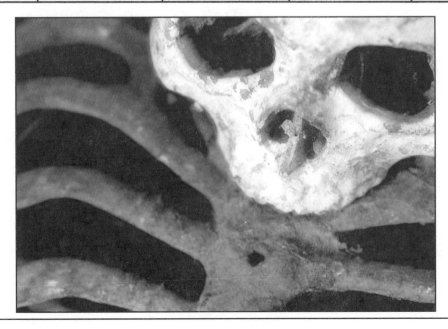

```
L S F R U P E L V I S Y H G P H K N H H V D O
E T T E R H O C H A V E R A C E P S Q X U F J
N S V I N M T N T D I K C O A U O L J N I O
N M W H I P I H T I R C A X N D N V U U M N K
R I P G H N O O P S M O O G T R B V E W H G O
E E C O O H N M S K U L L A J A L A P E N E C
F E R E W Q A B I I T L V G R Y E L I P N R I
O I A T I B I A E O O A O R A N K L E I I S E
O M N P B R N N S V E R P A E E D O Y B I I T
T A B N I I I A I T G B E C J A M T Y R I L Q
C A E G F I T B B V A O T I T A T O V B C A K
C A R E O A A A Y O W N V N H M E M V I V I I
I Q R A R P F J G O P E L N I L N A N S A N N
L A Y C E I L O C B L I Q A G A L T I O K E T
M F N U A T A N K P Q I N M H I L E C U G U E
C U U W R A T O N D A U N O P C I P G R I H I
H N T W M B B A U I C A A N U R S J A W D A W
A N N I C R R Q C B A N P R M A H S O O T G R
M Y R E N E E H K T R U I A P M M T A U G R I
S B G R E A A A L T D E B I E Q U O T G E R S
O O E A T D D O E Q B R T O E S F T H H I A T
W N S E E G F D E U I R L I N Y F I O Y T K P
E E W R A A U I H Z I N B N A R M H I A G U Q
```

Bones Word Search

HIP	FUNNY BONE	WRIST	FOREARM
PELVIS	FOOT	LEG	TOES
DISK	RIB	ANKLE	JAW
SKULL	KNUCKLE	THIGH	HEAD
FINGERS	ARM	COLLARBONE	TIBIA

```
L  S  F  R  U  P  E  L  V  I  S  Y  H  G  P  H  K  N  H  H  V  D  O
E  T  T  E  R  H  O  C  H  A  V  E  R  A  C  E  P  S  Q  X  U  F  J
N  S  V  I  N  M  T  N  T  D  T  I  K  C  O  A  U  O  L  J  N  O  F
N  M  W  H  I  P  I  H  T  I  R  C  A  X  N  D  N  V  U  U  M  I  N
R  I  P  G  H  N  O  O  P  S  M  O  O  G  T  R  B  V  E  W  H  N  O
E  E  C  O  O  H  N  M  S  K  U  L  L  A  J  A  L  A  P  E  N  G  C
F  E  R  E  W  Q  A  B  I  I  T  L  V  G  R  Y  E  L  I  P  N  E  I
O  I  A  T  I  B  I  A  E  O  O  A  O  R  A  N  K  L  E  I  I  R  E
O  M  N  P  B  R  N  N  S  V  E  R  P  A  E  E  D  O  Y  B  I  S  T
T  A  B  N  I  I  I  A  I  T  G  B  E  C  J  A  M  T  Y  R  I  L  Q
A  E  G  F  I  T  B  B  V  A  O  T  I  T  A  T  O  V  B  C  A  K
C  A  R  E  O  A  A  A  Y  O  W  N  V  N  H  M  E  M  V  I  V  I  I
I  Q  R  A  P  F  J  G  O  P  E  L  N  I  L  N  A  N  S  A  N  N
L  A  Y  C  E  I  L  O  C  B  L  Y  Q  A  H  L  T  I  O  K  E  T
M  F  N  U  A  T  A  N  K  P  Q  I  N  M  H  I  L  E  C  U  G  U  E
C  U  U  W  R  A  T  O  N  D  A  U  N  O  P  C  I  P  G  R  I  H  I
H  N  T  W  M  B  B  A  U  I  C  A  A  N  U  R  S  J  A  W  D  A  R
A  N  N  I  C  R  R  Q  C  B  A  N  P  R  M  A  H  S  O  O  T  G  I
M  Y  R  E  N  E  E  H  K  T  R  U  I  A  P  M  M  T  A  U  G  R  S
S  B  G  R  E  A  A  A  L  T  D  E  B  I  E  Q  U  O  T  G  E  R  T
O  O  E  A  T  D  D  O  E  Q  B  R  T  O  E  S  F  T  H  H  I  A
W  N  S  E  E  G  F  D  E  U  I  R  L  I  N  Y  F  I  O  Y  T  K  P
E  E  W  R  A  A  U  I  H  Z  I  N  B  N  A  R  M  H  I  A  G  U  Q
```

Bones Word Search

HIP	FUNNY BONE	WRIST	FOREARM
PELVIS	FOOT	LEG	TOES
DISK	RIB	ANKLE	JAW
SKULL	KNUCKLE	THIGH	HEAD
FINGERS	ARM	COLLARBONE	TIBIA

My Comfort Bears

See page 3 in the color section for finished project.

My Comfort Bears are wonderful for the Alzheimer's patients. They are soft and cuddly and their ears are shaped into hearts. I have many wonderful bear stories as I've traveled the country and handed out these stuffed bears. I've told the story of the bears in my *Elder Reflections for People Who Care* book on pages 12 and 13. Suggested fabrics for the bears are flannel, fleece, and cotton—or any other soft material.

These bears make great BINGO prizes!

Supplies needed:
Fabric (1 yard 36 inches wide is enough
   fabric for six bears)
Matching thread
Pinking scissors
Sewing machine
Poly foam stuffing
Needle and thread

Patterns shown pinned together.

Place right sides of the fabric together before cutting out the pattern. The pattern can be enlarged.

You can fold the fabric so you can cut four bear pieces at one time.

Lay pattern on the fabric and cut out using a pinking scissors.

Each bear requires one piece of fabric (10" x 18").

Sew left and right pieces together.

Sewing on the top (right side) of the fabric, then front and back pieces together following the edge of the pattern piece. Sew seam 1/4" from the edge around the bear.

Leave 3" along the back of the bear open for stuffing.

Stuff with poly foam.

Hand stitch the stuffing hole shut.

Note: My Comfort Bears (shown in color section on page 3) are four quarters sewn together.

Each bear requires one piece of fabric (10" x 18").

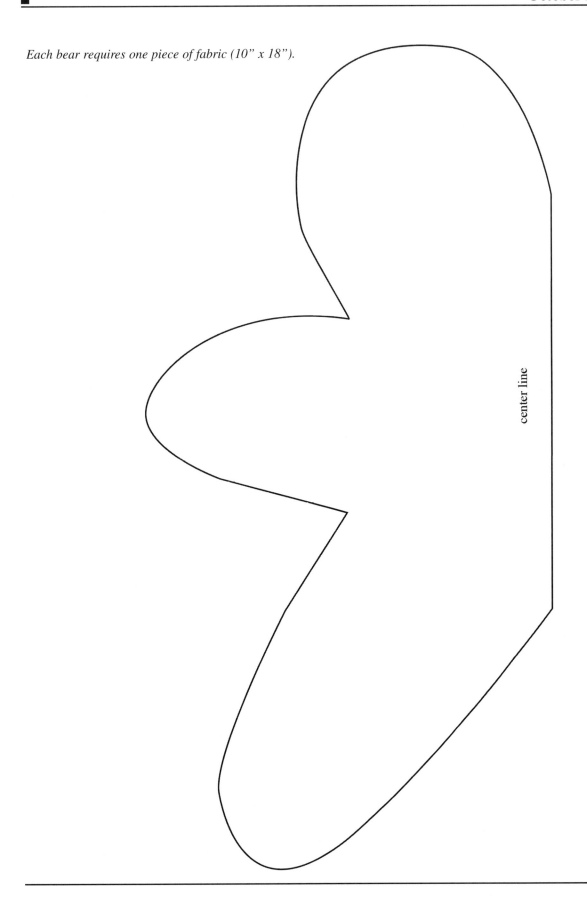

center line

Antonym Exercise

Antonyms are words with opposite meanings. Try to get the residents to tell the opposite of each word. *Webster's Dictionary* says, "A word that is opposite in meaning to another word". Example: sad is an antonym of happy.

1. hot	cold		26. freeze	melt
2. scalded	cool		27. crooked	straight
3. right	wrong		28. forward	backward
4. start	stop		29. late	early
5. shrink	stretch		30. hate	love
6. clean	dirty		31. back	front
7. wrinkled	pressed		32. cry	laugh
8. crisp	soggy		33. sickly	healthy
9. light	heavy		34. interact	withdraw
10. up	down		35. leave	stay
11. vertical	horizontal		36. help	hinder
12. rich	poor		37. rainy	sunny
13. simple	complicated		38. black	white
14. bad	good		39. sweet	sour
15. sad	happy		40. spicy	bland
16. run	walk		41. top	bottom
17. tear	mend		42. south	north
18. win	lose		43. east	west
19. slow	fast		44. closed	open
20. wet	dry		45. thin	fat
21. high	low		46. Christian	pagan
22. bass	soprano		47. lust	virtue
23. courteous	rude		48. in	out
24. empty	full		49. shiny	dull
25. large	small		50. lumpy	smooth

Famous People Trivia

1. She was a famous American movie star born in 1926 and died in 1962. Her initials are M. M.

2. He lived from 1889-1945 and was the leader of the German Nazi Party.

3. He was born in 1894 and died in 1971 and came up through the ranks of the communist party. His initials are N. K.

4. The name of the leader of Cuba. He was born in 1927 and his initials are F. C.

5. A famous French Jesuit Missionary. He was born in 1675. He joined Louis Joliet to explore and prove the Mississippi River flowed into the Gulf of Mexico. His initials are J. M.

6. The first American explorers to cross the North American continent in 1804-05.

7. What was the first name of the explorer Lewis of the Lewis and Clark team? It starts with an "M".

8. What was Clark's first name—from the Lewis and Clark team? It starts with a "W".

9. This man was born in 1451 in Genoa, Italy, and died in 1506. He was a sailor and a navigator and is given credit for discovering America.

10. A famous astronaut who was the first man to walk on the moon in 1969.

11. This man was born in 1822 and died in 1895. He discovered microscopic organisms and invented the method for pasteurization.

12. The famous record-breaking tennis player born in 1943. Her initials are B. J. K.

13. In 1943 the new war drama movie "Casablanca" was popular. Who were the stars in this movie? Their initials are: H. B. and I. B.

14. This famous gangster lived from 1899-1947. He was involved in the Valentine's Day Massacre in 1929.

15. A famous black singer who is known as the Queen of Soul.

16. This famous New Zealand opera singer was born in 1944 and appeared in 1970 in Mozart's "Marriage of Figaro".

17. This American engineer and businessman was born in 1955. By 2000 he was the richest man in the world.

18. She was the Princess of Wales. She died in a car accident in 1997.

19. This basketball player was born in 1959 and played for the Los Angeles Lakers in 1979.

20. This famous golfer was born in 1975. He was the youngest golfer to win the U.S. Masters tournament.

21. A famous explorer who reached North America five centuries before Christopher Columbus.

22. A famous nun who dedicated her life to helping the poor in India. She was born in 1910 and died in 1997.

23. He was born in 1868 and died in 1928. He was a famous Scottish architect and he designed a modern high-back chair in 1900.

24. She is famous for her violin teaching method called Montessori. She was born in 1870 and died in 1952. There are schools throughout the world teaching her method.

25. A famous comic strip in 1936 where the wife's name was Blondie. What was Blondie's husband's name?

26. He was born in 1935 in Tupelo, Mississippi, and died in 1977. He was known as the King of Rock 'n' Roll.

27. Who was Stan Laurel's partner in the motion picture comedies? His initials are O. H.

28. Can you name the four Marx brothers?

29. The comic strip character who loved spinach.

30. What singer and movie actor starred and sang the title song in "White Christmas"?

Famous People Answer Key:

1. Marilyn Monroe.
2. Adolf Hitler.
3. Nikita Khrushchev.
4. Fidel Castro.
5. Jacques Marquette.
6. Lewis and Clark.
7. Meriwether.
8. William.
9. Christopher Columbus.
10. Neil Armstrong.
11. Louis Pasteur.
12. Billie Jean King.
13. Humphrey Bogart and Ingrid Bergman.
14. Alphonse "Al" Capone.
15. Aretha Franklin.
16. Kiri Te Kanawa.
17. Bill Gates.
18. Princess Diana.
19. "Magic" Johnson.
20. "Tiger" Woods.
21. Leif Erickson.
22. Mother Teresa.
23. Charles Rennie Mackintosh.
24. Maria Montessori.
25. Dagwood.
26. Elvis Presley
27. Olive Hardy.
28. Chico, Harpo, Groucho, Zeppo.
29. Popeye.
30. "Bing" Crosby.

Christopher Columbus Program

My goal for the hour was to read the story of the Life of Christopher Columbus and ask the trivia questions. We played patriotic songs and had a sing-along. The elderly do so enjoy the music!

In the morning, or the day before, hand out the Word Search sheets and begin discussion about Columbus. You might also have maps of Genoa, Italy, and where he traveled available—or pin them up in the gathering area. Have beverages available for those who want to stay and work on the Word Search—or just discuss the topic.

The Story of Christopher Columbus

Christopher Columbus always had a passion for sailing and a real interest to discover the world. An enemy who was jealous of Columbus attached and burned his ship when he was 25 and some of Columbus' friends drowned. Christopher survived by hanging on to an oar and kicking his way to shore to save his life. He always believed things happened for a reason.

He lived in Portugal for nine years where he opened a store and sold maps. Many of his customers revealed secrets of traveling the world to him.

The king of Portugal insisted his sailors and vessels had to sail around the Cape of Africa to get to the Indies, but Columbus said there was a better way. He felt he could sail straight west to the Indies. Some people thought he was insane, but not everyone disagreed with his theory. He studied books and researched to gain incite into his theory. Columbus longed to go the Indies. He read all the books Marco Polo had written on the subject.

Even though he studied and researched, he turned to God to guide him. He was very sure that even his name "Christopher" meant "Christ bearing". Columbus felt God had led him to marry his wife in 1478.

In 1484 Columbus got the courage to ask the king of Portugal for ships to sail to the Indies and prove his theory, but the king refused. When Columbus' wife died he went to Spain along with his son, Diego, whom he placed in a monastery.

Then Columbus went to visit King Ferdinand and Queen Isabella of Spain. He had high hopes they would help him fulfill his dream.

It took one year before Columbus was able to finally meet with the Queen, and during this time he returned to Portugal to, again, appeal to the king. But, again, he was turned down. Columbus was now 41 years old and he felt the Queen of Spain would turn him down because she would think he was too old, so he traveled to France to find support for his venture. When the Queen discovered he was looking for help in France she decided to meet with Columbus because she didn't want France to gain the riches that would surely come to whomever sponsored Columbus' trip to the Indies.

Columbus sailed for the Indies with three ships on August 3, 1492. He was so happy to finally be on his way to fulfilling his dream. Due to bad weather conditions they made a stop at the Canary Islands where he picked up supplies and made ship repairs. On September 6, 1492, they pulled up anchor and headed due west to Japan (about 2,400 miles).

Columbus' crew became upset with him, as they felt so very far from home, but he had a way of calming them.

Columbus loved the stars and the sea. One day they saw four birds and Columbus felt it was a great sign. They also saw drizzling rain in the distance. Then they recognized land and they danced and cheered. On October 7, 1492, the *Nina* fired a cannon to announce they had found land. Later that night the *Pinta* also fired its cannon. They had been at sea for five weeks since leaving the Canary Islands.

Columbus named the island San Salvador. He and his crew were surprised to find naked natives, and the natives were puzzled with the dressed sailors. They didn't find Japan, but instead it was what we now call Cuba. Columbus had hoped to find gold, but the natives gave him parrots.

Columbus continued his voyage, next landing at Haiti. Here, he did find small amounts of gold (he knew the Queen expected him to bring gold).

About this time the *Santa Maria* began to leak, so they enlisted the help of the natives to remove their possessions from the ship before it sank. The king of the island gave Columbus a golden mask and gold coins. Columbus left to return to Spain, but some of the crew remained to continue to gather more gold. Columbus planned to bring another ship to get the gold the crew would find while he was gone. It was seven months from the time Columbus left Spain until he returned. The King and Queen greeted Columbus with open arms, and treated him very well for his accomplishments.

In June 1493 Columbus left Spain to return to the island of Hispaniola. This time he had seventeen ships and 1,200 men and five servants. There were also six priests to help convert the natives.

When he finally returned to Hispaniola on November 24, 1493, his 39 crewmen were dead. He learned a fierce tribe had killed his crew. The newly arrived crew became ill on the island, as they weren't used to the native's food.

As food was running low, Columbus decided to send some of the ships back to get more supplies. Twelve of the seventeen ships went back to Spain loaded with gold, cinnamon, and sixty parrots.

Then Columbus prepared to sail for China, but had to return to Spain empty-handed.

On May 30, 1498, Columbus set out on his third voyage. He dedicated this trip to the Holy Trinity. This time he found Trinidad and South America.

In 1500 Francis de Bobadilla arrived in Hispaniola to check on what was happening with the voyage. When he arrived he found seven of the crew had been hanged. He didn't investigate the problem, but just ordered Columbus to be put in chains. The only one of the crew that would do this was the cook. Columbus was returned to Spain in chains, but the Queen released him.

Columbus was suffering with arthritis, but he still yearned to sail on another voyage. The King and Queen agreed to another trip and provided four new ships and 135 men and an interpreter. Some of the rules they gave Columbus were that he could not stop in Hispaniola and could not bring back any slaves. Columbus wasn't very happy with the rules set down.

He called his fourth and final trip the "High Voyage". The fleet ran into a hurricane and only one of the fleet made it back to Spain. Columbus could not find the passageway to India. He did not realize how close he was to the passage.

Just north of Panama Columbus built a fort. The natives were very unfriendly in this area. In April of 1503 four hundred natives attached the fort and twelve Spaniards were killed.

Columbus was back on his ship sick with malaria, so he abandoned the land and headed back to Hispaniola. His ship was full of wormholes and falling apart. They traveled for two months while the crew bailed water. Finally the two ships landed in Jamaica. They were marooned here and Columbus was feeling sorry for himself, but he had to keep peace with the crew. Finally, Columbus got help to return to Spain. The Queen had died by the time he returned and Columbus, himself, was in very poor health.

It was unfortunate that Columbus had no idea of his accomplishment.

Ferdinand Magellan found the waterway that Columbus had been so close to finding, and Balboa claimed the Pacific Ocean for Spain in 1513.

Columbus had thought it was only 2,500 miles from the Canary Islands to Japan when in reality he was 10,000 miles away. In Columbus' mind the world was much smaller. He did not imagine the amount of water in the world, either.

Just think how Columbus would feel about his accomplishments if he could be here at our party today!

Christopher Columbus Trivia

1. What did Christopher Columbus' father do for a living?
2. What was the color of Christopher Columbus' hair?
3. What country was Columbus born in?
4. Why did Columbus want to take these voyages?
5. What did Columbus discover in 1492?
6. What kind of a hat did Columbus wear?
7. Did people believe the world was round or flat?
8. What three material goods did the people wish to find in the Indies in Columbus' time?
9. Which country decided to "pass" on sponsoring Columbus' exploration?
10. What were the names of Columbus' ships?
11. Which of the ships sank?
12. Why would they have cannons and muskets on Columbus' ships?
13. What were the names of Columbus' brothers and one son?
14. In which country did Christopher have a map store?
15. How many natives were dressed on the first island Columbus discovered?
16. How many voyages did Columbus make?
17. Did Christopher Columbus ever realize he had discovered America?
18. What was Columbus searching for on his trips?
19. Which of the following places was NOT one Columbus found in his travels? Haiti, Cuba, Jamaica, Dominican Republic, Portugal, South America, Canary Islands, Russia, Hispaniola.
20. How many feet in a nautical mile?

Christopher Columbus Trivia Answer Key:

1. Master weaver.
2. Red.
3. Italy.
4. To learn the secrets of the world.
5. America.
6. A red stocking cap.
7. Most believed it was flat— only a few forward-thinkers believed it was round.
8. Gold, jewels, and spices.
9. Portugal.
10. Nine, Pinta, and Santa Maria.
11. Santa Maria.
12. They needed protection from pirates and enemies.
13. Diego, Bartholomew, and his son was also named Diego.
14. Portugal.
15. They were all naked.
16. Four.
17. No.
18. Gold and spices for the Queen.
19. Russia
20. 800 feet.

```
N A N S I V A G A N C H O V I E S S O I T W A
L T I O W O T A S E N M S A M V E I L G S E E
R A I S I N S Q T A S B I I E L A B A H I L I
I P G R N E V A Y C I A H C A N N O N S C C W
C J A W E A E F N B E L L S T R V L L M B R R
E S O O H L C A N N I A L T G B C S R U A O R
P T A U Q N F I R E W O O D A O N E B S I S Y
U P T G B E A N N I M A Y O W O M A I K Q S H
S H E W N V M Y R E A N D O C A T B O E S B I
F A O S A R D I N E S O C B O M E I I T Y O N
N L I A I T O O E T A A K P M E R S N S R W K
A F E E R E E N S F T A L D P U P Q P H K S U
S H X U U H E R T O B C O T A R T U C E P G O
O O J N E L S T R O R H R B S N M I P A M E J
E U E R R E T R E D H E A T S I T T N E I R O
V R C O R N S S I A O E L T E I L S T R R C B
D G L H I N M C H D N S R Q S O A N J A R O C
L L P K I R I I A G E E E U I W V L R R O F I
L A I N R E E S O A Y P E Z I I L E M T R M B
O S B I K F E S E E L V F S Y B Q R E O S A E
T S R V A O I O T N E E D L E S N D J F N G A
O V B E O O M R P C A R G O I I N A T A J D N
P I N S L N A S L O H T I R C O G D H C E R S
```

Sailing With Columbus Word Search

PINS
KNIVES
RICE
RAISINS
CROSSBOWS
MIRRORS
SEA BISCUITS

WINE
SARDINES
HALF-HOUR GLASS
NEEDLES
HONEY
CHEESE
COMPASSES

CANNONS
MUSKETS
BELLS
WATER
ALMONDS
BEANS
SCISSORS

SALT MEAT
FIREWOOD
ANCHOVIES

```
N A N S I V A G  A N C H O V I E S  S O I T W A
L T I O  W  O T A S E  S A L T  M  V E I L G S E E
R A I S I N S  Q T A S B I I  E  L A B A H I L I
I P G R  N  E V A Y C I A H  C A N N O N S  C  C  W
C J A W  E  A E F N  B E L L S  T  R V L L  M  R  R
E S O O H L C A N N I A L T G B C  S  R U  U  A  O  R
P T A U Q N  F I R E W O O D  A O N  E  B I  S  I  S  Y
U P T G B E A N N I M A Y O W O M  A  B K  K  Q  S  H
S  H  E W N V M Y R E A N D O  C  A T  B  O E  E  S  B  O
F  A  O  S A R D I N E S  O C B  O  M E  I  I T  T  Y  O  N
N  L  I A I  T  O O E T A A K P  M  E R  S  N S  S  R  W  K
A  F  E E R E  E  N S F T A L D  P  U P  C  P H  K  S  U
S  H  X U U H E  R  T O B  C  O T  A  R T  U  C E  P  G  O
O  O  J N E L S T R O R  H  R B S  S  N M  I  P A  M  E  J
E  U  E R R E T R E D  H  E A T  S  I T  T  N E  I  R  O
V  R  C O R N S  S  I A O  N  E  S  E L T  S  R R  C  B
D  G  L H I N M  C  H D O N  E  S  R Q S  O  A N J A  O  C
L  L  P K I R I  I  A G E  E  E U I W V  A  L R R  F  I
L  A  I N R E E  S  O A Y  P E Z I I  L  E M T  R  M  B
O  S  B I K F E  S  E E L V F S Y B Q R E  O  R  S  A  E
T  S  R V A O I  O  T  N E E D L E S  N D J F  N  G  A
O V B E O O M  R  P C A R G O I I N A T A J  D  N
P I N S  L N A  S  L O H T I R C O G D H C E R  S
```

Sailing With Columbus Word Search

PINS	WINE	CANNONS	SALT MEAT
KNIVES	SARDINES	MUSKETS	FIREWOOD
RICE	HALF-HOUR GLASS	BELLS	ANCHOVIES
RAISINS	NEEDLES	WATER	
CROSSBOWS	HONEY	ALMONDS	
MIRRORS	CHEESE	BEANS	
SEA BISCUITS	COMPASSES	SCISSORS	

Health Fair Conference

This activity is a useful tool for the residents and their families. You can also get free newspaper coverage and involve your community in the project. Organize this project at least six months to a year in advance. I've found that Saturday is a good day for such an event as this. Start at 9 a.m. and end by 3:30 or 4:00 p.m.

Here's a list of possible professional health and social people to invite to your conference, it can include anyone with helpful information or activities for your residents.

1. A local fitness center to come and exercise with the group.
2. Massage therapist to do chair massage.
3. Aroma therapist.
4. Music therapist.
5. Art therapist.
6. Health care provider.
7. Doctor.
8. Geriatric social worker.
9. Representative from AARP.
10. Veterans Administration personnel.
11. Social Security personnel.
12. Someone knowledgeable about Medicare.
13. A pharmacist or pharmaceutical representative.

Of course, you may not be able to get everyone to participate, but hopefully you will get a range of individuals who will make the time interesting for your audience.

This activity is best with your higher functioning residents, but the aroma, music and art therapy, and the massage will be interesting for all.

Set up booth areas with chairs so attendees can feel comfortable as they move from area to area. But also save some open areas for the wheelchair bound residents. Set up tables so each participant will have space to show off their brochures and products.

Make a schedule and print off copies so people can plan which presentations will interest them. Take reservations so your dietary staff will know how many to plan for. Have the kitchen make up lunch boxes and have beverages available for break time in the morning and afternoon.

Start the day with a continental breakfast consisting of sweet rolls, croissants, butter and jams, donuts, juice, fruit, coffee, and tea.

You will need to ask staff, family members, and people from the community to volunteer to help with the conference.

Set aside a dining area for the breakfast and lunch. (Most of the residents will eat their regular lunch and breakfast.) The continental breakfast is for the presenters and family members.

World Food Day

October 16 is World Food Day. Nations throughout the world honor the founding of the Food and Agriculture Organization of the United Nations in 1945. This day is set aside to remind the world that millions of people go hungry every day. The first World Food Day was commemorated in 1981. One hundred fifty nations celebrate the day. Over 400 organizations in America are involved.

Schools and organizations study food and hunger programs in over 100 countries and set goals to work in their own way toward the common goal of providing food for the world.

For example, in Barbados people help farmers improve farming techniques.

Canada and the U.S. export two-thirds of all the food aid sent throughout the world.

Contact your local teacher's organization and work with them to get the students to make banners with the residents in your facility for World Food Day. You could also ask local church youth groups or Scouts to get involved. Set up a food donation project and have the children involved in collecting the donations. Your collection points can be at the school, churches, and your facility. When all the collections have been made try to have them brought to your facility so the residents can see how much has been collected, or you might get transportation and take your residents to the church or school so they can be involved in the community. (They really enjoy getting involved with the young people—it's good for both generations!)

Plan coffee and dessert as the final activity and include everyone involved in the project. Then pack up the food and deliver it to your chosen charities.

Indian Summer Party

This is a simple activity, but it creates good memories.

Webster's Dictionary defines Indian Summer as, "a period of mild, warm, hazy weather following the first frosts of late autumn."

In Wisconsin mid-October to the last week of October is a break and a tease to have warm weather again for three to five days. Leaves are falling and people are beginning to anticipate the cold of winter. As I travel to various care facilities I am always aware of how much the residents appreciate the sun.

If the weather permits, take a group outside onto the patio for morning or afternoon coffee. Do a few exercises and read some poetry to them about the Sun.

Another suggestion is to invite a local meteorologist from your radio or TV station to discuss Indian Summer with the residents.

Poetry:

The Splendid Sun
Author unknown

It is a treat to feel the rays of the sun.
The sun gives me splendid light to see birds in flight.
The sun brightens the gardens of flowers and vegetables.
The sun gives me the gift of having fun outdoors with my family.
The sun brings joy and comfort to my heart.
The sun brings outdoor events that can be enjoyed by all.

In Alaska I long for the Sun during the long, cold, winter months. But in Wisconsin I find the Sun all year 'round, on most days. It is wonderful to witness the rays of the splendid sun!

The Sun
Author unknown

The Sun brings light,
The Sun makes me feel so bright!
The Sun lets my grandson ride his bike.
Joy comes from focusing
My eyes on the Sun!

Songs to Sing with the Residents
"You are my Sunshine"
"Red Sails in the Sunset"
"When Autumn Leaves Start to Fall"
"Down by the Riverside"
"Under the Shade of the Old Apple Tree"
"Oh! Susanna"
"Red River Valley"
"She'll be Comin' 'Round the Mountain"
"St. Louis Blues"
"Sidewalks of New York"
"Take Me out to the Ballgame"
"Let the Rest of the World Go By"

Give the residents a chance to discuss their memories of Indian Summer.

One lady said she got all of her kids to help her clean the windows, then they grilled out and gathered around the table to play cards.

A man said he took his son fishing.

Others said they weren't at home because they worked when their children were in school.

The residents enjoyed the sun discussion and the music.

Family Chili Supper

The purpose of the chili supper is to have a time and purpose for families and friends to come together for a social time. Be sure to let the families know that neighbors and friends are welcome at this event. You might have a staff member available who will be happy to take any newcomers through your facility for a tour and get their name for your mailing list so they can be aware of upcoming events. It will create goodwill and residents will have an opportunity to show off their family and friends.

Menu

Chili

Cheese Cubes

Crackers

French Bread and Butter

Cookies and Brownies

Coffee, Tea, and Milk

Generally one pound of dry macaroni yields 2 to 2 1/2 pounds of cooked macaroni. Some people may not like macaroni in their chili. The following recipe with macaroni will yield 24 pounds (or 60 servings) of chili, without the macaroni you will get 22 pounds (or 50 servings) of chili. I don't add salt to my chili as you get plenty from the canned ingredients.

One loaf of French bread will serve 6 to 8 people and one box of soup crackers will serve 12 people. A four-pound tub of margarine will serve 50 people—but you might need one tub for each table.

Ask the staff and family members to contribute to the supper by bringing dessert. If you plan to do the brownies and cookies yourself, my recipes are in *Picnics, Catering on the Move* on pages 141-144 for cookies and page 120 for brownies, or make the Peanut Butter Honey Cookies on page 183 of this book.

Family Chili

Yield: 40 to 50 servings.

1	pound uncooked elbow macaroni, optional
6	pounds ground chuck
2	medium onions, diced
4	quarts tomato juice
6	pounds canned diced tomatoes with juice
6	pounds mild chili beans with sauce
2	cans (15 ounces each) kidney beans, drained
2	cans (15 ounces each) black beans, drained
2	cans (15 ounces each) great northern beans, drained
1	tablespoon garlic powder
3	tablespoons cumin
4	tablespoons chili powder

Brown the meat with the onions and drain well.

Cook macaroni in a large saucepan (add 2 teaspoons olive oil to the water, bring to a boil, add macaroni and cook until tender. Drain and rinse. Reserve and add to chili last).

Place browned meat and onion in large stockpot and add all the other ingredients except the macaroni. Stir together and simmer for one hour. Chili tastes best if you cook it the day before and then reheat it at serving time. If you want the macaroni add it during the reheating process.

Granny's Soup Kitchen

Corn Harvest Tasting Day

Corn Chowder was made with salt pork, hot milk, and fresh corn. It was served at least once a week because it was easy on the budget and very nutritious.

Chicken Corn Chowder

Yield: 18 to 20 servings.

2	pounds chicken breasts, cubed
2	cups water
2	teaspoons olive oil
1	medium onion, diced
1	quart 99% fat-free chicken stock
1/2	gallon whole milk
2	pounds frozen corn, thawed
1	red pepper, diced
1	green pepper, diced
1	cup diced celery
1	package (3/4 ounce) fresh cilantro leaves, chopped
2	teaspoons garlic pepper
2	teaspoons cumin

Thickener:

1 can (14 ounces) chicken stock
7 tablespoons cornstarch (almost 1/2 cup)

Sauté chicken in water and oil until cooked through. Drain chicken and place in a large stockpot add the onion, chicken stock, milk, corn, red and green pepper, celery, cilantro leaves, garlic pepper, and cumin. Cook over low heat for 45 minutes to one hour.

To thicken, stir cornstarch into the can of chicken stock until blended well and smooth. Bring soup to a boil and slowly add the thickener, stirring constantly. Serve immediately.

Corn Fritter Pie

Yield: 1 9-inch deep-dish pie. 8 servings.

1 1/2   cups canned corn, drained
1/2   teaspoon pepper
1/2   teaspoon salt
3/4   cup flour
2   teaspoons baking powder
3   eggs, slightly beaten

Mix corn, pepper, salt, flour, baking powder, and eggs.

Grease deep-dish pie pan. Pour dough into pan and bake at 400 degrees for 20 to 30 minutes, or until a toothpick comes out clean. Serve warm with butter and honey.

Creamed Corn

Yield: 4 or 5 servings.

1   can (14.75 ounces) cream-style sweet corn
1   egg, beaten well
1/2   teaspoon salt
1/2   teaspoon garlic pepper
1/2   cup Italian-style bread crumbs
1   tablespoon butter, melted

Topping:

1/4   cup Italian-style bread crumbs

Mix egg, salt, and garlic pepper into the corn, add 1/2 cup bread crumbs and melted butter. Mix well. Top with the additional 1/4 cup bread crumbs.

Cover and bake at 350 degrees for 20 to 30 minutes, or until bubbly.

Popovers

Yield: 8 servings.

1 1/2   cups flour
1/4   teaspoon salt
3   eggs
1 1/2   cup whole milk

Note: Popovers taste best warm. If you need to make them a day ahead, place back into custard cups or muffin tins and reheat in a 300- to 350-degree oven for 5 minutes. Popovers do not need to be refrigerated. I like the popovers with the Corn Chowder soup.

Mix flour and salt together. Beat eggs and add to milk. Gradually stir the liquid mixture into the flour mixture until you have a smooth batter, then beat thoroughly with a mixer.

Fill greased custard cups or muffin tins a little over half-full.

Bake in a very hot oven (450 degrees) for 15 minutes, then reduce temperature to 350 degrees and continue to bake for 20 to 30 minutes more. Serve warm with butter and honey.

✧

Bee Sweet Party

Gather the residents to make one or two recipes made with honey. Have a bake sale so the residents will have quarters for BINGO, or give the money to a worthy cause of their choice, such as the Cancer Society or Arthritis Foundation. Let the residents vote on where to make the donation.

Tell the story of honey and work on the Honey Word Search. Music you can work into the program includes: "Put Your Arms Around Me, Honey" and "Be My Honey". There is enough material included here for several days' activities.

The Story of Honey

Out of a total of 20,000 species of bees, only five honeybee species exist in the entire world. Bees are vegetarian. They are a valuable source of honey and wax.

Beehives contain three types of bees: Queen, Drone, and Worker.

Worker bees are small female bees that can't lay eggs. Worker bees protect the hive and store the honey in the cone. They will completely cover the cone until all the cells are filled.

The male bees are the drones.

The Queen bee stays in the hive. The worker bees always surround the Queen to protect her. The Queen only leaves the hive to mate and then she will return to lay her eggs in the center part of the honeycomb. She is capable of laying hundreds of eggs daily—one egg per cell. Cells are the size of a pin. It takes three days for the eggs to grow into larvae that look like soft, white worms. The larvae then change into a pupa. A bee is fully grown in three weeks and then it chews its way through the wax and emerges. It takes four days for the bee's body to become hard. A Queen bee is grown in a larger cell, thus being a larger bee when hatched. When a larger bee is in the larva stage the worker bees feed the larva with royal jelly. It takes two weeks for the Queen to grow before hatching. Once a new Queen is hatched the old Queen exits with some of the worker bees and finds a new home. The group of bees is called a swarm and the worker bees surround the Queen and protect her until they find a new home.

My mother had an expression she used with us when she wanted us to do our homework. If we were dilly-dallying and not getting our work done she would say, "What do you children think you are? Queen bees? Now get rolling and get this work done."

My mother-in-law came to visit us one time and we took her to the Proud Popover Restaurant. They served honey with their popovers and she just had to purchase one of their honey dippers to take home to show her friends.

The people of Africa especially value the honey when there are food shortages.

Honey is known as far back in history as 300 A.D. The Bible speaks of the land of milk and honey.

Australia, Canada, and Mexico are the major exporters of honey. The yearly crop is worth millions of dollars.

In apple orchard and fruit farm country farmers place hives in their orchards. A person having bees is called a beekeeper. In Europe beekeepers decorated their beehives. Folklore says that if a beekeeper died a family member would go tell the bees about the death so they could prepare for a new keeper.

Bee's wax is used in candles and lipstick.

Bees have enemies. In West Africa the carmine bee-eaters kill thousands of bees. In the Kalahari Desert in southern Africa the honey badger will break open the nests and eat the larvae and honey. The honey badger also lives in India. Bears are also very fond of honey.

Honey was used to cure ailments and Kings kept honey at their bedside for good health. Honey contains minerals, but very few vitamins. Roman doctors believed honey was a good laxative. Babylonians kept bees in their gardens and ate a mixture of rich cream mixed with flour, dates, sesame seeds, and honey.

There are many honey recipes. Coconut Shrimp is dipped into honey, rolled in coconut, and then baked or fried. Duck is very tasty with honey, orange juice, and fresh ginger root. There are many tasty salad dressings made with honey. Honey-glazed ham is a Christmas favorite. Crepes and popovers are served with honey. The Greek pastry Baklava is made with filo dough, nuts, and honey. Honey is an ingredient in candies such as divinity and fudge.

Some varieties of honey are: single flower, multi-flower, honey dew, blended honey, creamy honey, runny honey, crunchy honey, and honey in the comb.

People enjoy peanut butter and honey. I have a friend who was a hot-lunch cook at school and she tells of receiving government subsidies of both peanut butter and honey. She couldn't figure out how to get the kids to eat the honey, so she mixed it with the peanut butter and made up sandwiches. Parents called her asking for the peanut butter sandwich secret, but she never shared the proportions. She is 90 and she has never shared the secret. I believe she will take it with her to her grave.

Recipes:

Honey Peanut Butter Cookies

Yield: 3 1/2 dozen cookies.

1/2	cup shortening
1/2	cup butter, softened
1/2	cup brown sugar
1/2	cup white sugar
1/2	cup honey
2	eggs
1	cup peanut butter
1/2	teaspoon salt
1	teaspoon baking soda
4	cups flour
1	teaspoon vanilla

Cream shortening, butter, brown and white sugar, and beat. Add honey and eggs and beat again. Add peanut butter and beat again. Mix salt and baking soda with flour. Add one cup at a time to the creamed mixture and beat until smooth. Stir in vanilla. Form dough into 2-inch balls and press down with a fork.

Place 12 cookies on a 14 x 17-inch lightly greased cookie sheet, sprinkle sugar on cookie tops if you wish. Bake at 350 degrees for 8 to 10 minutes.

Honey Pumpkin Ice Box Pie

Yield: 8 servings.

1	9-inch deep-dish pie crust
8	ounces cream cheese
1	cup pumpkin
1/2	cup honey
1/2	cup brown sugar
1/2	cup evaporated fat-free milk
3/4	teaspoon cinnamon
1/2	teaspoon cloves
1/2	teaspoon ginger
1/2	teaspoon salt
1	envelope unflavored gelatin
1/4	cup cold water

Prick the pie crust with a fork to prevent blisters while it bakes and bake at 400 degrees for 8 to 10 minutes, or until golden brown.

Beat cream cheese until smooth and add pumpkin and honey and beat again. Add brown sugar, mixing again. Add evaporated milk and spices, mixing again.

Mix the unflavored gelatin and cold water in a small bowl and let set for 2 minutes, then microwave for 40 seconds, cool slightly and add to pumpkin mixture. Beat until smooth.

Pour mixture into baked pie crust. Refrigerate until set. Serve with whipped cream or mix 3/4 cup chocolate sauce with 1/2 cup coconut and spread over the top of the pie. Top with 3/4 to 1 cup nuts on top of pie. Garnish each slice with a maraschino cherry with a stem.

Honey Cinnamon Pecan Pie

Yield: 8 servings.

1	9-inch deep-dish pie crust
1/2	cup honey
1/4	cup white sugar
1/4	cup brown sugar
3	eggs, beaten
1/4	cup butter, melted and cooled slightly
1	teaspoon vanilla
1/2	teaspoon cinnamon
1 1/4	cup whole pecans

Mix honey and both sugars together. Add eggs and beat. Add butter, vanilla, and cinnamon and beat. Fold in pecans carefully so as not to break them.

Pour into unbaked pie shell and bake at 350 degrees for 55 to 60 minutes, or until a knife inserted comes out clean.

Note: This Chocolate Honey Sauce is very tasty on ice cream and in milk shakes.

Chocolate Honey Sauce

Yield: 1 1/2 pint.

1	package (12 ounces) chocolate chips
1	tablespoon water
1	cup honey
1	cup evaporated milk at room temperature
1	teaspoon vanilla

Add water to the chocolate chips and microwave for 1 to 2 minutes until chips melt. Remove from microwave and stir to blend. Add honey, evaporated milk, and vanilla and stir again until well blended. Store in refrigerator in two airtight pint jars.

Honey Apple Loaf Cake

Yield: 1 loaf.

2	cups flour
3	teaspoons baking powder
3/4	teaspoon salt
4	tablespoons butter
1/2	cup honey plus 1/3 cup (added at one time to recipe)
1	egg
1	cup evaporated milk
3	Granny Smith apples, peeled and thinly sliced
1	teaspoon cinnamon
1	teaspoon lemon juice
2	teaspoons plus 3 tablespoons sugar (divided)

Glaze:

1 1/2	teaspoons softened butter
1	teaspoon cream cheese
1 1/2	cups powdered sugar
1/2	teaspoon almond flavoring
1	tablespoon honey
2	tablespoons evaporated milk
1/8	teaspoon salt

Grease loaf pan.

Mix the flour, baking powder, and salt. Mix the butter, honey, and evaporated milk. Add to the flour mixture. Mix well.

Spread half of the dough into the bottom of the loaf pan and sprinkle 2 teaspoons of sugar over the dough.

Toss apple slices in lemon juice and pat dry. Mix together cinnamon and 3 tablespoons of sugar, add to apples and toss to coat. Place apple slices in a row down into the dough mixture. Cover the apples with the remaining dough mixture.

Bake at 375 degrees for 45 to 60 minutes, or until a toothpick comes out clean. Cool.

Prepare the glaze by mixing the butter and cream cheese. Add the powdered sugar and almond flavoring, honey, evaporated milk, and salt and beat until smooth. Spread over the top of the cake loaf before serving.

Microwave Honey Fudge

Yield: 16 to 20 pieces.

1	pound powdered sugar
1/2	cup cocoa
1/4	cup evaporated milk
2	tablespoons honey
6	tablespoons butter
1	teaspoon vanilla
1/2	cup pecans (optional)

Optional Topping for Fudge:

1	cup white chocolate chips
2	tablespoons evaporated milk
1/2	teaspoon vanilla
1/2	cup chopped pecans (optional)

Place powdered sugar, cocoa, evaporated milk, honey, and butter in a microwave bowl. Do not stir. Microwave for 2 1/2 minutes. Beat with a mixer until smooth and creamy. Add the vanilla and stir.

Line the bottom and sides of an 8 x 8-inch square pan with waxed paper and butter the bottom and sides of the waxed paper. Spread the fudge in the pan.

Topping:

Add evaporated milk to the white chocolate chips and microwave for 1 to 2 minutes, or until the chocolate melts. Wire whip to a smooth consistency. Add the vanilla, mix and spread over the fudge in the pan. Sprinkle pecans over the top if you wish.

Place the fudge in the freezer for 10 minutes. Remove and cut into pieces.

Note: If you choose not to have the topping, then stir pecans into the fudge after adding the vanilla.

References:
Honey from Hive to Honey Pot by Sue Style. 1993.
This book takes you through the history of honey and has many wonderful recipes. I found it at my local library.

```
H O N E Y S B R V W L M B R T C D O C E O E Q
I T R E T S R S W A R M A O B E E K E E P E R
V S H I O V B O N S B S I S E L K P M I V C I
E M O R P I U O M P U P A S D L L D P W O B E
R I N H A N M A T B O E S B I C O T A I T N I
E E E N T I B M E I I T C O L O N Y S N R E W
F E Y L A I L E R F L Y I N G E A T S E E I N
O I C R P G E U P Q P H K S U E L T E H E E A
O M O I J A B R T U C E P G O S R Q S Q T E S
N A M C S F E N M I P A M E J R E V I B R W S
E G B E Q A E I T T N E I R Y O E E I N U O T
C A S P U T G R L S T R R C N C F G Y A N R Y
T Q T U E E W O T N J A R O R K D E E I K K S
A A Y F E O S W V I R R O F O F G T O R S E M
R F N N N I A I L E L I Z E H A I A B U H R E
G A N A B E E B Q R E Q S A K C V R C E L B L
U I P O L L I N A T I O N G N E A I I R A E L
I N O O O J I I N A T A J D I S R A C R O E Y
D Y L E U E C O G D H C E R A H C N E I E N L
E I L V·R C E S S O M E A D O W S T A I T C E
O O E D G L V E I L G S E E A L T G N R P O A
E N N L L P L A B A H I L I O O D A S K L C H
E R S L A I N N O N S C C W A Y O W V A N N H
```

Honey Bee Word Search

FLYING	TREE TRUNKS	HONEYCOMB	MEADOW
WORKER BEE	PUPA	ROCK FACES	POLLEN
SWARM	CELL	BEEKEEPER	NECTAR GUIDE
NASTY SMELL	QUEEN BEE	HIVE	HONEY
VEGETARIAN	POLLINATION	FERTILIZE	
WASP	BUMBLEBEE	COLONY	

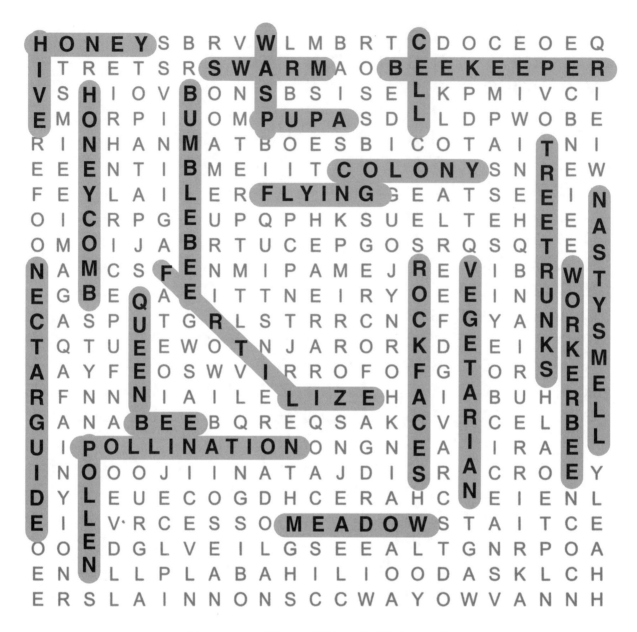

Honey Bee Word Search

FLYING	TREE TRUNKS	HONEYCOMB	MEADOW
WORKER BEE	PUPA	ROCK FACES	POLLEN
SWARM	CELL	BEEKEEPER	NECTAR GUIDE
NASTY SMELL	QUEEN BEE	HIVE	HONEY
VEGETARIAN	POLLINATION	FERTILIZE	
WASP	BUMBLEBEE	COLONY	

Halloween with Children

Invite young children from your school or church to the care facility and suggest they come dressed in their Halloween costumes. Be sure to find out from their teacher how many will be attending.

The residents met ahead of the program and stuffed Halloween bags with candy and an apple. (We used brown lunch bags.)

Trace and cut out pumpkin shapes from orange construction paper and decorate them with markers or crayons. Punch a hole in the top of the pumpkin and thread a black ribbon through the hole. Use this cute tag to tie the bag shut.

Or here's another Treat suggestion:

Take clear plastic gloves and fill them with popped popcorn. Tie the glove top shut with the pumpkin tag or black and orange ribbon. Place a spider ring on one of the fingers of the glove. The kids will love the spider rings! (See page 4 in color section.)

The residents should be waiting in the meeting room when the children arrive. Work with the teacher ahead of time to have the children make cards to give to the residents. Then encourage the residents and children to exchange treats and cards.

A sing-along always works well in these inter-generational programs. Also invite the children to present their own songs or a play or poems for the elders.

The residents talked for days about the children and how cute the costumes were.

Pumpkin Centerpiece

See finished centerpiece on page 5 of color section.

While attending an Alzheimer's Association conference in Canton, Ohio, I met Trudy. She was the chairman of the conference and we had a great time.

I shared my activity programs with the attendees and I met many wonderful people. We had a very memorable experience.

Trudy had made the centerpieces for the tables at the conference and they were so nice I asked if I could have one to take back with me.

This type of centerpiece is especially nice on a table where people are carrying on a conversation as the centerpiece is low and people around the table can see over it.

Trudy had gotten the ceramic pumpkins and a bag of leaves at a discount store. You will make three rows of leaves around the pumpkin. Fourteen large leaves make the bottom row, row two has ten large leaves, and the final row has ten smaller leaves. Glue the rows of leaves into a wreath shape and glue the wreath onto the pumpkin with a hot glue gun. If your pumpkin has a stem, glue some leaves on to it. If it doesn't have a stem, make one out of grapevine.

Pumpkin Heart Pin Art Project
for Higher Functioning Residents

See page 4 in the color section for finished project.

Supplies needed:

Tacky glue or hot glue.
Hearts 2 inches in diameter, made of wood.
Paint brushes.
Acrylic paint in orange, green, and black.
Black marker to make face.
Pin back.

Use patterns on next page to copy shapes.

Place damp paper toweling on the table to limit the heart from sliding while it is being painted.

Paint the heart and make facial features with the marker. When dry glue on the pin back.

Pumpkin Pin Art Project for
Lower Functioning Residents

See page 4 in the color section for finished project.

Supplies needed:

Green fun foam.
Orange fun foam.
Black fun foam.
Black marker.
Multi-purpose glue.
Pin back.
Hot glue

Lay out pattern and cut pieces for the pumpkin, stem, and mouth using the appropriate color of foam for each pattern.

Glue stem to the top of the pumpkin and glue the mouth and nose to form a face. Mark the eyes with a marker.

Glue on pin back—and you're done!

Pumpkin (Upside Down) Heart Pin Pattern
For Higher Functioning Patients

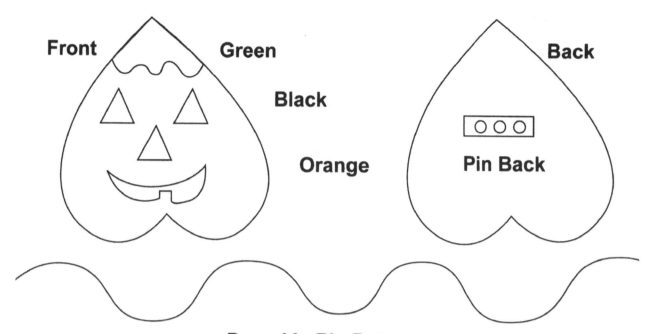

Front   **Green**

Black

Orange

Back

Pin Back

Pumpkin Pin Pattern
For Lower Functioning Patients

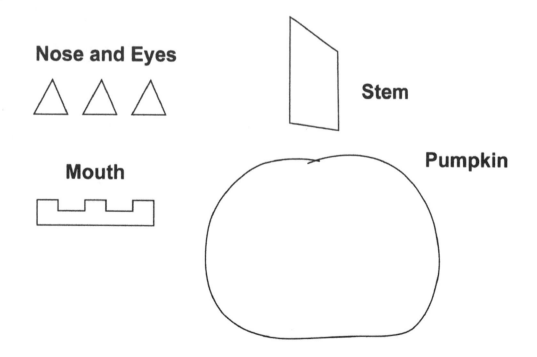

Nose and Eyes

Stem

Mouth

Pumpkin

Halloween Magnet

See page 4 in the color section for the finished project.

This is an excellent project for Independent Living residents. We made and sold them at our craft fair. This magnet looks great on your refrigerator at Halloween time.

Supplies needed:

4 tongue depressors (1 for the cat and 3 for the ghosts)

Orange felt for the pumpkin.

Green felt for the stem.

Green ribbon 1/8-inch wide for the bow.

1 black pipe cleaner for ears and tail of the cat.

1 miniature pink ball for the cat's nose.

Black and white craft paint.

Black marker.

White marker.

Multi-purpose glue.

Magnet strip one inch long and one-half inch wide.

Suppliles. Be sure to glue the magnet to the back of the tallest stick.

Lay out 3 tongue depressors and cut them to the lengths of the ghost patterns. Paint the depressors white for the ghosts on front and back (give them two coats of paint, as it soaks in). Using the marker, make 2 dots for eyes on the ghosts.

Cut the 4th tongue depressor the correct length for the cat from the pattern. Paint both sides of the depressor black (also give this two coats of paint). Using a white marker, or the white paint, make the cat's eyes. Glue the pink ball on for the nose.

When the painting is complete for the ghosts and cat glue the magnet backs on them 1/2 inch from the top.

See the diagram on how to glue the 3 1/8-inch and 2 1/2-inch ghosts onto the tallest ghost (3 3/4 inch) on page 193.

Glue the ears and tail onto the cat and then glue the cat on top of the ghosts (see the diagram).

Trace the pumpkin pattern and cut it out from orange felt, the stem from green felt, and the bow from the green ribbon. Now assemble the pumpkin with glue and glue the pumpkin to the stick ghosts and cat.

Halloween Magnet

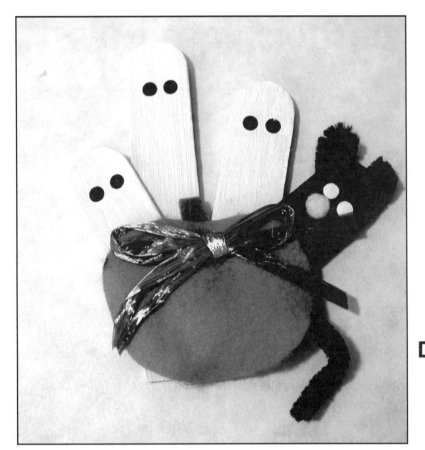

**Size
of
Tongue
Depressor**

G
H
O
S
T

3 3/4"

G
H
O
S
T

3 1/8"

G
H
O
S
T

2 1/2"

C
A
T

2 1/4"

November Activities

Granny's Soup Kitchen
Squash Soups

Spaghetti Squash Soup

Yield: 18 to 20 servings.

1	large spaghetti squash
2	cans (14 ounces each) onion seasoned 99% fat-free beef broth
1	quart tomato or vegetable juice
2	jars (26 ounces each) traditional spaghetti sauce
2	cans (14.5 ounces each) diced tomatoes with juice
1	package (38 ounces) ready-to-serve 1/2-ounce Italian-style meatballs
2	bunches scallions with tops, chopped
2	leeks, sliced into ringlets
1	package (8 ounces) sliced mushrooms
1	package (3/4 ounce) fresh basil, minced
2	tablespoons minced garlic
2	tablespoons dried rosemary
1	teaspoon black pepper
1	cup Marsala cooking wine
2	packages (9 ounces each) fresh reduced-fat cheese ravioli
2	teaspoons olive oil

To prepare spaghetti squash:

I find spaghetti squash very interesting. The outside skin is very stiff and the cavity is filled with seeds and string like spaghetti. Always cut the squash lengthwise and remove the seeds. Fill a large pan half full of water and place the squash face down in the water. Bring to a boil and boil for 10 to 12 minutes, or until the squash is tender. You can also microwave the squash if you wish. Microwave for 8 to 10 minutes, remove from microwave and when cooled remove the outer skin. When you do this, the squash will shred into spaghetti-like strings.

Note: I purchase ready-made half-ounce meatballs to speed up the preparation time of this soup. You can cut the meatballs in half, but I like them whole. Purchase ravioli in the dairy department, or the frozen food's section of your supermarket (you can omit the ravioli if you are watching your carbo -

hydrates). I use 99% fat-free onion seasoned beef broth, but you can use plain beef broth if you wish. The Marsala cooking wine in this recipe is optional, and you may **use tomato juice instead of vegetable juice***, but it is less spicy. The elderly may like the less spicy taste of tomato juice. This is a very hearty and filling soup.*

Prepare squash according to method in introduction.

Using a large stockpot, add beef broth, diced tomatoes, tomato or vegetable juice, spaghetti sauce, meatballs, scallions, leeks, mushrooms, and basil, garlic, rosemary, and black pepper. Mix together well and then add the squash. (You may need to divide the soup into two pots at this time.) Cook over medium heat for 1/2 hour and then reduce heat to low, add wine and continue cooking for 1 1/2 hours. Stir occasionally to prevent sticking.

Before serving bring water and olive oil to a boil in a medium saucepan and cook the ravioli until tender. Drain and rinse and add ravioli to the soup (if you have two pots, divide the ravioli evenly between the two.)

Serve with crackers and French bread.

Note: You can cut the size of this Butternut Squash Soup in half and it will turn out just fine. The Butternut flavor is enhanced with apple juice, chicken stock, and milk or cream. I prefer to not use wine in this soup as it gives it a very different taste. This is a very rich soup. You can use 2% milk, half and half, or whipping cream (don't whip it). The 2% milk will be best if you're watching you diet.

Butternut Squash Soup
Yield: 26 to 28 servings.

4	tablespoons butter
2	butternut squash (4 pounds each) peeled and chopped
2	tablespoons garlic
1	bunch scallions with tops, chopped
2	pounds boneless, skinless, chicken breast tenders
2	cups milk (2% or half and half)
1	medium onion, diced
2	cans (14 ounces each) 99% fat-free chicken broth
4	cups apple juice
4	Granny Smith apples, peeled, cored, and diced
2	teaspoons allspice
1	teaspoon cinnamon
2	teaspoons pepper

Garnish:

1	apple slice per serving
	toasted almonds

Melt the butter in 2 large skillets and divide the following ingredients between the two. Add squash, garlic, scallions, and onion, and sauté until slightly cooked.

Add 1/2 cup of the chicken stock to a fry pan and cook the chicken tenders. When cooked, cut into small pieces and divide the cooked chicken between two crockpots, add the squash mixture to the crockpots and mix together.

Add the apple juice, milk, and remainder of the chicken broth equally to the two crockpots and mix thoroughly. Add the allspice, cinnamon, and pepper.

Cook on low heat for 4 to 5 hours.

When ready to serve, garnish each bowl with an apple slice and toasted almonds and serve with cranberry nut bread (recipe follows). Or serve the Buttermilk Biscuits (recipe follows).

Cranberry-Orange Bread

Yield: 1 loaf.

2	cups flour
1/2	teaspoon salt
1 1/2	teaspoons baking powder
1/2	teaspoon baking soda
1/3	cup shortening
1	cup sugar
3/4	cup orange juice
1	egg
1/2	cup chopped pecans
1	cup raw cranberries

Note: You may substitute blueberries for cranberries.

Preheat oven to 350 degrees. Grease a 9 x 5 x 3-inch loaf pan.

Cut cranberries in half.

Combine flour, salt, baking powder, and baking soda. Cut the shortening into the flour mixture until it is fine particles. Add the sugar and mix well. Stir in the nuts and cranberries.

Mix the orange juice and beaten egg together and add to the dry mixture, combining with a folding motion just until the dry ingredients are moist.

Pour into the greased and floured loaf pan and bake for 45 to 60 minutes, or until a toothpick comes out clean.

Granny's Old-Fashioned Buttermilk Biscuits

Yield: 9 to 12 servings.

For instant mashed potatoes used in biscuit recipe:

2/3	cup water
1/8	teaspoon salt
1	tablespoon butter
1/4	cup milk (either 2% or whole)
2/3	cup instant potato flakes

My grandmother used her leftover mashed potatoes to make these delicious biscuits. I just use instant mashed potatoes to save time and for convenience.

Heat water, butter, and salt just to boiling. Add the cold milk and stir in the potato flakes until moistened. Let stand until the liquid is absorbed.

Biscuits:

2	cups flour
2	teaspoons baking powder
1/2	teaspoon baking soda
3	tablespoons sugar
1	cup buttermilk
1	tablespoon plus 1 1/2 teaspoons butter, melted and slightly cooled
1	cup cooked instant mashed potatoes, warm

Preheat oven to 400 degrees.

Combine flour, baking powder, baking soda, and sugar in a large mixing bowl. Mix in buttermilk, butter, and potatoes.

Drop batter onto a non-stick cookie sheet to form biscuits.

Bake 15 minutes or until lightly brown. Test with a toothpick for doneness.

Serve warm with butter and honey.

```
S Y H G P W N J S A N D W I C H D A Y R N N I
V E T E R A N S D A Y V B C A K B N R I I A B
F I K C L H T A M E M V I V I I E G E I T M Y
R I A X E A V I L N A N S A N N R E B A A I G
M A R G N B O G A L T I O K E T R A E P F S C
U L S S N Y O H U L S C U G U E Y C N I P C K
T L T G T E B P C Y P A R I H I N U L T R H N
A S I A E F P U R S F A I D A W U W I A E I U
Z O R R F E L M A H S A O N G R T W C B S E C
A U U M O S Q I M M T A W G T I N I H R I F K
U L P I O T B E G U O T G K R S R E T E D N L
N S S S T I T E S H T H H I E T D R E A E I E
G D U T C V T N Y F T O Y T K S E A R D N G E
D A N I C A Q A R M H I A G U Q D E Y G T H H
A Y D C I L U H K N H H N D O E W A A A K T I
I U A E L A Z T P S Q X U A J F R U Y E E H A
N A Y D M F E L E C T I O N B T E R H O N T D
G N P A C U N D N V U U M N K A I N M T N T I
A U I Y H N T R B V E W H G O W L I P I E P S
R E B I ' A N J A L A P E N E C P G L N O D S K
D R T H A N K S G I V I N G I C O O O N Y I I
B R L I S B A N M I C K E Y M O U S E O B E O
I N B N O Q E E D O Y B I I T A T I B I N S C
```

Famous Dates in November Word Search

VETERANS DAY	MICKEY MOUSE	REBENLICHTER
ALL SAINTS' DAY	MISCHIEF NIGHT	STIR UP SUNDAY
TAZAUNGDAING	ARMISTICE DAY	FIRST FLIGHT IN A BALLOON
THANKSGIVING	GUY FAWKES DAY	PRESIDENT KENNEDY
SANDWICH DAY	HABYE FESTIVAL	
ALL SOULS' DAY	ELECTION	

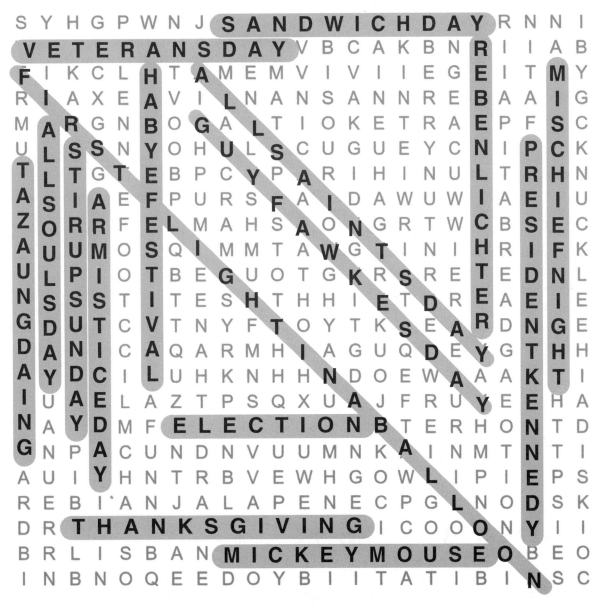

Famous Dates in November Word Search

VETERANS DAY

ALL SAINTS' DAY

TAZAUNGDAING

THANKSGIVING

SANDWICH DAY

ALL SOULS' DAY

MICKEY MOUSE

MISCHIEF NIGHT

ARMISTICE DAY

GUY FAWKES DAY

HABYE FESTIVAL

ELECTION

REBENLICHTER

STIR UP SUNDAY

FIRST FLIGHT IN A BALLOON

PRESIDENT KENNEDY

National Sandwich Day

I presented this program in November. The residents enjoyed watching me assemble a Dagwood Sandwich. I used square sourdough buns and used butter, mustard, mayonnaise, ham, turkey, roast beef, Swiss cheese, lettuce, tomatoes, pickles, pepper rings, and black olives as ingredients. I let each resident choose which ingredients they wanted on their Dagwood sandwich and it was inter-esting to see the combinations. I also made up sandwiches with odd combinations and had a taste-testing contest.

Webster's Dictionary defines a sandwich as "two or more slices of bread with a filling of meat, fish, cheese, jam, etc. between them."

Do you know that a "sandwich man" walked the streets wearing signboards on both the front and back with advertising on the boards? (Thus he was the filling of the sandwich!)

Do you know a sandwich bar specializes in serving sandwiches? Do you know a sandwich shop is a small restaurant with a limited menu of sandwiches?

How did the sandwich come to be?

It is believed that John Montague (born on November 3, 1718), the 4th Earl of Sandwich, was responsible for the invention. The Earl enjoyed gambling and he didn't want to leave his games, so he sent his servant out to bring him a piece of meat between two slices of bread. "Make the food so will not be messy," said the Earl. He ate it quickly so he could continue gambling. Soon, many people were adopting this new style of food. The name has stuck with this food all through the years. There are many success stories connected with sandwiches.

- When my husband attended school he looked forward to a lunch of a peanut butter sandwich with two slices of dill pickle tucked inside. This is still one of his favorite snacks.
- Scouts make a treat called S'mores, which is really a sweet sandwich made of graham crackers with chocolate and toasted marshmallows for filling.
- Then there are ice cream sandwiches made with vanilla ice cream between two chocolate cookies.
- McDonald's is only one of the fast-food chains that sell billions of hamburger sandwiches each year.

- The comic strip "Blondie" first became popular in the 1930s. Blonde's husband, Dagwood, loved to make a Dagwood sandwich as a midnight snack. He used three thick slices of white bread and put everything imaginable on his sandwich until the sandwich was so tall the thing teetered and was hard to balance to eat.

The Ziploc® Company started National Sandwich Day. Each year the company sponsors a contest for the best sandwich recipe. Their address is: National Sandwich Contest, Dow Brands Food Care Division, P.O. Box 78980, New Augusta, IN 46278.

Blondie and Dagwood Night at the Movies

Since the residents enjoyed the Dagwood sandwich activity and talked about the comic strip so much we decided to have a movie night with Blondie and Dagwood movies and popcorn as a snack.

Before you present this activity consult with your residents and see if they are interested in watching the video on Blondie and Dagwood. Personally, I find it rather funny, but I enjoy the old-time movies. I bet your residents will, too.

I enjoy the styles of clothes, appliances in the home, cars, and how they raised a family, all very interesting. It shows how people lived in that era and their attitudes at the time. But, no matter what era a person lives in it is interesting to view the styles, personal values, and family life of that time.

The two videos we viewed are:

"Blondie—It's a Great Life". It is 75 minutes long and was created in 1943. It is distributed by Bridgestone Multimedia Group in Chandler, AZ. The story line is about Dagwood buying a horse instead of a house and you know how Dagwood stories go—one thing leads to another!

"Blondie in Society". The story line here is about a Great Dane dog. Dagwood acquires the dog from a friend who owed him $50 and didn't have the cash, so he gave him the dog. The dog is a big nuisance. He eats Dagwood's favorite stew and gets into all kinds of trouble with the neighbors. In the end the Great Dane wins Dagwood $500, but not without a lot of hassles.

My library has a large selection of Blondie and Dagwood videos. Check at your library—if they don't have them in their own collection maybe they can get them through the traveling library.

Reference:
The Bridgestone Multi Group, Chandler Arizona. © MCMXCIX B.M.G.

```
S H B U T T E R S A M E A T L O A F R I N N S
V A T H R A N S D E M V I V I I E G E I I A I
P M K A F I S H P O R K R O A S T E B A T M B
E A A M E A V B R A T S O C H E E S E B A I Y
A N R B N B O G D L S A O N I O N S N P L S G
N D S U N Y P H U Y P C B C H I N A L I I C C
U C T R T E B I C S F N I Q A W U L I C A H K
T H I G E F P U C K D A F H S R T A B K N I N
B E M E F E L M U K J C C O L I P D A L S C U
U E U R O S Q I C T L B A R I S E D R E A K C
T S S S O T B E U U E E M S C T P R B R U E T
T E T S H I T E M R T O S E E S P E E E S N O
E S A L A M I N B K T I N R D Q E S C L A S M
R A R I M A Q A E E U H D A B E R S U I G A A
H Y D C A L U H R Y C X K D E F O I E S E L T
B U N S N A Z T S C E I N I E T N N S H N A O
D A Y D D F E L N V U U Y S F A I G A T Y D E
J N P A C U N D B R E A D H C W G L U I W T S
E U I Y H N M A Y O N N A I S E A P C B E T S
L E B I E N J A R S V I N G M C O O E O D P K
L R T P E P P E R S C K E Y Q O U S B N Y S I
Y R L I S B A N D M A R G A R I N E R O B I Z
I N B N E Q E H O T D O G S H D A Y O I N E O
```

Sandwich Fixings Word Search

PEANUT BUTTER	MEATLOAF	TOMATOES	SALAD DRESSING
JELLY	PEPPERS	BREAD	TURKEY
HAM AND CHEESE	PICKLE RELISH	MARGARINE	PEPPERONI
MUSTARD	BRATS	SLICED BEEF	ITALIAN SAUSAGE
BUNS	HORSERADISH	CHEESE	BARBECUE SAUCE
BUTTER	SALAMI	CUCUMBERS	
FISH	PORK ROAST	MAYONNAISE	
HOT DOGS	LETTUCE	HAMBURGER	
PICKLES	CHICKEN SALAD	ONIONS	

Sandwich Fixings Word Search

PEANUT BUTTER	MEATLOAF	TOMATOES	SALAD DRESSING
JELLY	PEPPERS	BREAD	TURKEY
HAM AND CHEESE	PICKLE RELISH	MARGARINE	PEPPERONI
MUSTARD	BRATS	SLICED BEEF	ITALIAN SAUSAGE
BUNS	HORSERADISH	CHEESE	BARBECUE SAUCE
BUTTER	SALAMI	CUCUMBERS	
FISH	PORK ROAST	MAYONNAISE	
HOT DOGS	LETTUCE	HAMBURGER	
PICKLES	CHICKEN SALAD	ONIONS	

National Alzheimer's Month

Note: Refer to the October Activities for the Bears project page 164-165. Complete the bear project before November so you will have bears available to give to the Alzheimer's residents. I have had some great experiences handing out bears to Alzheimer's sufferers. One lady always carried her doll with her and when she was given a bear, she gave it to her doll as a gift. This woman was still being a Mother with a loving heart. When distributing the bears be sure to spend some time with each person.

A number of the facilities I work with have held fundraisers and given the money to the Alzheimer's Association to help with research into the disease. One project that always is well received is a pizza sale. Sell the pizza by the slice for the residents to purchase, and take orders for pizza "to go". There is nothing like a good homemade pizza. If you don't want to make the crust you can buy ready-made crusts. The following is information on quantities of ingredients for pizza toppings based on a pizza pan size of 8 1/2 x 12 1/2 inches.

- 1 16-ounce can of grated Parmesan cheese will make 9 or 10 pizzas.
- 2 small onions equal 8 tablespoons and is enough for 4 pizzas.
- 12 ounces of sliced mushrooms equals 9 1/2 cups and will make 11 pizzas.
- 3 cups shredded mozzarella cheese will make 3 pizzas. Each 12-ounce bag holds 3 cups.
- 1 very large green pepper equals 2 cups chopped pepper. This is enough for 16 pizzas.
- 1 pound pizza sausage sautéed will make 4 pizzas.
- 1 8-ounce package of sliced pepperoni equals 100 slices. This will make 8 or 9 pizzas.
- Each batch of pizza sauce (recipe on next page) will make 4 1/2 cups. That is enough for 4 1/2 pizzas.
- The dough for a single pizza crust weighs 3/4 pound. The dough (recipe on next page) is enough for one pizza. Use a scale and weigh the dough so each crust is uniform.
- Pizza pans can be sprinkled with cornmeal instead of spray oil.
- Pizza dough will stretch.

Set up an assembly line for assembling the pizzas. Assign each person a job. Make up the dough first and let it rise while preparing the rest of the ingredients, or the dough can be made up, placed on the pizza pans, and frozen. If you freeze the dough be sure you have covered the dough tightly with plastic lids or wrap. Chop the green pepper, onions, and mushrooms. Make the sauce ahead of time. Place the cheeses in separate bowls for easy access when assembling.

S.M.O.P. Pizza *(Sausage, Mushroom, Onion, and Pepperoni)*

Yield: topping for one pizza.

1	cup pizza sauce
1/2	cup grated Parmesan cheese
1/3	cup pizza sausage
2	tablespoons green pepper
2	tablespoons chopped onions
1/2	cup fresh, sliced, mushrooms
1	cup mozzarella cheese
12	slices pepperoni, 3 across and 4 down

Pizza Dough

Yield: Four 8 1/2 x 12 1/2-inch pizzas cut into 6 large slices per pizza.

2	cups lukewarm water
2	packages (1/2 ounce each) active dry yeast
2	teaspoons sugar
2	teaspoons salt
5 to 6	cups flour

Mix water, yeast, and sugar together and let stand until a foam forms on the top. Slowly add the salt and flour. Knead dough until it is smooth and elastic, adding flour until you reach the right consistency. Divide dough into 4 equal balls of 3/4 pound each. Place each dough ball in a separate bowl, cover with a towel and let rise in a warm area.

Grease the pizza pans with spray oil, or flour with cornmeal.

Roll out each dough ball on a floured board until it fits the pizza pan. The dough will stretch to fit the pan. Bring the dough up the side of the pan at least 1/4 inch so it will hold the toppings.

Pizza Sauce

Yield: Sauce for four pizzas.

2	cans (15 ounces each) tomato sauce
1	can (6 ounces) tomato paste
5	leaves fresh basil, finely chopped
1	tablespoon Italian seasoning
1/2	teaspoon onion powder, or granulated white onion
1	teaspoon garlic, minced

Mix tomato sauce, tomato paste, and seasonings together. Cook over low heat for 30 minutes, stirring every 5 to 6 minutes. Set aside and let it cool down.

Pizza Sausage

Yield: Four pizzas.

1	pound bulk pizza sausage
1/2	cup water

Add water to sausage and sauté until there isn't any pink color left in the sausage. Drain, rinse with cold water, and dab dry with a paper towel. Set aside to add to the assembly line.

Top the crust with pizza sauce, spreading to an even consistency. Sprinkle Parmesan cheese over pizza sauce, dot sausage over top of cheese, sprinkle the individual chopped vegetables evenly over the sausage, sprinkle mozzarella cheese over vegetables and top with the pepperoni.

Bake at 400 degrees for 15 to 20 minutes, or until the crust is golden brown and the cheese is melted.

Veterans Day Breakfast Gathering
November 11

This project is to honor any veterans that are residents in your facility. You might also include veterans who are spouses of any of your residents.

Decorate the area in red, white, and blue and place American flags around the room. If you can locate a large flag in a stand have it in the front of the room and use it when you recite the Pledge of Allegiance.

Have a poppy to present to each veteran and pin it on their shirt or sweater so they can wear it all day and receive some well-deserved recognition. Explain how the poppies are sold by veterans groups to raise money for the disabled veterans.

Include the veterans in the program by having them talk about their time in the armed services. Where they served; what branch of the service they served in; their rank; how long they served; what their job was; etc. Give them plenty of time to tell their stories. After the Pledge of Allegiance is recited share a moment of silence to remember those who gave their lives for their country. Some songs you might include in the program are:

"Anchors Away"
"The Marine's Hymn"
"Caissons Song"
"Battle Hymn of the Republic"
"God Bless America"
"America"

Involving Students or Scouts in the Veterans Day Program

Suggest the teacher or scout leader review the history of Veterans Day with the students before they come to visit your facility. This is a good activity for children 10 to 12 years of age. See my reference list at the end of this activity for some poetry books the children can use to read poetry to the veterans. The children might make cookies or some other treats to bring with them to give to the veterans. Run off copies of the Veterans Day Word Search and pair up a child with a veteran and have them work the puzzle together. It's a good way for them to get acquainted and is a great sharing experience. The children could also have a bake sale at their school or some public place to raise money they can donate to the Disabled American Veterans Association.

History of Veterans Day

World War I began in 1914. Before the war ended 30 countries were involved in the conflict, and ten million soldiers were killed with over twenty million injured. At first the United States didn't get involved in the conflict, but then Germany began sinking American ships so the U.S. joined our allies (France, Britain, and Russia) in fighting the axis powers of Germany, Austria-Hungry, and Turkey.

The surrender of Germany took place on the 11th of November at 11 a.m. (It was called the 11th hour.) President Woodrow Wilson set aside November 11 as a holiday to commemorate the end of the fighting. He named the holiday Armistice Day (which meant "to stop fighting"). On Armistice Day people wore red poppies as a reminder of the bloody battle fought at Flanders Field, which was a poppy field. The battlefield was made into a cemetery and the wild poppies bloomed among the grave markers. John McCrae, a Canadian soldier, wrote a poem about the courage of the soldiers at Flanders Field. He was killed in action in 1918 so he never knew his poem became so famous. The poem was first published in the British magazine *Punch* on December 9, 1919.

Flanders Fields
by John McCrae
1872-1918

In Flanders fields the poppies blow
Between the crosses, row on row,
That mark our place; and in the sky
The larks, still bravely singing, fly
Scarce heard amid the guns below.

We are the dead. Short days ago
We lived, felt dawn, saw sunset glow,
Loved and were loved, and now we lie
In Flanders fields.

Take up our quarrel with the foe;
To you from failing hands we throw
The torch; be yours to hold it high.
If ye break faith with us who die
We shall not sleep, though poppies grow
In Flanders fields.

The peace after World War I didn't last, and the United States was again drawn into war on December 7, 1941, when the Japanese bombed Pearl Harbor in Hawaii. World War II was certainly a "world war". There was fighting in Europe, Africa, and the Pacific. Once again we were fighting with Germany and Italy in Europe, and Japan in the Pacific due to cruel dictators of those countries. World War II ended with the United States' bombing of Hiroshima in Japan, and the defeat of Hitler and Mussolini in Europe, in 1945.

The name of Armistice Day was changed to Veterans Day in 1954.

References:
The Oxford Book of War Poetry, edited by Jan Stallworthy. This book contains the following poems suitable for Veterans Day.
"Range-Finding" by Robert Frost, pg. 169.
"Death of a Soldier" by Wallace Stevens, pg. 169.
"On Being Asked for a War Poem" by W.B. Yeats, pg. 171.
"Returning We Hear the Larks" by Isaac Rosenberg, pg. 187.
"Two Canadian Memorials" by Rudyard Kipling, pg. 215.
"When a Beau Goes In" by Garvin Ewart, pg. 272.
"The Middle of a War" by Roy Fuller, pg. 272.
"A Front" by Randall Jarrell, pg. 278.
"The Heroes" by Louis Simpson, pg. 283.
"Flanders Fields" by John McCrae, pg. 165.
"The Hero" by Siegfried, pg. 176.

Favorite Poems Old and New by Helen Ferris and illustrated by Leonard Weisgard. This book contains the favorite poem "Trees" on pg. 207. This poem was first recited during World War I and has deep meaning for many people. This poem has also been set to music.

Trees
by Joyce Kilmer

I think that I shall never see
A poem as lovely as a tree.

A tree whose hungry mouth is pressed
Against the Earth's sweet flowing breast.

A tree that looks at God all day
And lifts her leafy arms to pray.

A tree that may in summer wear
A nest of robins in her hair.

Upon whose bosom snow has lain;
Who intimately lives with rain.

Poems are made by fools like me,
But only God can make a tree.

```
B I C A N D E A R A D I C T A T O R S L S C S
V P E A C E R Y D L A D G D P M C O B W A R M
L E U E M V A C U S T O M S S Q O U E R U C A
Q I T A L Y B X Y F S U R R E N D E R E D S N
B E A E T S D N I U K E S O L D I E R L A P D
T E R L R D R U I S R G A N S O A F I I G O C
E N M Y P A E E B N P I C N I I E G P S E P H
L F I G F R N R T P A O L O B S T E E H N P E
E L S E S M S S L D I V W V Y E E S A T T I E
V A T R L E I N O E R O A E G O N S R T O E C
E N I M E D Y B U F O C H M R I N A L R E S R
N D C A T F E T H E F G I B K S U S H E S T O
T E E N T O I W A A O O H E N R T I A E S R S
H R D Y U R I A M T I N R R U I P N R S K L S
H S A E C C A R B E H G S E C S E G B I I E A
O F Y Y E E L S U D O N L L I T P L O N Z N B
U I S C T S L T E Y R G I E O G P P R T O N Y
R E N V U U S I F H S K C V M Q N O R R R T E
S L B R E T R O O P S I E E A E R W V E G E C
S D Y T E N S E S I A T D N E F O E A E E F U
I S R S V U L S H O N O R T E A R U S R I A E
S E A I C T S T I X I A Y H F I C R U S S I A
H U D V E T E R A N S D A Y C R G E K L A N D
```

Veterans Day Word Search

HONOR	NOVEMBER ELEVENTH	ARMED FORCES	SOLDIER
TROOPS	VETERANS OF FOREIGN WARS	VETERANS DAY	RUSSIA
TENSE	ELEVENTH HOUR	DEFEATED	AIR
PEACE	FLANDERS FIELDS	GERMANY	LAND
ITALY	PEARL HARBOR	AXIS POWERS	WAR
SEA	SURRENDERED	TREES	CUSTOMS
CROSS	ARMISTICE DAY	POPPIES	DICTATORS

Veterans Day Word Search

HONOR	NOVEMBER ELEVENTH	ARMED FORCES	SOLDIER
TROOPS	VETERANS OF FOREIGN WARS	VETERANS DAY	RUSSIA
TENSE	ELEVENTH HOUR	DEFEATED	AIR
PEACE	FLANDERS FIELDS	GERMANY	LAND
ITALY	PEARL HARBOR	AXIS POWERS	WAR
SEA	SURRENDERED	TREES	CUSTOMS
CROSS	ARMISTICE DAY	POPPIES	DICTATORS

Be Happy Party

This activity is designed for 2nd Stage Alzheimer's patients.

This activity is a good one to plan for morning coffee time. We invited Crackers the Clown to come to entertain the residents with some magic and balloon animals for them. I bet you have someone in your community that can be a Crackers Clown—ask around!

We talked about what makes us all happy. Let the residents who will, join in the discussion about what makes them happy. Many in my group said their family made them happy.

Many times small things are just as important as a big, elaborately planned party. Just go with the flow and make memories and smiles for your Alzheimer's patients. Our residents loved the clown and responded very well.

Election Day Coffee Klatsch

Election Day is always held the first Tuesday after the first Monday in November. There are other special and primary elections, but the November voting day is always on the same day and is the final election for local, state, and federal offices.

Sometimes people take the right to vote for granted and forget how long it took for it to be possible for everyone over 18 years of age to be able to vote. Some countries still don't have this right to help choose their leaders. When the United States was a young country only the men were allowed to vote. It took many years for women and African Americans to gain that right.

In larger towns and cities people vote on a voting machine. However, there are still rural areas where people cast a paper ballot that they mark by hand. The ballots are then deposited in a ballot box and when the polling place closes at the end of the day the ballots are counted to find out who has been elected. In larger cities people have to register to be able to vote on election day, and their name is checked against a list of eligible voters. Everyone is allowed to vote an absentee ballot if it is impossible or difficult for them to go the actual polling place to cast their ballot. In facilities where I work we always give the residents the opportunity to vote an absentee ballot. If you contact the county courthouse they will get you in touch with the correct person to talk to about getting your residents absentee ballots. Sometimes they will even send an election official to your facility to assist the residents with their voting.

When you gather your residents for coffee discuss if any of them would like to vote and follow through with getting them a ballot. Encourage the discussion to include past elections and whom they think are the best candidates running in this election. Talk about the two political parties. You might even ask them about the first time they voted.

```
B A I U R M L G E V O T I N G B O O T H J N G I
S M A Q I M K O X S W V S B A L L O T B O X M E
D E R T W R S V Z W E B D B I D U H C Z W A K L
L R E W E E V E A E R C P A R T I E S A U M B E
F I P E L P P R N R E G I S T E R E D C N E A C
K C R W E U A N P A X M E D H M W H M P I R L T
J A E C C B O M D S T Z B I K B O N K L T I L R
H N S I T L S E E D F O Z Q G V I M J M E C O O
V C E T I I L N M F X C R O E H U X U K D A T N
B I N Y O C F T O A V G C S T A T C N O S N J I
D T T E N A N P C C Y P O U R O R E H C T C P C
E I A L D N C U R V B O F V L S T Z E O A I O M
M Z T E A I M N A E T I R D E L J X T N T T L A
O E I C Y U X H T S S U J F J R K C G G E I I C
C N V T S V Z Y I F P O L L S K N V B R S Z T H
R X E I X R O T C G A D I I E F A O F E G E I I
A C U O C T C T G M S F A U R N S Q R S M N C N
C V S N N J P R E S I D E N T C D E V S N R A E
Y F D S J K W F R C L P D T L E A D E R C S L K
I H F J D A Q R F A F O F W S A K T E F A X R D
U J V I C E P R E S I D E N T V W Y C V M F R E
S D I E E D R D H I J U J W C N X S W H I D E F
```

Election Day Word Search

PRESIDENT

MAYOR

VOTE

ELECTION DAY

CONGRESS

REPRESENTATIVE

SENATORS

LAWS

GOVERNMENT

VOTING BOOTH

DEMOCRATIC

REPUBLICAN

CITY ELECTIONS

BALLOT BOX

REGISTERED

EIGHTEEN

LEADER

UNITED STATES

GOVERNOR

POLITICAL

PARTIES

POLLS

BALLOT

ELECTRONIC MACHINE

DEMOCRACY

VICE PRESIDENT

AMERICAN CITIZEN

```
B A I U R M L G E V O T I N G B O O T H J N G I
S M A Q I M K O X S W V S B A L L O T B O X M E
D E R T W R S V Z W E B D B I D U H C Z W A K L
L R E W E E V E A E R C P A R T I E S A U M B E
F I P E L P P R N R E G I S T E R E D C N E A C
K C R W E U A N P A X M E D H M W H M P I R L T
J A E C B O M D S T Z B I K B O N K L T I L R
H N S I T L S E E D F O Z Q G V I M J M E C O O
V C E T I I L N M F X C R O E H U X U K D A T N
B I N Y O C F T O A V G C S T A T C N O S N J I
D T T E N A N P C C Y P O U R O R E H C T C P C
E I A L D N C U R V B O F V L S T Z E O A I O M
M Z T E A I M N A E T I R D E L J X T N T T L A
O E I C Y U X H T S S U J F J R K C G E I I C
C N V T S V Z Y I F P O L L S K N V B R S Z T H
R X E I X R O T C G A D I I E F A O F E G E I I
A C U O C T C T G M S F A U R N S Q R S M N C N
C V S N N J P R E S I D E N T C D E V S N R A E
Y F D S J K W F R C L P D T L E A D E R C S L K
I H F J D A Q R F A F O F W S A K T E F A X R D
U J V I C E P R E S I D E N T V W Y C V M F R E
S D I E E D R D H I J U J W C N X S W H I D E F
```

Election Day Word Search

PRESIDENT	LAWS	REGISTERED	POLLS
MAYOR	GOVERNMENT	EIGHTEEN	BALLOT
VOTE	VOTING BOOTH	LEADER	ELECTRONIC MACHINE
ELECTION DAY	DEMOCRATIC	UNITED STATES	DEMOCRACY
CONGRESS	REPUBLICAN	GOVERNOR	VICE PRESIDENT
REPRESENTATIVE	CITY ELECTIONS	POLITICAL	AMERICAN CITIZEN
SENATORS	BALLOT BOX	PARTIES	

Craft Bazaar

At our facility we always hold a craft bazaar in November, usually on the first weekend of the month. I have found it is best to try to always hold the bazaar on the same weekend year after year, so people will remember when it is scheduled and will make plans to attend.

Our bazaar gives residents and community members a chance to purchase items for Christmas gifts, and is a nice social occasion for seeing old friends and having refreshments.

Invite area crafters and quilters to rent a table to sell their items. Charge a small rental fee so that everyone can attend. You should include the Bazaar date on your facility calendar and you might even send invitation notes to family members to encourage attendance. One lady in our community made 50 lap robes and donated them for the craft bazaar. We sold them for $5 each which gave us some money for our other projects and we even donated some to the Christmas fund for needy children.

Don't forget to send the information to your local newspaper and buyer's guide. They will most likely give you some free advertising. Also, your local radio and TV station will do the same. Contact local churches and they will include the date and time in their bulletin.

Try to set aside a place where visitors can buy a cup of coffee and a treat, and sit and visit with your residents, staff, and friends.

Have a great day!

Men's Group Lunch

Set a time after Thanksgiving for the men's lunch and arrange with the kitchen to bring their lunch to their special room or designated area.

To get the conversation going try making a "big" deal about what they want for Christmas—even to the point of making a list so "Santa" will know what to bring. You never know who might be wanting to buy a little gift for one of them—and you'll know "exactly" what it is they want! In fact, try to see that everyone gets something they mention—it causes such interest and happiness!

Some of the wishes were for:
- A beer with the Christmas lunch.
- That children would come and spend the day.
- That they could go out for lunch and select whatever they wanted.
- Being able to go to church on Christmas.

After the fun of the Christmas list, I changed the conversation to anything they had concerns about. Many were worried about health issues and money concerns. I tried to alleviate the concerns and console them that the staff at the facility will always be there to take good care of them. I encouraged them to have faith and trust and the staff would do the rest. I came away from that lunch very determined to make each man's Christmas wish come true. We worked together to make it happen and it was so worthwhile!

Deer Hunting Season

Gather the men for a morning coffee and conversation. Start the discussion by encouraging the men to talk about when they went, or didn't go, deer hunting. You might also have an invited guest to talk about hunting experiences. A warden from the DNR might also be an interesting person to invite. They can discuss the newest hunting rules, how many deer they estimate there are, the tagging and registration process, etc.

Here are a couple of my deer stories:

My female friend loves to go deer hunting. Each year she travels to her family farm in western Wisconsin to hunt deer. She has a daughter who goes hunting, too. This past year she shot a buck and a doe. She sat very quietly for several hours before she saw the buck. She was so excited as she related the experience to me.

The husband of one of my friends loves to deer hunt. He goes with three other guys. They had been hunting for four days and he still had no deer. Finally, one of the men said, "I'll help you get a deer." So he climbed a tree to watch for the deer and when he saw one he signaled that the deer was coming in behind the hunter. When the luckless hunter saw the signal he turned around and shot the deer. The moral of the story is you need to look all around for your deer.

I'm sure your resident hunters will have some good tales to tell.

References:
25 Years of Deer & Deer Hunting by the Original Stump-Sitters Magazine. Edited by Daniel E. Schmidt.

Heart and Blood, Living with Deer in America by Richard Nelson.

John F. Kennedy Discussion

As I traveled the country in 2003 I noticed almost every library had a display about President Kennedy for the 40th Anniversary of his assassination.

I remember making a poster in my high school history class during his campaign for President. He also visited nearby Ball State Teachers College (now Ball State University) when he was campaigning.

The thing that always amazes me is almost every person can remember where they were and what they were doing when Kennedy was shot on November 22, 1963. I was a junior in college. It was a Friday, and I had just finished taking an exam and had walked with a friend to get a sandwich at one of our local restaurants. I was stunned and could not believe this could happen in the U.S.

Gather the residents for coffee and discussion. I told my story—but you tell your story about what you remember of that day. Then ask the residents to tell their stories and feelings of that sad time in our country.

A Few Important Points:
*   Kennedy's most famous quote from his inaugural speech: "Ask not what your country can do for you, but what you can do for your country."
*   In his younger years he had poor health and was always in the shadow of his older brother, Joe, who was killed in World War II.
*   His father encouraged him to go into politics.
*   He was a Congressman and Senator from Massachusetts before running for President.
*   He became President in 1961, and served for only 1,000 days. Much was accomplished in this short time. He dealt with the civil rights movement, Cuban missile crisis, Southeast Asia, and the Bay of Pigs issue in Cuba. He is known for shaping American policy and left an unforgettable legacy to this nation.

References:
There are many references on Kennedy in your library. The book that fascinated me the most was:
High Treason, The Assassination of President John F. Kennedy, What Really Happened by Robert J. Groden, Harrison Edward Livingstone, and an article by Colonel Fletcher Prouty.

John F. Kennedy by Judie Mills.

The Oregon Trail Activity

Share this story with your residents.

The Story of Raymond Nekka

It was the year 1850, I was ten years old. The people in our town were all talking about the gold mines out West. Pa was really intrigued by all the stories. For more than five years Pa had wanted to travel the Oregon Trail and make a fresh start out West. The Oregon Trail was started in 1840, so it was about the same age as I was.

Pa woke us up on a brisk April Sunday morning. It seemed too early to get up. But he kept after us to clean up, dress quickly, and come to the kitchen for a family meeting. This was going to be an unforgettable morning.

Mary was eight and Ana Samantha was six. (Ana always insisted she was six and one-half when I teased her about her age.)

Pa began the meeting by stating, "This is a most glorious day in my life!" Then he blurted out, "We're going to Oregon." I couldn't believe what Pa was saying. Wow! Are we really going to Oregon? Pa had talked about this for at least five years.

He continued saying, "Today will be the last Sunday service we'll attend in Boston, so say farewell to your friends and family. We're going to get a new start in life."

Ma said, "Pa has had these plans for years. Now it's finally going to happen."

"We can get a big parcel of land and build up an apple orchard. We'll grow the finest apples in Oregon," Pa continued, his eyes sparkling. "I have plans for building a new house, too. Everyone will have to work hard to make our dream come true." Pa gave us the opportunity to share our thoughts and ideas on this big change in our lives. He really felt it would be a better life for all of us. Pa always said if you can dream it you can do it. He explained that we must leave soon as it would take four to six months to travel to Oregon and we wanted to get there before winter set in.

Pa was tired of paying the high taxes in Boston. A fresh start to a better life and to build up a home and some financial success was what spurred him.

But Ma had a different idea. She said we were settled and had our wonderful family and friends around us. We had roots and we were safe. The idea of traveling West in a covered wagon was very scary to her. The unknown bothered Ma greatly. "If we stay here we're not immigrants. If we go to Oregon *we will be*, because Oregon is not even a part of the United States. So that will make us immigrants."

"Oh!" said Ana Samantha. "Is that bad to be an immigrant?"

Pa jumped in quickly, "No, it is not bad to be an immigrant. It's just a term people use; don't worry your pretty little head about that."

Mary and Ana Samantha really didn't understand Pa's thinking—nor Ma's, either, for that matter.

Ana Samantha was the adventuresome one in our family. She was always running and tumbling and being pretty rough for a girl. She loved to climb trees and roll in the grass. Ma said she thought Ana should have been a boy. Pa called her "Sammy". Ana Samantha loved to hear Pa tell stories of the West.

Mary was a very dainty girl and was sickly as a baby. She worried Ma so. Ma was afraid she might lose her when she was a baby. Mary liked to read and have tea with Ma. Mary always helped

Ma in the kitchen and the two of them sang hymns as they worked.

After a long discussion it was decided the Nekka family would make the trip to Oregon.

We said our last goodbyes to friends and family at church that morning and returned home to our favorite Sunday breakfast of pancakes and real maple syrup. Later that day we began packing up our things for the long trip. Our Aunt Sarah (Ma's sister) would be staying in our house to watch over things and if we wanted to return to Boston we'd have our place to come back to.

Ma wanted to take the beautiful grandfather clock her father had made for Ma and Pa as a wedding gift, and she also wanted to take her good china. Pa didn't think it was a good idea to take these things, but he finally gave in to Ma's wishes. The rest of us packed only the necessities.

Soon we were on our way.

When we arrived in Independence, Missouri, we celebrated completing the first part of the journey. We stayed there a few days to rest and prepare for the rest of the trip.

Independence was a booming town with many folks heading West just like our family. "Go West Young Man" seemed to be the motto of the travelers. The talk was that there was gold in the West and you could strike it rich. Pa just wanted land and a new life for us.

People were wheeling and dealing on covered wagons and buying supplies for the long trip ahead. Pa purchased a covered wagon, two oxen, tools, boots, warm clothes, and other supplies for the trip. Ma made sure there was plenty of food for us. They also purchased a barrel for storing water. All of those supplies had to fit into the wagon—and where were we all going to ride?

Pa purchased a horse for Mary and me to ride. Ana would have to sit up front on the wagon seat with Pa. Ma would walk some, or drive the wagon and Pa would walk. That was when Ma decided to shorten her skirts a little so the walking would be easier.

Pa knew the oxen were steady and sturdy, and it cost less to use oxen because they required only grass for a meal. Some people purchased mules to pull their wagons, but it took four mules to a wagon and even though they were faster they were also stubborn. Horses were the other choice, but they wore out more easily. So Pa made the choice of oxen to pull our wagon. Oxen could travel 12 to 15 miles a day.

We could hardly sleep once the purchases were made—we were so excited! Finally, we were on our way. Little did we know the *real* adventure was still ahead! Could we make it to Oregon before winter? Pa was optimistic.

The trail was rugged and the wagon had no brakes and often seemed to have a mind of its own. As the days went by trail water became scarce. Some people drank dirty water full of bacteria and contracted a disease called cholera. It caused many deaths. We always tried to plan our trip so we would get to a water stop by noon or sunset. Sometimes the water tasted so bad that even the small children drank coffee instead.

Some families took time to hunt buffalo, antelope, and deer for meat on the trip. Salt was used to preserve the meat.

When we stopped to rest, or in the evening, Ma always encouraged us to gather buffalo chips (also called meadow muffins). We used these chips to help kindle a fire. Sometimes we used the chips to entertain us. We'd throw them back and forth. Once Ana laughed so hard in our game that she wet her pants! Ma made it clear to us that the buffalo chips were for lighting a fire!

We met caravans of white, canvas-covered wagons as we traveled. From a distance they looked like a stream of sailing ships, and people called them "prairie schooners". Our trip took us to

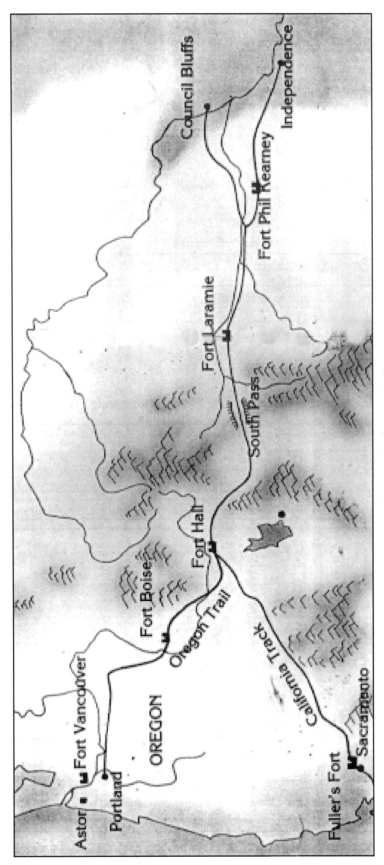

Map of the Oregon Trail

Fort Phil Kearney and then to Fort Laramie, where we stopped and purchased more supplies.

We came to a river and, of course, there was no bridge for crossing. It was raining by this time, and Ma pleaded with Pa to wait to cross until the rain stopped. Thankfully, he listened to Ma.

One of the men in our group crossed the river on his horse and put markers where he thought it was safe to cross, but the rain just kept coming down harder. Two other wagons were determined to cross and they started across the water. But the water was so deep that it ran inside the wagon and it sank to the bottom. Those poor people lost all their worldly possessions. The second wagon tipped over and all but two small children drown. Pa and Ma took in the two little ones and assured them they would be taken care of.

It was hard to wait for the rain to stop, but finally after four days we got to cross the river. We hugged each other in triumph as we reached the other side.

We traveled in a group of wagons now, and at night we would park the wagons in two big circles with our campfires in the middle. The Indians were hunting buffalo in this area and once the buffalo stampede just missed our camp.

Pa loved the scenery and weather. He often remarked about the fresh air and wide-open spaces. The sky was so blue and the sunrise and sunset so beautiful. Our family made new friends on the Oregon Trail, and became even closer as a family.

On August 14, the right, front wheel on the wagon broke. Others in our wagon train helped Pa fix the wheel. Everyone in the wagon train worked together to help each other succeed, and the safety for everyone was much better when we traveled and worked together.

The trip ahead was very treacherous. We had to climb a steep hill with humongous boulders. The trail was loosely-packed dirt and we knew if it rained we'd never be able to make it up. It was also getting very windy with the dirt blowing in our eyes and mouths and making it very hard to see. Pa said he felt like he'd eaten a bucket of dirt! But our trusty oxen just keep plodding ahead.

We gazed in disbelief at the snow-capped Rocky Mountains. They were so majestic and Ma said the beauty just made her shiver—only God could create something so beautiful!

After we crossed the mountains the wagons fanned out in a valley. The tall grass made it more difficult for us to follow the trail. It was hot all night and the grass was covered with dew in the morning.

As we moved along we heard a loud scream that didn't stop. We took the horse and followed the scream and found a woman in labor. We hurried back to our wagon and got Ma and she went to help the woman. Soon Ma helped deliver a beautiful baby boy. He was named Raymond after me! I was so proud. Ten babies were born on the way to Oregon. I questioned how these babies would know where they were born. I guess they could proudly say, "I was a pioneer baby born on the way to Oregon on the Oregon Trail."

Soon we made it to Fort Hall and then to Fort Boise. Our poor horse died on the trail of heat exhaustion. We prayed a prayer that he would "rest easy" and traveled on to our destination. Finally, we made it to Fort Vancouver.

A tall, handsome man named Ben greeted us at Fort Vancouver. He was dressed as a lumberjack. "Where are you from?" he asked.

"Boston," was our reply.

"Are you looking for land?"

"Yes."

He showed us where there was vacant land available for homesteading. We chose a spot and began to settle in. We had exactly one month before bad weather, but Pa was confident we could make it all work out. Here we were in Oregon at last! We were tired but we all felt the trip was worth it. Now it was up to our whole family to work on our dream.

That dream came true. I am now forty, and I've never left Oregon. My wife and I have witnessed many pioneers coming through the Oregon Trail that was in use until the 1880s. Twenty thousand people died on the trail, mostly to disease and drowning. There are many businesses here such as blacksmiths and suppliers that help the new settlers with supplies and advice.

Ma, Pa, and Mary have all been laid to rest in the last three years. We miss them. However, it was Pa's dream that brought us here to a better life. Last year we expanded the apple orchard. Ana Samantha, my wife, and I are running the Nekka family orchard and we're doing fine. People come from all over to buy our apple pies and preserves, and we owe it all to Pa and Ma.

Oh, by the way, I am now the proud Grandpa of a baby boy named Raymond. My daughter married the baby boy Raymond from the wagon train and her baby is also named Raymond!

Remember—If you can dream it, you can do it!

Reference:
Website: http://www.isu.edu/~trinmich/Oregontrail.html
"The Oregon Trail" by teachers Mike Trinklein and Steve Boettcher, creators of the award-winning documentary film.

```
C N M S O U T H P A S S E L N V E P L S A P
E O C U O N K S O D A S P R I N G L W I R H
R R O E X I R N Y O K E S G D C E A A S L Y
O T V D M S Y A D E C W T E I M U D H U H D
C H E T D I A K C C E S U O A L Y T I G A C
K P R Y A D T E G R T Y V A N T S K H A R H
Y L E K W F O R T B O I S E S R D I R R I I
M A D K S E S I R A Y U X C U P A N S W N M
O T W A K E E V S D B P Y G G F R G L E D N
U T A P I O N E E R S C Z M P S E D I A E E
N E G L P R N R F O R T L A R A M I E D P Y
T R O A A E N B L U Q H S S A E A M E U E R
A I N I I G R A W G S A N N I T Y S X S N O
I V R N R O V U A H O L B B R T A W Y T D C
N E H S O N E G H T I L I Y I U P E L Y E K
S R O H F T M A I C X I R N E C S E E T N D
C D E E P R I V E R U J A A G E E T M R C A
A E S S M A P L E O R C H A R D L W F A E V
M L E L H I R C K A X L A A V U S A G I D A
B U F F A L O C H I P S A A R E I T E L P T
I G E C R K X C C H V O E E T E B E S S S C
R E O N T I E S E R B M A C S V D R S P T A
E M S O U T N L U W S P T A P P I G R A S S
```

Oregon Trail Word Search

SOUTH PASS	OREGON TRAIL	CHIMNEY ROCK	FORT HALL
SODA SPRING	BUFFALO CHIPS	DEEP RIVER	SWEET WATER
SNAKE RIVER	DROUGHT	FORT LARAMIE	COVERED WAGON
FORT BOISE	OXEN	DUSTY TRAILS	ROCKY MOUNTAINS
PIONEERS	GRASS	INDEPENDENCE	NORTH PLATTE RIVER
PLAINS	MUD	PRAIRIE	

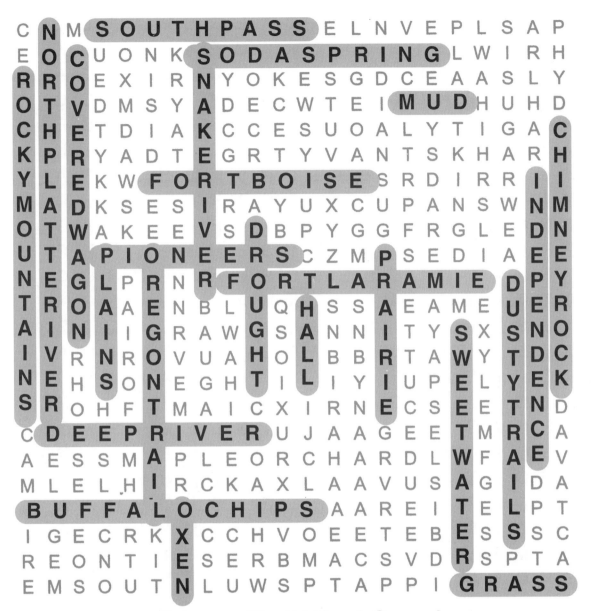

Oregon Trail Word Search

SOUTH PASS	OREGON TRAIL	CHIMNEY ROCK	FORT HALL
SODA SPRING	BUFFALO CHIPS	DEEP RIVER	SWEET WATER
SNAKE RIVER	DROUGHT	FORT LARAMIE	COVERED WAGON
FORT BOISE	OXEN	DUSTY TRAILS	ROCKY MOUNTAINS
PIONEERS	GRASS	INDEPENDENCE	NORTH PLATTE RIVER
PLAINS	MUD	PRAIRIE	

```
C A D K A D S C L C R A C K E R S W A T L E
E T W A W F R T S O A L R I C E A A I R E K
R T A P S U Q H N R I E T N D U L H L W C A
O A G L K B A C O N R M R C A Y T I K A C C
C M O A C O A L I M I F H O R S E S I T S E
A M B K P O I O X E N G I D A D I R T E L U
I U L Y A T X J A A G E L P V A B S T R P A
N N A I L S U C H L D S S S I R A L K B O D
S I N O R O R L A A R S P T N E K I R A Y O
C T K D O A X S A A I R I S E M I E Y R D E
A I E N F M U L E S E S C P G A N E S R C C
M O T T P H V M A C D I K H A Y G P U E G R
B N S S M R B P T A F S L A R D P O G L T B
D G E L H W S E L N R U E D U P O T A I R A
R R O F A S S P R I U G S C C S W A R V S D
E M I C R A S S G D I A R H E E D T N E E F
N G R E A S E T E I T R B I S L E O N R F I
O C U O D C W U O A L W N M A S R E N B L R
R O E O U B S V A N T E D N L I T S R A W E
T V D O N T E S C O F F E E T B E O V U A A
H F L O U R I A C U P D P Y V D R N E G H R
P R Y M S Y U Y N G F U E R P I G T M A I M
L E K D I B P Z M S S S N D E P K N I V E S
```

Oregon Trail Supplies Word Search

KNIVES	CORN MEAL	SALT	WATER BARREL
AMMUNITION	CRACKERS	PICKLES	LARD
NAILS	DRIED BEANS	DRIED FRUIT	FIREARMS
BLANKETS	OXEN	HORSES	MULES
BOOTS	GREASE	VINEGAR	POTATOES
RICE	FLOUR	TEA	COFFEE
BACON	COAL	BAKING POWDER	SUGAR

```
C A D K A D S C L C R A C K E R S W A T L E
E T W A W F R T S O A L R I C E A I R E K
R T A P S U Q H N R I E T N D U L H L C A
O A G L K B A C O N R M R C A Y T I K A C C
C M O A C O A L I M I F H O R S E S I S E
A M B K P O I O X E N G I D A D I R T E L U
I U L Y A T X J A A G E L P V A B S T R P A
N N A I L S U C H L D S S S I R A L K O D
S I N O R O R L A A D S P T N E K I E Y O E
C T K D O A X S A A R I C I S E M I R D E
A I E N F M U L E S R S K P G A N E S C C
M O T T P H V M A C D I K H A Y E S U G R B
B N S S M R B P T A D F S L A R D P A G T B
D G E L H W S E L N R U E D U P O R I R A
R R O F A S S P R I U G C C S W T A V S D
E M I C R A S S G D T A R H E E D O N E E
N G R E A S E T E I R B I S L E S N R F F
O C U O D C W U O A L W N M A S R E N B L I
R O E O U B S V A N T E D N L I T S R A W R
T V D O N T E S C O F F E E T B E O V U A E
H F L O U R I A C U P D P Y V D R N E G H A
P R Y M S Y U Y N G F U E R P I G T M A I R
L E K D I B P Z M S S S N D E P K N I V E S M
```

Oregon Trail Supplies Word Search

KNIVES	CORN MEAL	SALT	WATER BARREL
AMMUNITION	CRACKERS	PICKLES	LARD
NAILS	DRIED BEANS	DRIED FRUIT	FIREARMS
BLANKETS	OXEN	HORSES	MULES
BOOTS	GREASE	VINEGAR	POTATOES
RICE	FLOUR	TEA	COFFEE
BACON	COAL	BAKING POWDER	SUGAR

Thanksgiving Activities

Contact your local elementary school or church group and invite a class of students for a turkey day lunch. The students should bring their own brown bag lunch and prepare a game to play with the residents, such as checkers, cards, etc. Supply the drinks for your residents and the children and maybe a cookie or brownie.

You can expand the time, entertainment, and food to fit your personal situation. Just include the children in the lives of your residents.

This simple activity brings much joy to both generations.

Turkey Pins Art Project

Supplies needed per pin:

See page 5 in the color section for finished project.

1 miniature straw hat
4 or 5 small feathers
1 brown miniature-size ball
2 miniature eyes
1 red pipe cleaner
1 light brown pipe cleaner
1 pin back
Hot glue

Hot glue the feathers on the top back of the hat to form the tail of the turkey. Hot glue the miniature ball on the front top of the hat to form the turkey's head. Glue the eyes on the ball to form the turkey face.

Cut 1/4-inch of the brown pipe cleaner for the beak and glue on to the head ball to form the beak. To form the turkey's waddle, cut 1/2-inch strip from the red pipe cleaner and fold back and forth. Hot glue the red pipe cleaner on the hat underneath the beak.

Hot glue the pin back to the back of the hat under the feathers.

Thanksgiving Lunch or Dinner with the Families

We announced we would have a special Thanksgiving dinner for residents and their families and took reservations, so we'd know how many to plan for.

My husband and I helped with the preparation and serving. The dietary department should be involved in the planning and be responsible for the food ordering and in charge of the preparation.

We helped with peeling potatoes, and preparing the other vegetables. We also prepared the coffee and made sure we have plenty of beverages for our guests. I set and decorated the tables and we played soft dinner music. As this was a fairly small facility, we had plenty of room for the invited guests to have a sit-down dinner, and we served the meal on nice china. I have a friend at this same facility now and they have over 200 residents! So now they serve the meal buffet style. Family members are encouraged to go with their resident through the serving line and help with food selection and trays.

Whatever you do, whether a lunch, coffee time, or a full dinner, make your invited guests feel like part of the larger facility family. Your residents will feel so special to have their family present and enjoy the time together.

FAVORITE HYMNS BINGO

B	I	N	G	O
How Great Thou Art	Amazing Grace	Softly and Tenderly	Abide with Me	Jesus Loves Me
Let There Be Peace on Earth	The Prayer of St. Frances	Blessed Assurance	Joyful, Joyful We Adore Thee	How Great Thou Art
Holy, Holy, Holy	Whispering Hope	FREE	Old-Time Religion	Rock of Ages
Crown Him with Many Crowns	The Old Rugged Cross	What a Friend We Have in Jesus	The Lord is My Shepherd	Were you There?
Joshua Fought the Battle	Swing Low Sweet Chariot	In the Garden	God Bless America	America

December Activities

Granny's Soup Kitchen

Holiday Lobster Soup
Yield: 18 servings.

4	tablespoons butter, melted
2	(8 ounces each) lobster tails without shells, diced (makes 1 cup)
20	cooked and peeled jumbo shrimp without tails, diced (makes 1 cup)
	juice from one fresh lime
2	teaspoons olive oil
1	quart 100% fat-free chicken broth (reserve 2 cups)
2	bunches asparagus tips (2 cups)
1	leek, diced (1/2 cup)
1	cup sliced fresh mushrooms
1	large red pepper, chopped (1 1/2 cups)
1	package (3/4 ounce) fresh basil chopped (1/3 cup)
1	bunch scallions, chopped (1 1/2 cups)
2 1/2	cups diced celery
1	clove garlic, minced
1	cup half and half
1/2	cup sherry cooking wine
1	teaspoon onion powder
1	teaspoon Chesapeake Bay style seafood seasoning
1	teaspoon pepper
3	cups Penne Rigate (see following recipe for cooking pasta)

You may get donations to help you with the cost of the shrimp and lobster used in this recipe. If you cannot afford the shrimp and lobster you can substitute poor man's lobster. If you use cod in the soup recipe, substitute whole milk for the half and half and eliminate the butter completely. The recipe for the Poor Man's Lobster is on page 229. Not only will you save fats with the Poor Man's Lobster, but also calories—not to mention the cholesterol!

You can substitute low-carbohydrate pasta for the Penne Rigate. It does have a very different taste and texture.

Decorate the serving tables with a Christmas theme. The decorations and presentation mean so much to the residents and their families and friends. Eye appeal is very important!

Serve this soup with assorted cheese and crackers, nine-grain, and whole-wheat sourdough bread. I purchased my bread at the Market City bakery in the Milwaukee area. I am sure you have a local bakery that can supply your needs.

Melt butter in a large stockpot and sauté lobster and shrimp. Set aside and squeeze lime juice over the seafood.

Using a wok add olive oil and heat to medium heat. Add 2 cups of chicken broth, and stir. Add asparagus, leek, mushrooms, red pepper, basil, scallions, celery, and garlic and cook vegetables until barely tender.

Add partially cooked vegetables to the seafood in the stockpot. Add the remaining chicken broth, half and half, wine, onion powder, seafood seasoning, and pepper. Cook over low heat for about one hour.

For cooking pasta:

3	cups raw Penne Rigate (low carbohydrate, optional)
2 1/2	quarts water
2	teaspoons olive oil
1	teaspoon salt

Add olive oil and salt to water and bring to a boil. Add the pasta and boil until the pasta is tender. Drain and set aside.

When soup is heated through, add the cooked pasta to the soup. Heat to serving temperature and serve immediately.

Poor Man's Lobster

Yield: *6 servings.*

1	pound frozen cod loin
2 1/2	quarts water
1	tablespoon lemon juice
1/2	teaspoon salt

Bring water to a boil; add the lemon juice and salt and stir until mixed. Add the frozen cod to the water, boiling for 8 to 10 minutes, or until cod is cooked through.

Drain off the water and place cooked fish on a paper towel and dab dry. Flake the fish to use in your recipe.

Saint Nicholas Coffee

Include your cafeteria staff in the preparations for this activity. Have coffee, tea, milk, and juice available for refreshments.

Gather the residents and invite school children to make a visit to celebrate Saint Nicholas' Day on December 6. Fifth and Sixth grade children are a good age for this activity. Ask the children to dress up as elves and have them sing "Jolly Old St. Nicholas" and also recite some Christmas poems. Practice with the children, or have them practice at school so they have the song and poems familiarized. If they have trouble memorizing the poems, make copies for them to use. Several of our residents broke into tears when the children presented them with candy and shook their hand.

I remember when I was a child our pastor, dressed as Saint Nicholas, came to our school every year on Saint Nicholas' Day. All through the semester our teacher would say, "Saint Nicholas knows who is naughty and who is nice. He will pass you by and you will not get your bag of candy if you are naughty." The bags of candy were big bags so I tried hard to be nice—I didn't even like the candy. Truthfully, it was the thought of being told I was a bad child and I did not want to be singled out in front of my classmates for being bad. I always gave my candy away, and sighed with relief that one more year had gone by with me being a good child. I even got all the children on the playground to gather together and sing, "Santa Claus is Coming to Town". I made it through all eight grades being nice!

Just last Christmas my husband and I were attending his work Christmas party and we sang that very song. My husband confessed to me that he, too, was told to be good or there would be no candy. He loves candy. I asked him if he was nice just to get the candy, or due to fear—I never did get an answer from him. Oh well!

I told that story at our facility and one of the residents started to snicker. He didn't care if he was a good child or not because he got others to give him their candy. He said he enjoyed being mischievous. I didn't quiz him on what kind of trouble he stirred up in the classroom, as I was happy he came to our activity. He said his wife always kept him in line. He enjoyed having a good time. He was a very pleasant man.

Throughout the entire Christmas season I gave programs including poems and music. To my surprise even the second- and third-stage Alzheimer's patients could complete my sentences. I would start a verse of poetry and pause, and the residents would complete the verse. This always brought big smiles. I would always decorate a table with a tree and decorations to set the mood for the activity. It is an attention getter and the residents will talk about the decorations while they are waiting for the start of the program.

Jest 'Fore Christmas
by Eugene Field

Father calls me William, sister calls me Will
Mother calls me Willie, but the fellers call me Bill!
Mighty glad I ain't a girl—ruther be a boy,
Without them sashes, curls, an' things that's worn by Fauntleroy!
Love to chawnk green apples an' go swimmin' in the lake—
Hate to take the castor-ile they give for belly-ache!
'Most all the time, the whole year 'round, there ain't no flies on me,
But jest 'fore Christmas I'm as good as I kin be!

Got a yeller dog named Sport, sic him on the cat;
First thing she knows she doesn't know where she is at!
Got a clipper sled, an' when us kids goes out to slide,
'Long comes the grocery cart, an' we all hook a ride!
But sometimes when the grocery man is worried an' cross,
He reaches at us with his whip, an' larrups up his hoss,
An' then I laff an' holler, "Oh, ye never teched me!"
But jest 'fore Christmas I'm as good as I kin be!

Gran'ma says she hopes that when I git to be a man,
I'll be a missionarer like her oldest brother, Dan,
As was et up by the cannibals that lives in Ceylon's Isle,
Where every prospeck pleases, an' only man is vile!
But Gran'ma she has never been to see a Wild West show,
Nor read the Life of Daniel Boone, or else I guess she'd know
That Buff'lo Bill an' cowboys is good enough for me!
Excep' just 'fore Christmas, when I'm good as I kin be!

And then old Sport he hangs a round, so solemn-like an' still,
His eyes they keep a-saying': "What's the matter, little Bill?"
The old cat sneaks down off her perch an' wonders what's become
Of them two enemies of hern that used to make things hum!
But I am so perlite an' 'tend so earnestly to biz,
That Mother says to Father: "How improved our Willis is!"
But Father, havin' been a boy hisself, suspicions me
When, jest 'fore Christmas, I'm as good as I kin be!

For Christmas, with its lots an' lots of candies, cakes, an' toys,
Was made, they say, for proper kids, an' not for naughty boys
So wash yer face an' bresh yer hair, an' mind yer p's and q's,
An' don't bust out yer pantaloons, and don't wear out yer shoes;
Say "Yessum" to the ladies, an' "Yessur" to the men,
An' when they's company, don't pass yer plate for pie again;
But, thinkin' of the things yer'd like to see upon that tree,
Jest 'fore Christmas be as good as yer kin be!

Reference:

From *Favorite Poems Old and New*, selected by Helen Ferris, illustrated by Leonard Weisgard (1957). Doubleday Book for Young Readers, published by Delacorte Press. ("A Visit from St. Nicholas"—following—is also from the same book.)

A Visit From St. Nicholas

by Clement Clarke Moore

'Twas the night before Christmas, when all through the house
Not a creature was stirring, not even a mouse;
The stockings were hung by the chimney with care,
In hopes that St. Nicholas soon would be there.
The children were nestled all snug in their beds,
While visions of sugar-plums danced in their heads;
And mamma in her 'kerchief, and I in my cap,
Had just settled our brains for a long winter's nap,
When out on the lawn there arose such a clatter,
I sprang from my bed to see what was the matter.
Away to the window I flew like a flash,
Tore open the shutters and threw up the sash.
The moon on the breast of the new-fallen snow
Gave the luster of midday to objects below,
When, what to my wondering eyes should appear,
But a miniature sleigh, and eight tiny reindeer,
With a little old driver, so lively and quick,
I knew in a moment it must be St. Nick.
More rapid than eagles his coursers they came,
And he whistled, and shouted, and called them by name:
"Now Dasher! Now, Dancer! Now, Prancer and Vixen!
On, Comet! On, Cupid! On, Donder and Blitzen!
To the top of the porch! To the top of the wall!
Now dash away! Dash away! Dash away all!"
As dry leaves that before the wild hurricane fly,
When they meet with an obstacle, mount to the sky,
So up to the housetop the coursers they flew,
With the sleigh full of toys, and St. Nicholas, too.
And then, in a twinkling, I heard on the roof
The prancing and pawing of each little hoof.
As I drew in my head, and was turning around,
Down the chimney St. Nicholas came with a bound.
He was dressed all in fur, from his head to his foot,
And his clothes were all covered with ashes and soot;
A bundle of toys he had flung on his back,
And he looked like a peddler just opening his pack.
His eyes—how they twinkled! His dimples how merry!
His cheeks were like roses, his nose like a cherry!
His droll little mouth was drawn up like a bow,

And the beard on his chin was as white as the snow;
The stump of a pipe he held tight in his teeth,
And the smoke it encircled his head like a wreath;
He had a broad face and a little round belly
That shook, when he laughed, like a bowlful of jelly.
He was chubby and plump, a right jolly old elf,
And I laughed when I saw him, in spite of myself;
A wink of his eye and a twist of his head,
Soon gave me to know I had nothing to dread;
He spoke not a word, but went straight to his work,
And filled all the stockings; then turned with a jerk,
And laying his finger aside of his nose
And giving a nod, up the chimney he rose;
He sprang to his sleigh, to his team gave a whistle,
And away they all flew like the down of a thistle.
But I heard him exclaim, ere he drove out of sight,
"Happy Christmas to all, and to all a good night."

Men's Lunch for Pearl Harbor Day

Ask the kitchen staff to bring the men's lunch to a separate room you can use for this activity. Announce the program to the men in advance and remind them in the morning of the men's lunch. Remind any personnel that help the men to bring them to the special lunch.

History

Pearl Harbor in Hawaii has been used by the Navy since 1887. On December 7, 1941, there were 94 ships in the harbor—it was a peaceful Sunday morning until the Japanese attacked at 7:55 a.m.

People did not think Japan would bomb the U.S. But Admiral Isoroku Yamamoto wanted a surprise attack that would cripple the U.S. Navy. Japan wanted to conquer Southeast Asia. They had worked out their plan very well, even including special code words to send messages to their flyers. "Rain" meant to carry out the attack and "Tora, Tora" meant the Japanese flyers were to kill the soldiers on the ships in the harbor and wherever they saw them on land.

U.S. Colonel William E. Farthing predicted the bombing of Pearl Harbor. His theory was the Japanese were not afraid to come into the harbor, even though they knew full well they would die in the attack. Others in the armed service and administration in Washington believed Hawaii had the strongest naval base and could withstand anything—this was foolish on their part.

Farthing suggested that Hawaii should receive long-range torpedo bombers, but nothing was done. The U.S. was short on B-17s as they had been sent to the Philippines and Britain so the U.S. was caught off guard and suffered the consequences. The ships and airplanes were all lined up very neatly that morning and it made it very easy for the Japanese planes to take out the whole fleet.

Eight battleships were lost during the raid, and the *Arizona* remains at the bottom of Pearl Harbor to this day. It was fortunate that the dry dock, gasoline storage, and naval repair shops were not damaged and they were all able to operate the day after the bombing.

President Franklin D. Roosevelt convened both houses of Congress and made a Declaration of War on December 8, 1941, against not only Japan but also Germany and Italy. The leaders of the two later nations were Adolph Hitler in Germany and Bernito Mussolini in Italy.

Admiral Chester W. Nimitz was the commander of the Pacific Naval forces for the majority of the war.

Anyone who visits Pearl Harbor cannot help but be touched by the loss of all those young lives in this brutal attack.

Pearl Harbor Questions:

1. What was the name of the main city at Pearl Harbor?

2. How long did it take to destroy the ships and bomb Pearl Harbor?

3. Name the five out of seven battleships that were hit.

4. How many service men and women died on December 7, 1941?

5. Which ship was able to head out to sea?

6. Which ship was hit in the second round of bombing by the Japanese planes?

7. Where were you the day Pearl Harbor was attacked?

8. Name the U.S. President when Pearl Harbor was bombed.

9. What was the name of the U.S. ship that sank in the harbor and is still there as a monument to all those who died that day.

10. Which bay did the Japanese Imperial Naval fleet sail from?

11. Name the islands where Tankan Bay is located.

12. What three foods represent the symbols "to fight, win, and be happy"?

13. What act finally made the U.S. enter World War II?

14. Which city and state is the location of Pearl Harbor?

15. Does any one know the code message flashed by the Japanese Navy commander Mitsus in the surprise attack on Pearl Harbor?

16. Name the Emperor of Japan at the time of the bombing of Pearl Harbor.

Pearl Harbor Answer Key:

1. Pearl City.
2. 1 hour and 45 minutes.
3. *Arizona, West Virginia, Oklahoma, Tennessee, Nevada.*
4. 2,000 armed forces men and women lost their lives that day.
5. *Nevada.*
6. *Pennsylvania.*
7. Ask your residents to tell what they remember about that day.
8. Franklin D. Roosevelt.
9. *Arizona.*
10. Tankan Bay.
11. Kurile Islands.
12. Dried chestnuts, shellfish, and seaweed.
13. After the bombing of Pearl Harbor.
14. Honolulu, Hawaii.
15. "Mitsuo Fuch, Da Tora, Tora, Tora."
16. Hirohito.

B	I	N	G	O
Blue Christmas	Jingle Bells	Hark! The Herald Angels Sing	A Holly, Jolly Christmas	Oh Christmas Tree
We Three Kings	Frosty the Snowman	Toyland	It Came Upon the Midnight Clear	Silent Night
Santa Claus is Coming to Town	God Rest Ye Merry Gentlemen	**FREE**	Deck the Halls	Christ was Born on Christmas Day
The Twelve Days of Christmas	Silver Bells	Winter Wonderland	We Wish You a Merry Christmas	The First Noel
Jolly Old St. Nicholas	Let It Snow!	The Most Wonderful Time of the Year	A Marshmallow World	Angels We Have Heard on High

```
A Y H G R A V Y C H S E I V I I P G E I W A I
V R T E L D E T R O I T S A N N H E B A E M B
F I I C E A R A A U O T O K T T O A E P S I Y
R I A Z O B S I V H T R N   A E E C N I T S D
M A R G O R T G E F T A R I N I N U L T V C O
U L S S T N A L R M H L I D G W I W I A I H W
T T C M E F A P S N H E O N I R X W C B R I N
A E I A F E P U T S Q I W G E I N I H R G E E
Z N R R L S L M A S S G G K R S R E T E I V S
A N U Y O I Q I E V U H H I E T D R E A N E K
U E P L T I F E I V E O Y T K S O L R D I N L
G S S A C V T O N A P I A G U Q K E Y G A I E
D S U N C A T N R I V H N D O E L A A A T G E
A E N D I L Q A L N C X U A J F A U Y E K H H
I E D E L A U H W O I I O N B T H R H O E T I
N U A D M F Z T A D A A M N K A O N M T N H A
G A Y A C U R T I S S W H G O W M I P I N T D
A N P Y H N N D E M V E N S O L A C E O E T I
R U I I A H E L E N A I N G H C O G L A L A S
D E U H A B J A L T I K E Y M A U S E O Y S K
B R T I S T P S F O W B I I T A W I B I B I R
I R A N O Q E A Y P D W I C H D A Y R N N E I
I N H P W N E V A D A B C A K B N R I I N S P
```

Pearl Harbor Word Search
U.S. Ships on Battleship Row in Pearl Harbor

NEVADA	CALIFORNIA	DETROIT	OGLALA
PHOENIX	TANGIER	SOLACE	SHAW
OKLAHOMA	UTAH	TENNESSEE	DOWNES
WEST VIRGINIA	CURTISS	MARYLAND	ARIZONA
VERSTAE	RALEIGH	HELENA	

Pearl Harbor Word Search
U.S. Ships on Battleship Row in Pearl Harbor

NEVADA	CALIFORNIA	DETROIT	OGLALA
PHOENIX	TANGIER	SOLACE	SHAW
OKLAHOMA	UTAH	TENNESSEE	DOWNES
WEST VIRGINIA	CURTISS	MARYLAND	ARIZONA
VERSTAE	RALEIGH	HELENA	

A Family Gathering to Light the Christmas Tree and Sing Christmas Carols

This event is a very simple, but effective activity. I sent invitations to families to attend the lighting ceremony—I asked each person to bring an ornament for the tree (if they wished).

The day of the event we bought a tree and placed the lights on it, along with the ornaments we'd saved from previous years.

We asked the residents to gather in the meeting room a few minutes before the families were to arrive, and as the guests arrived we encouraged visiting until everyone was in attendance. When everyone was there we asked people who had brought ornaments to come to the tree and hang their ornament and then we lighted the tree. I played my accordion and we sang Christmas carols.

Hot cocoa, punch, and Christmas cookies were served.

This was a great way to get families to participate in our facility's Christmas activities and share the Christmas spirit.

The "Q" Word Game

Answers should be words with the letter "Q" in them.

1. Look into or try to find out about a place or thing.

2. Silent

3. Resign from a job.

4. Having the same rank as someone else.

5. Two people, statements, or things that are not equal.

6. A type of bedcover.

7. Being the same.

8. Selling out to pay a business debt.

9. Alcohol such as gin, rum, or vodka.

10. A fluid substance.

11. A flavored drink high in alcohol content.

12. Pertaining to horses.

13. A mathematical expression.

14. The circle around the center of the Earth.

15. A person who attends a royal family.

16. All angles of a diagram are equal.

17. Having to do with balance.

18. Fairness in legal procedures.

19. Personal gear you might carry on an outing.

20. A fine carriage.

21. A statement used to find out the truth.

22. A vegetable family that includes zucchini, butternut, spaghetti, and acorn.

23. Four of these coins equal a dollar.

24. Two pints make a _____.

25. A fight or dispute between people.

26. Isolation for the public's protection to a contagious disease.

27. A large hole in the ground where stone is extracted.

28. If there are 12 months in a year, what is 3 months called?

29. To stop a rebellion or an objection.

30. A province in Canada.

31. To search for a treasure.

32. To ask about a fact or situation.

33. The wife of a King.

34. A certain size of bed.

35. Taking a drink to stop your thirst.

36. This dish is made of eggs, meat, and cheese in a pie shell.

37. To argue over a petty fact.

38. Fast moving.

39. A bread item such as a muffin, or banana bread.

40. Large stiff wing or tail feathers of a bird.

41. To shake or tremble.

42. A short written or oral test.

43. A pecular trait.

44. A riding whip with a short handle.

45. To reach an allotted amount.

46. A passage quoted in literature.

47. Unfair.

48. A port located on the Pacific Ocean in Chile.

49. This country is in the Middle East. Its people are mainly Muslim and they have large oil reserves.

50. A native of Iraq is called by this name.

51. An American Indian tribe.

52. A puzzled expression.

53. Someone you know.

54. Strange or peculiar.

55. A box or drawing with four equal sides is said to be _____.

56. To use foolishly.

57. To cry or scream loudly.

58. A serious, noisy argument.

59. Bend down by bending your hips and knees.

60. Wife of a North American Indian.

61. A person living on government land in hopes of gaining title to the land.

62. To wrinkle up your eyes to a slit.

63. Apply pressure to something.

64. The title of an English country gentleman.

65. A type of sea mollusk.

66. A small firecracker that burns with a hissing noise before exploding.

67. This rodent creature has a busy tail, is gray or red, and loves trees.

68. A Mediterranean plant.

69. Not being able to sit still.

70. A dance where four couples make a dance group and a caller calls out directions for the dance.

71. A car used by police.

72. A unit of the cavalry, army troops, or tanks.

73. To treat fairly.

74. Very dirty and unorganized due to neglect.

75. A British description for a short, fat person or thing.

"Q" Word Game Answer Key:

1. Inquire	17. Equilibrium	33. Queen	49. Iraq	65. Squid
2. Quiet	18. Equitable	34. Queen-size	50. Iraqi	66. Squib
3. Quit	19. Equipment	35. Quench	51. Iroquois	67. Squirrel
4. Equality	20. Equipage	36. Quiche	52. Quizzical	68. Squirting
5. Inequality	21. Equivocate	37. Quibble	53. Acquaintance	cucumber
6. Quilt	22. Squash	38. Quick	54. Queer	69. Squirm
7. Equal	23. Quarter	39. Quick Bread	55. Square	70. Square dance
8. Liquidate	24. Quart	40. Quill	56. Squander	71. Squad
9. Liquor	25. Quarrel	41. Quiver	57. Squall	72. Squadron
10. Liquid	26. Quarantine	42. Quiz	58. Squabble	73. Square deal
11. Liqueur	27. Quarry	43. Quirk	59. Squat	74. Squalid
12. Equestrian	28. Quarterly	44. Quirt	60. Squaw	75. Squab
13. Equation	29. Quash	45. Quota	61. Squatter	
14. Equator	30. Quebec	46. Quotation	62. Squint	
15. Equerry	31. Quest	47. Inequity	63. Squeeze	
16. Equiangular	32. Question	48. Inquique	64. Squire	

Children Caroling

I plan this activity every year in our facility. In fact, my husband has become involved also. We create the Christmas spirit for the moment for everyone, but we've found the Alzheimer's patients especially enjoy this activity. Remember—it is music that touches the inner soul.

Contact a church youth group, or a music teacher at your local elementary school and invite them to come to your facility for Christmas caroling. You can make a regular program out of it, or just have them walk through the halls in the evening singing carols.

If you are making a regular program out of it meet with the group to practice the songs and the order of presentation before the planned entertainment. Maybe someone from the group, or a teacher or parent, will play a guitar to add to the program.

No matter how you present this activity your residents will enjoy it immensely. It will even bring tears to the eyes of some, as they remember earlier Christmases. Maybe they even did the caroling when they were young.

If you make this a regular program for your residents be sure to serve refreshments at the end of the program. It doesn't have to be fancy, or a lot—just a drink and a Christmas cookie.

Bake Sale to Raise Money for Toys for the Disadvantaged Children in Your Community

We asked our employees and their friends to contribute baked goods for this event. Many people also responded by bringing a small toy to add to our collection for the children. We raised $100 from our bake sale, and interestingly enough, we also collected 100 toys. We made a list of children we knew could benefit from is project, but if you don't know who should receive the toys your local Social Services Department can help you, or your elementary school secretary may know of some children.

We had a number of volunteers who wanted to help so they took the list and went to purchase the toys and bring them to our facility. Some of them even helped our residents with the gift wrapping of the toys.

Wrapping Presents for Disadvantaged Children Coffee

We requested donations of wrapping paper and ribbon for the gift wrapping. You can even use newspaper for a different look if you need to. Department stores and gift shops may donate to this cause.

Gather your residents and volunteers and set up teams or an assembly line for wrapping. If you have wallpaper samples one group can cut out tags from it. You will need to mark the packages somehow with whether it is for a boy or girl and the appropriate age. If you have a "Merry Christmas" stamp you can use it on the tag.

It's amazing how residents take such pride in this project.

Once the gifts are all wrapped, you will need to find people to deliver the toys to the children, or maybe your local Social Services Department or Fire Department can help with this.

Everyone involved will feel so good for making Christmas for these children. If you have a local Childrens' Hospital you can also deliver gifts to them for the sick children.

I am a firm believer in making the elderly feel needed and keeping them involved in their local community projects does this very well. It helps your residents to feel vital and emotionally healthy. This is some of the best medicine for your residents!

Christmas Spelling Bee

Simple Words:

Baby Jesus	Scene	Feast	Legend
Parties	Chimney	Yule Log	Elves
Magi	Christmas	Caroling	Star
Three Kings	Wrapping Paper	Noel	Manger
Silver Bells	Stockings	Gold	Advent
Candy Cane	Customs	Wise Men	Goodwill

Challenging Words:

Poinsettias	Tradition	Wassail	Ceppo
Ornament	Epiphany	Nativity Scene	Hanukka
King Herod	Gingerbread	Myrrh	Bethlehem
King Wenceslas	Santa Claus	Frankincense	Mistletoe
Figi Pudding	Christianity	Jultomen	Entertainment
Kris Kringle	Medieval Gifts	Julklapp	Yorkshire Pudding

```
N E B C K S M O C I S A R C R E A M E D S K H
S N T U S P I C E D T E A A S T O M A S M H O
I T H C T O S T S H O C M N A O N O N P O T L
Y A O U T S O S E E P B A D H M Q N D I K G I
E E T M R S N A E N T R R I C S O O J N E A D
I S B B O T I L T T I A Z E A E F P E A D D A
R B U E A U E M E A D I I D A E A E R C S C Y
S K T R S F E O B E S S P G N F I N R H A G P
P I T F T N N O S T E A R C C R G Y R L M U
I Z E I E E F D A B E D N A H T W R Y S M R N
C O R N D D L G O K L R F P O O O A R C O A C
E R E G C M A L I I E A R E V Q T V S G N A H
C A D E H U A A N Z N B U F Y D L T S S I C H
O E R R E S T Z T O G B I R D D I E O N A L O
O S U S S H E E R R A I T U I O C V G D V I V
K T M A T R D E W A R T M I P C K E I G D S L
I R S N N O Y E E E N U D T P S A D R N N Y M
E R B D U O H V L I D E F P O E M M I R I O B
S T O W T M P E O S E S U E P I I G I M V T G
C U R I S S L E B R U C H E N H T E A N E R Y
E M A C C H O T C H O C O L A T E S R R P S U
N I E H E G L A Z E D H A M N R T S P O S T R
I F O N D A N T C A N D I E S I R O M A K I K
```

Christmas Beverages and Holiday Foods Word Search

WASSAIL	ALMOND GLAZE	SPICE COOKIES	HOT BUTTERED RUM
HOT TODDY	HOLIDAY PUNCH	CREAMED SPINACH	STUFFED MUSHROOMS
DIVINITY	EGGNOG	SMOKED SALMON	MARZIPAN FRUIT
LEBRUCHEN	HOT CHOCOLATE	FONDANT CANDIES	
SPICED TEA	ANCHOVY DIP	ROASTED CHESTNUTS	
ROMAKI	TOM AND JERRY	CUCUMBER FINGER SANDWICH	
BRAISED RABBIT	GLAZED HAM	CANDIED GRAPEFRUIT PEEL	

Christmas Beverages and Holiday Foods Word Search

WASSAIL	ALMOND GLAZE	SPICE COOKIES	HOT BUTTERED RUM
HOT TODDY	HOLIDAY PUNCH	CREAMED SPINACH	STUFFED MUSHROOMS
DIVINITY	EGGNOG	SMOKED SALMON	MARZIPAN FRUIT
LEBRUCHEN	HOT CHOCOLATE	FONDANT CANDIES	
SPICED TEA	ANCHOVY DIP	ROASTED CHESTNUTS	
ROMAKI	TOM AND JERRY	CUCUMBER FINGER SANDWICH	
BRAISED RABBIT	GLAZED HAM	CANDIED GRAPEFRUIT PEEL	

An Old-Fashioned Christmas Tea

I remember when I was in college we gave an old-fashioned Christmas tea each year. I enjoyed it so much that I carried on the tradition during my teaching and catering careers.

I enjoy this simple, but elegant tea. Here are some of my favorite recipes.

To decorate the serving table place candles and candleholders on a Christmas tablecloth. Arrange the breads, butter, fruits, and beverages on the buffet table. Serve food on festive china or crystal and enjoy!

Holiday Coffee Cake

Yield: 8 servings.

3/4	cup sugar
1/4	cup shortening
1	egg
1/2	cup 2% milk
1 1/2	cups flour
1/2	teaspoon salt
2	teaspoons baking powder
1/3	cup candied fruit, cut up

Topping:

1/2	teaspoon cinnamon
3	tablespoons sugar

Garnish:

red and green maraschino cherries

Grease a 9-inch round pan. Heat oven to 350 degrees.

Cut shortening into fine particles; add sugar and mix thoroughly.

Mix flour, salt, and baking powder. Set aside.

Mix egg and milk. Add shortening to mixture. Add dry ingredients and mix until moistened. Stir in candied fruit.

Mix cinnamon and sugar and sprinkle on top of the batter in the baking pan.

Bake for 30 to 35 minutes, or until toothpick comes out clean. Garnish with maraschino cherries.

Streusel Filling:

1/2	cup brown sugar
2	tablespoons flour
2	teaspoons cinnamon
2	tablespoons butter, melted
1/2	cup chopped pecans

Pour half of the coffee cake batter (above recipe) into the baking pan and sprinkle half of the Streusel mixture on the cake batter. Add the remaining cake batter and sprinkle remaining Streusel mixture over top of cake. Bake per the directions above.

Orange Tea Biscuits
Yield: 20 miniature biscuits.

    2   cups all-purpose flour
    3   teaspoons baking powder
  1/2   teaspoon salt
  1/2   cup butter
  2/3   cup 2% milk
  1/2   cup orange juice concentrate (undiluted)
   20   small sugar cubes

Preheat oven to 400 degrees.

Combine dry ingredients thoroughly. Cut butter into the flour mixture until it resembles coarse cornmeal. Pour in milk and mix lightly with a fork.

Turn dough onto a lightly floured countertop. Knead. Roll out to 1/2-inch thickness. Cut 1-inch diameter biscuits. Place on cookie sheet.

Dip sugar cubes into the orange concentrate and press into the center of each biscuit.

Bake until golden brown, about 10 to 14 minutes.

Pecan Fruit Bread
Yield: 1 loaf.

  1 1/2 cups finely chopped candied fruit
    1/2 cup finely chopped pecans
      3 tablespoons butter
    1/2 cup boiling water
         grated rind of 1 orange
    1/3 cup orange juice
      1 cup sugar
      1 egg, beaten
    1/2 teaspoon almond flavoring
      2 cups flour
    1/4 teaspoon baking soda
      2 teaspoons baking powder
    1/2 teaspoon salt

Preheat oven to 350 degrees. Spray non-stick coating on a loaf pan measuring 9"x5"x3".

Mix flour, baking soda, and salt together.

Place butter in bowl and pour boiling water over it. Add the orange rind and juice, sugar, almond flavoring, beaten egg, fruits, and nuts.

Add the dry ingredients, stirring only to moisten the batter.

Pour into prepared loaf pan. Bake 55 to 60 minutes, or until toothpick comes out clean.

Banana Nut Bread

Yield: 1 loaf.

      1/2   cup shortening
        1   cup sugar
        1   cup mashed ripe bananas
        3   eggs, well beaten
        1   tablespoon sour milk
        2   cups flour
        1   teaspoon soda
      1/4   teaspoon salt

Heat oven to 350 degrees. Spray non-stick coating on loaf pan 9"x5"x3".

Cream shortening, add sugar and cream until light and fluffy. Add eggs and beat well.

Mash bananas and add to egg, shortening/sugar mixture, mixing thoroughly.

Add soda and salt to flour.

Add flour mixture and milk and mix until batter is moistened.

Pour into pan and bake for about 1 hour, or until toothpick comes out clean.

Note: Once a friend called me and said, "My banana bread did not turn out."
I asked, "Did you use ripe bananas?"
"No, I used green bananas!"
She learned the hard way that she needed to use yellow or very ripe bananas. I like the banana peel to become black before I use them for banana bread. At this stage the banana is very sweet and perfect for tasty banana bread.

Date Nut Bread

Yield: 1 loaf.

        2   cups chopped dates
        2   teaspoons soda
        1   cup boiling water
        2   eggs, beaten
      1/2   teaspoon vanilla
        2   cups flour
      1/2   teaspoon baking powder
      1/2   teaspoon salt
      1/2   cup shortening
      1/2   cup sugar
      1/2   cup chopped pecans

Heat oven to 350 degrees. Spray non-stick coating on a 9"x5"x3" loaf pan.

Sprinkle dates with soda and add boiling water. Cover and cool.

Mix flour, baking powder, and salt together.

Cream the shortening and sugar together. Add the beaten eggs, vanilla, and date mixture. Add salt to flour. Gradually add flour mixture to the liquid batter. Add nuts last and beat until smooth. Pour batter into pan and bake for 60 to 70 minutes, or until toothpick comes out clean.

See recipe for **Cranberry-Orange Bread** in the November chapter, page 196. This is my most favorite Christmas bread. Not only do I make it in November and serve it with soup, I serve it at my Christmas Tea, too.

Apricot Bread
Yield: 1 loaf.

1/2	cup milk
2	eggs, beaten
2	tablespoons grated orange rind
2	cups flour
4	teaspoons baking powder
1/2	teaspoon soda
1	teaspoon salt
1/2	cup shortening
1	cup sugar
3/4	cup whole wheat flour
1	cup finely chopped dates
1	cup finely cut dried apricots

Heat oven to 350 degrees. Spray non-stick coating on 9"x5"x3" loaf pan.

Mix flour, baking powder, soda, and salt together. Cut in shortening. Add sugar, whole-wheat flour mix, and fruit.

Moisten the batter with the milk and eggs.

Pour into prepared loaf pan and bake for 45 to 55 minutes, or until toothpick comes out clean.

Always let your breads rest one day before slicing and serving them.

Stuffed Dates

Yield: 10 servings.

    1   box (12 ounces) pitted dates
    1   package (8 ounces) cream cheese
    1   teaspoon vanilla
    1   tablespoon powdered sugar
    1   package (8 ounces) pecan halves

Beat cream cheese, vanilla, and powdered sugar together. Slit dates and pipe in the cream cheese with a number 28 star tip. Place one pecan half in the middle of the cream cheese.

Serve on a platter lined with a paper doily, or on a glass mirror.

Candied Grapefruit Peel

Yield: 10 servings.

    2   grapefruit
        water for cooking peel
    1   cup sugar
    1/2 cup water
        granulated sugar

Peel the two grapefruit and cut the peel into strips about 1/4-inch wide. (Be sure to leave the white pulp on the peel.) Cover the peel with water and cook until tender. Drain.

Make a syrup of 1 cup sugar and 1/2 cup water by boiling in a large bottom kettle until it begins to thicken. Add the cooked grapefruit strips and continue cooking until all the syrup has been absorbed. Remove pan from heat. Roll peels in granulated sugar. Be careful not to get excess sugar on the peel strips. Dry and arrange on platters for serving.

Spiced Tea

Yield: 6 servings.

    1 1/2 cups water
      1/2 cup sugar
        1 cup orange juice
        1 cup pineapple juice
           juice from one lemon
        3 (2-inches each) cinnamon sticks
   7 or 8 whole cloves
   7 or 8 allspice
        4 teaspoons tea leaves, your choice of flavor.

Place the cinnamon sticks, cloves, and allspice in a tea ball or cheesecloth. Combine sugar, water, and juices. Add the spices in the tea ball and bring to a boil. Remove from heat when it starts to boil and add the tea leaves (also in a tea ball). Steep 3 minutes. Remove the tea but leave the spices in until the flavors are blended to your desired strength.

Reception French Cocoa

Yield: 8 servings.

      1/2 cup sugar
      1/2 cup cocoa
        2 cups water
        5 cups milk

Mix dry ingredients and add the water and cook over direct heat for 5 minutes, or to a thick syrup. Add hot milk and heat to almost boiling. Keep hot. Wire whip before serving. Serve with whipped heavy cream as a garnish and sprinkle cinnamon sugar on top.

```
B E A O L O B E S R S R S V U L S H N R H S R
A N I V W G O S T O E A I C T S T I U I K S S
C F R W S I A S N O W M A N R E C A R O L S T
M H S E H F O K L D C A N D E A H A I O Y S A
O A A A I T I I E C A R O L S I R H O S E H R
R A N R H S N Z N H U E M V A C I C M A G O O
E T T E I R T O G R T S T O N E S A S I O L F
R N A M S T R R A I A E T S D N T S E N D Y B
L A C S A E Y A R S R L P R E I M T E T E F E
E T L G I G K E N T M Y J A E E A F F N C A T
V I A K C V I C D M I G A O N R S O C I O M H
U V U H E E C S U A S E S M Y S T L T C R I L
R I S T O N K A N S D R A E I N R K M H A L E
G T T G R U S L E C T V N D Y B E L Q O T Y H
A Y H Y E H D E R A A O E F E T E O N L I E E
R S R U D O L P H R E N M N I K A R D A O S M
R C E L T A E S K D D Y U S T A M E O S N B N
I E E E D P G P D S A E C C A W B I I K S E G
S N K L S S E O C F E Y E E L S R B S S S R F
O E I O R E N P H I S P T S L T E E E M E R E
N S N G P E D T E R S V E U S I F G A D F I R
I R G A N T S I S H E E P R K N I G H T G B M
E P S C H O P E D V H A D V E N T K S T H A O
```

Christmas Word Search

JOY	SHEEP	LEGENDS	FOLKLORE
HOPE	CHARITY	SANTA CLAUS	NATIVITY SCENES
ADVENT	HOLY FAMILY	GIFTS	CHRISTMAS TREE
THREE KINGS	MAGI	CAROLS	CHRISTMAS CARDS
RUDOLPH	SNOWMAN	DECORATIONS	ADVENT WREATH
YULE LOG	CUSTOMS	SAINT NICHOLAS	STAR OF BETHLEHEM

Christmas Word Search

JOY	SHEEP	LEGENDS	FOLKLORE
HOPE	CHARITY	SANTA CLAUS	NATIVITY SCENES
ADVENT	HOLY FAMILY	GIFTS	CHRISTMAS TREE
THREE KINGS	MAGI	CAROLS	CHRISTMAS CARDS
RUDOLPH	SNOWMAN	DECORATIONS	ADVENT WREATH
YULE LOG	CUSTOMS	SAINT NICHOLAS	STAR OF BETHLEHEM

Santa's Secret Gift Exchange

While presenting programs at various facilities I've learned that so many people need small items such as stockings, or a tube of lipstick, or deodorant. Throughout the year many of us documented the needs and desires of the residents. We raised enough money among ourselves to purchase these small items. We gathered our group of "Santas" together on our own time and wrapped these small gifts—marking each gift with a small card that said, "To: Mary   From: Santa"

One morning very near Christmas we gathered the residents for a morning coffee (after we had placed the gifts under the Christmas tree). As we handed out the gifts we told about Santa stopping by early with these gifts for them. We played Christmas music while they opened their gifts. When all the gifts were opened we served coffee and donuts and the group sang Christmas carols. At the close of coffee time we shook everyone's hand and wished everyone a Merry Christmas!

Christmas Trail Mix

Yield: 3 pounds

1 package (15.25 ounces) bite-size honey-nut biscuits cereal
1 can (10 ounces) salted peanuts—you can use low-salt if you have people who should not have too much salt
2 packages (6 ounces each) cherry-flavored sweetened dried cranberries
1 package (12 ounces) white chocolate chips

Combine the ingredients in a large bowl. Fill Christmas cupcake liners with the trail mix, so each resident has their individual portion.

Serve and enjoy—anytime!

Christmas Customs Around the World

The purpose of the custom's gathering is to have the residents share their personal family customs and to learn about other people's customs.

You can use all of the following customs, or pick out the ones that are connected with your residents. (Example: If you have several people from Sweden in your group include the Swedish customs in your program.)

History of Some General Customs

The legend of the **Christmas Stocking** began with Bishop Nicholas. He provided dowries for three daughters of a nobleman who had lost his fortune in a failed business. The Bishop filled three bags with gold coins and dropped them into the stockings hung by the chimney.

Christmas Seals originated in Denmark. A postal employee there started the idea of selling the seals to raise money to help people suffering from tuberculosis and needing hospital care. The U.S. joined in the effort and sold the seals here also to help those suffering from the disease.

The **Star of Bethlehem** is associated with the three wise men who followed the star and it led them to the manger where the baby Jesus lay. The song "We Three Kings" tells the story. Play the song and review the words with the group.

Santa Claus has many different names in different countries. However, he is usually dressed similarly from country to country. Here are the different names and countries:

Austria	Santaklausen
Britain	Father Christmas
China	Dun Chelaroren
Germany	Pelnickel
Holland	Saint Nicolas or Sinter Klaas
Norway	Father Frost
Russia	Saint Nicholas
Sweden	Jultamten
U.S.	Santa Claus

Your residents may have other country Santa names to add to this list—ask them!

Africa

Many of the African natives are not Christians and they are unaware of the holiday.

In the Congo many people sing Christmas carols while others tell the nativity story.

In Ethiopia there are Christian groups that came from Europe such as the Reformed Church of Holland. Missionaries have helped bring Christianity to the people.

Christians work hard during the year to save for gifts to offer during the Christmas season. They carry their offerings in a basket on their head as they file into church. This is a large colorful procession leading to the church.

Many non-Christians live in fear, but these gifts warm the hearts of these people and reveal Jesus. The hard work of the missionaries shows love to the people, and they, in turn, learn to love Jesus.

Australia

It is very warm in Australia at Christmas time. Families celebrate Christmas with a picnic lunch.

Austria

Austria does not have a Santa Claus that comes with gifts on Christmas day, but instead Saint Nicholas comes on December 6. He is called "Santaklausen". This country is the home of the Christmas song, "Silent Night".

Belgium

My grandmother was born in Belgium. She came to the United States when she was 19.

Belgium celebrates Christmas with a procession. In Antwerp bells ring all over the city. After the procession people gather at the church, and when the services are over the people journey home where they light candles and sing Christmas songs.

Britain

England does Christmas in a big way. The people living in castles in the olden days really feasted with plum pudding and boar's head.

Children hang up their stockings above the fireplace on Christmas Eve. If they don't have a fireplace they hang them on their beds.

Parents decorate the tree on Christmas Eve after the children are in bed.

Christmas Day includes attending church and family dinners with turkey, roast, mince pie, plum pudding, candies, nuts, and fruits. At afternoon tea fruit cake with almond paste icing is served.

Christmas cards and Mistletoe both originated in Britain. Holly is also a part of an English Christmas.

Caribbean

The people of Tobago celebrate Christmas by attending church. They decorate their homes and make a meal of mashed sweet potatoes and ham. Some homes make a wreath out of bread dough.

Trinidad has a mixture of English, Spanish, and French influences. There are a variety of foods such as fruitcakes, minced pies, potato salad, and deep-fried pastilles. Groups go through the streets singing Christmas songs in Spanish. Almost every country bakes breads, pastries, and cookies to whet the appetite of family members.

China

Families decorate their houses with colorful paper lanterns, and tree branches with paper chains and paper flowers. A lantern also hangs from one of the branches.

Santa Claus is called Dun Chelaroren ("dwyn-chuh-lah-oh-rum"). Children are hopeful that Santa will come and bring them presents. They also hang their muslin stockings on paper chains.

Germany

The German people celebrate Christmas beginning on Christmas Eve. It is called Weihnacht, or "watch night".

The Weihnchtsmann or "Christmas man" brings in the Christmas season. The "Christmas man" is described as an old man carrying a tree on his shoulder. He has the image of being exhausted.

Holland

St. Nicolas (Saint Nicholaus) brings gifts on December 6 to all good children.

Children in Holland put their shoes in the chimney corners the evening of December 5 and hope that St. Nicholas will soon be there. The gifts are wrapped in several layers of pretty paper. The children try to guess what is inside the package—this is half the fun of getting a gift in Holland.

Iran

Iran calls Christmas "Little Feast". The families take time to have a quiet time and celebrate with prayers. A chicken stew (Harosa) is served and children receive new clothes—but giving of gifts is not part of their tradition.

Iraq

In Iraq families gather together and each member holds a lighted candle while they read about the Christ Child's birth. When the reading is finished they build a bonfire and the family watches as the thorn bushes burn to ashes. They sing while the fire is burning. When the fire turns to ashes they jump over the ashes three times and each member makes a wish. This ceremony is for good luck in the coming year.

Families attend church the following day and they light another bonfire in the churchyard. The bishop carries the figure of baby Jesus on a red pillow. He selects one person to bless with a touch, and that person turns and touches (blesses) the next person. It is called the "touch of peace".

Ireland

Irish folks place candles in their window on Christmas Eve. This is an invitation to show all are welcome.

The Irish tradition features "Feeding the Wrens". One wren is killed and carried door to door while young boys sing and collect money to feed all the starving wrens.

Italy

Christmas Day in Italy is a family going to church day. Many families participate in midnight mass. There are nativity scenes all over Italy. They celebrate Jesus' birthday. They also celebrate on January 6 (Epiphany or Three Kings' Day). Did you know that Saint Frances of Assisi made the first nativity scene in Greccio?

Mexico

The poinsettia originally came from Mexico.

Children dress up and march in a procession called the "posada". In Spanish the word means "lodgings". The first posadas come on December 16. People decorate their homes with evergreen, moss, and paper lanterns.

A board is used to carry the clay figures of Mary riding on a donkey, Joseph, and an angel guiding them to find a place to stay. Children carry lighted candles while others carefully carry the clay figures on the board. They continue the procession by knocking on doors asking for a place to stay— "Sorry, there is no room." Finally, someone at the next door says, "Yes, there is room in the Inn," and the children say a prayer of thanks that there is really room for the posadas.

Christmas is celebrated with zest in Mexico. Pinatas are decorated in shapes such as goats, lambs, or snowmen. The piñatas are filled with goodies.

There is a quiet time preceding fireworks.

The children receive their gifts on January 6 (Epiphany Day).

New Zealand

Christmas in New Zealand is very similar to Christmas in England or the U.S. However, in this country Christmas comes in the middle of summer, so their menu is a warmer weather menu with fruits and ice cream served along with the plum pudding.

Norway

In Norway Santa Claus is called Father Frost. A Christian Christmas was first established in the Scandinavian countries in the tenth century.

Rome and Greece

Wreaths were also worn as crowns in ancient Rome and Greece. People believed the wreaths gave them divine power. Some wore wreaths of olives to show peace. The Bible mentions wreaths many times. Generally the wreath was associated with honor, joy, and triumph. Sometimes wreaths are thought of as a symbol of eternity.

In Greece, the main holiday is Easter. On Christmas families go to church and gather to share fine foods. They do not put up a tree or give gifts—the gifts come on Saint Basil's Day. Some people still have the superstitious practice of throwing a little cross into the water on Epiphany Day, which is the end of the Christmas season.

Russia

In Russia there is the snegurochka "snow maiden" assigned to pass out the gifts. The snow maiden is the grandfather's first granddaughter.

The story of the snow maiden:

There was an older couple who had no children. One day, they found the snow maiden and took her home. They loved her very much. When spring arrived the snow maiden melted and went away. The old couple was very sad. When the winter season came again the snow maiden returned to her mother and father, and they realized she would return year after year.

South America

In Brazil people roast pork over an open fire. They celebrate Christmas with their families and go to church.

Chile and Argentina use food readily available in their region.

Spain

In Spain the feast of the Immaculate Conception is celebrated on December 8 each year. It is a holiday that celebrates the purity of Mary, the mother of Jesus.

The children dress in elaborate costumes. The choir sings and there is dance in front of the altar. All the markets in Spain are decorated with greenery. The people decorate their homes and also place a nativity scene in their home. In some parts of Spain people put up a Christmas tree.

The people make marzipan and roasted chestnuts during the Christmas season.

Most people attend church on Christmas Day and afterward, family and friends gather for a meal and fellowship. The people gather together with an urn in the center of a table. Each person writes his or her name on a piece of paper and they put the papers in the urn. A person is assigned to draw out two names at a time. It is then predicted that each pair will become best friends for the coming year.

Another Spanish custom is children place wheat in their shoes and hope it will be replaced with candy and, maybe, joy.

Sweden

The family prepares a special dinner on Christmas Eve. It consists of ham and fish. After the meal the family opens gifts. They attend church on Christmas day.

The Swedes celebrate Saint Lucia's feast day or the Festival of Light on December 13. The oldest daughter in the family carries a wreath on her head with seven lighted candles. She takes coffee and buns to her family members while they are still in bed.

Saint Lucia lived in the fourth century. At that time many people didn't like Christians so they would hide their Christmas celebration. Thus, wearing the candles on her head as she carried the food to the Christians in hiding.

Santa Claus is Jultomten in Swedish. In early times givers tossed their presents at the front door.

United States

Christmas in the U.S. is a big deal. Between Christmas shopping, trimming the tree, and outdoor lights people are very busy. Christmas is a family day in the U.S. Everyone prepares favorite foods for the holiday, and many of the dishes are traditions families brought with them when they immigrated from other countries.

Did you know that stockings were first hung from the mantle in the Victorian era of the 19th century?

Christmas cards did not become popular in the U.S. or England until 1860. The first Christmas card was printed in England in 1843.

Santa comes by sleigh and reindeer, with the legend of Rudolph leading the pack.

About two-thirds of the population will light a Christmas tree during the season.

In New England the children helped make bread stuffing for the turkey. The herbs from the gardens were hung in the attic to dry. Herbs such as sage and thyme were used in the dressing.

Saint Stephen's day is celebrated on December 26 in the U.S. Stephen means "the crowned one".

```
S E I G P I C K L E D H E R R I N G A Q S C O
P T R S L A N C H U T N E Y U S M A M R R H L
O F O B W C F R T R N P A E A A I S B D S R D
P K A L S M K S E N C F E Y E L N D R T D I F
P I G T L O I A C D E E S P T M C G E U T S A
Y N T I I E N N N E Y F S V E O E O F X H T S
S G O L N E N T E S E F A E P N D L E Z O M H
E E B S I G W O L S N E T Y S A M D E C L A I
E R C R H L E U I A A R E A S N E E H H I S O
D M H S I R N R P T I N H I C D A N E R D B N
W A O T I O I H B E R U M A N D T F P I A R E
R N R A C U C M P R D S A N D I T R L S Y O D
E B O R E R N H P M E E H O L L A U U T L C F
A U A O O G L P E C N A O M V L R I M M O C R
T T S F R A A E S O C E D D O W T T P A B O U
H T T Z O R S C D C I A A T D R L C U S S L I
R E D U O R C A A K N T N P R E E A D C T I T
I R U R T I E N S T G S A D A A T K D O E S C
S C C I D S N P F A B I G P Y T S E I O R A A
O A K C S O E I E I E M A I D H L A N K S L K
N K K H R N S E W L R D R C E N K S G I O A E
I E I G P I R S P I C E D P E C A N S E U D A
E A N A N H O L I D A Y C O M P O T E S P Z X
```

Christmas Foods Around the World Word Search

PFEFFERNUSE	ROAST DUCK	CHRISTMAS COOKIES
STAR OF ZURICH	CANDY	SALMON AND DILL WREATH
GOLDEN FRUITCAKE	STOLLEN	CHRISTMAS BROCCOLI SALAD
POPPY SEED WREATH	GINGERBREAD	PECAN PIE
PLUM PUDDING	SPICED PECANS	OLD FASHIONED FRUITCAKE
PICKLED HERRING	SHRIMP COCKTAIL	GERMAN BUTTER CAKE
HOLIDAY LOBSTER SOUP	BRIOCHE	MINCEMEAT TARTLETS
HOLIDAY COMPOTE	CHUTNEY	

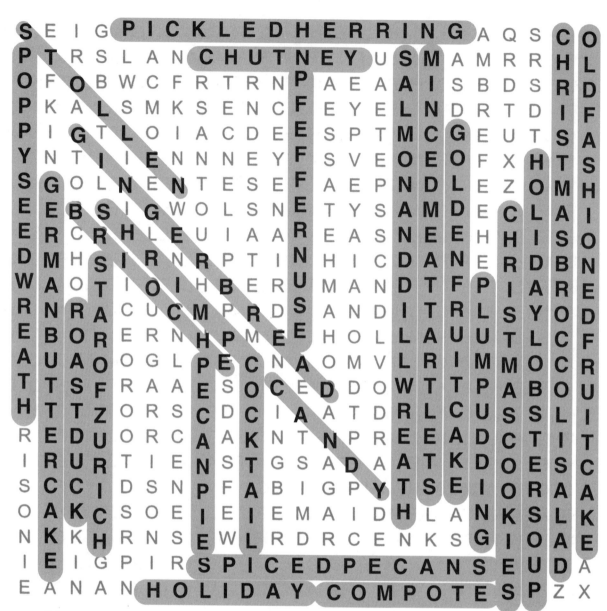

Christmas Foods Around the World Word Search

PFEFFERNUSE	ROAST DUCK	CHRISTMAS COOKIES
STAR OF ZURICH	CANDY	SALMON AND DILL WREATH
GOLDEN FRUITCAKE	STOLLEN	CHRISTMAS BROCCOLI SALAD
POPPY SEED WREATH	GINGERBREAD	PECAN PIE
PLUM PUDDING	SPICED PECANS	OLD FASHIONED FRUITCAKE
PICKLED HERRING	SHRIMP COCKTAIL	GERMAN BUTTER CAKE
HOLIDAY LOBSTER SOUP	BRIOCHE	MINCEMEAT TARTLETS
HOLIDAY COMPOTE	CHUTNEY	

The Story of the Glass Pickle Ornament

The pickle ornament was considered a very special tree decoration by many families in Germany.

There, the fir tree was traditionally decorated on Christmas Eve. For good luck, the pickle always was the last ornament to be hung on the tree—with Mother and Father hiding it in the green boughs among the other ornaments.

When the children were allowed to view the splendor of the decorated tree on Christmas morning they would gleefully begin searching for the pickle ornament. They knew that whoever found that special ornament first would receive an extra little gift left by Saint Nicholas for the most eager child.

The Christmas Pickle

To start a tradition

That surely will last,

Here's a story

About the pickle of glass.

The night before Christmas

It's hung on the tree

While everyone's sleeping

It's done secretly.

And on Christmas morning

When you arise

The first one to find it

Will get a surprise.

A family tradition

For all to endear

You'll look for the pickle

Year after year.

A Victorian Christmas

Christmas celebrations in the 1800s were a quiet day at home. Families would gather for church and then prepare a meal in celebration. Giving of gifts was not part of the day. Sometimes the children would be given an extra piece of fruit or a handmade toy.

In the 19th century the Christmas celebration changed. This was the time of Queen Victoria, who ruled from 1837 to 1901. It was the beginning of the Industrial Age and people were making more money working in factories, so they could afford to buy gifts for their family. Fancy decorations appeared in homes and the festivities became more elaborate.

In the 1800s people believed children would become spoiled if they were given too much attention, but Queen Victoria disagreed. She started to change this idea and children received more attention. Children began to look forward to a Christmas with pretty decorations and gifts and families gathered together to trim a tree and exchange presents.

Prince Albert (Queen Victoria's husband) is the person who made the Christmas tree popular in Britain and America. The Queen and her family would place a small tree on a table and decorate it with lighted candles and a star on the top.

Christmas became very popular when the Royal family was featured in the *American* magazine standing around the candle-lit tree.

In general, Victorian homes were lavishly decorated with lace curtains, wallpaper, ornate furniture, table coverings, and colorful draperies. People even began to decorate their doors one or two weeks before Christmas, and decorated angels were placed in the windows. Victorian advent wreaths came into fashion and nativity scenes of Jesus, Mary, and Joseph were displayed in homes.

The Christmas tree was set up in the parlor on Christmas Eve and taken down on January 6. This time frame represented the twelve days of Christmas. The star on the top of the tree represented the coming of the Wise Men. Other tree decorations were hand-dipped candles, strings of berries and popcorn, nuts, pinecones, tiny dolls, and children's mittens. The custom of hanging Christmas stockings was very popular during this time.

Every year the Victorian Christmas became more elaborate. The Christmas Eve festivities included charades, dancing, a family member playing the piano, and the reading of a Christmas tale or play. Some people went on hayrides, sipped hot cider, and sang Christmas carols.

The churches were decorated with evergreen boughs and lighted candles glowed in the windows. Church bells rang and people gathered to celebrate Jesus' birth.

On Christmas day church bells rang and gifts were exchanged. There was usually a huge Christmas dinner consisting of turkey, goose, ham, yams, corn, potatoes, stuffing, cranberry sauce, and gravy. Of course, plum pudding was always served for dessert. Wines, cakes, and candies were also a part of the feast. After dinner people went from house to house visiting friends and family.

There were parlor games for the children. One such game was "Bag and a Stick". A paper bag was filled with candy and tied with ribbons. A child would be blindfolded and given a stick. The object of the game was to poke the bag with the stick until it broke open and the candy spilled out. Then the scramble was on as the children raced to pick up the candy.

Christmas Crackers were popular at this time. A paper tube was filled with candy and wrapped with a tie at each end. Two people would pull on the ends of the "cracker" until it cracked and they could get the candy.

Wassail was prepared to greet the Christmas visitors, and the custom of sharing a drink of punch and wishing a person good health became known as "wassailing". Wassail contains sherry, cider, ale, lemons, roasted apples, and spices.

Manufactured Christmas ornaments became a big industry. In Germany blown glass balls known as krugels were shipped to America. Other ornaments included: cornucopias filled with candies, nuts, and fruit; ornaments shaped into cradles, carriages, boats, and animals were made from cotton batting and covered with thin crinkled and punched metal; and Dresden ornaments made from cardboard and shaped into animal shapes.

The first Christmas cards, in 1840, were sent and the receiving person paid the postage. The first fine art cards were made by Louis Prang in 1875. Pictures of angels, birds, and children were often featured on the cards.

Elf Tins for Goodies or a Gift

See page 6 in color section for the completed project.

Supplies needed:
Soup can (10 3/4 ounce size)
Peanut can (small size)
Nut can (large size)
9 black buttons (3 for each can elf)
Black felt
Fabric large enough to fit around top of can and tie for
    a hat
Hot glue
Twine
Pinking shears

Remove all labels and glue from the cans.

Measure around the can for size. Use Pinking shears to cut out felt pieces. Wrap felt around can. Glue piece to can with seam in back of can.

Hot glue fabric around top edge of can top, and tie with twine to form the hat.

Hot glue buttons on for the eyes and nose, cut out some black felt for the mouth and hot glue on also.

Fill the cans with candies or other goodies for a gift.

```
W A S S A I L I N G I C D A N E R D B R F A A
P M A T K Q U E E N V I C T O R I A R G E I E
O E G I I A C S N A N D I T D R E S D E N S S
D R O L N N L P C O E L A B O R A T E P I R
E I C S N T E I A O M V L R I M M O C R A D S
C C C R W O L N E R D H W T T P S B O L R N P
O A H H P U I O A N T D O L C U A S L V L A I
R N R R R P O T U P R E L A D N T I I O T C
A M I O I I R T S C D S A T L D T E S C R I K
T A S U N M S D I O P Y T S E Y A R A T G V L
E G T R C H A T M P I D H A A N C S L O A I E
D A M G E P D R M I C E N K R G L O A R M T O
W Z A A A E V P E A P E C A N S A U D I E Y R
I I S R L C E N Y S S M P O T E U P Z A S S N
N N S R B A N I E R C C N G A Q S C O N T C A
D E T I E N T A E Y A S R A M R R H L T E E M
O C O S R P W C A E R A G A R L A N D R R N E
W A C O T I R M E Y D L N D C T D I F E M E N
S N K N S E E O S P S M C G E K T S A E C C T
I G I I R S A E S V E O E O F X E T L S O I A
E E N H O L T E A E P N D L E Z O R R D C N S
E L G C K L H G T Y S A M D E C L A S A K G D
T R B N C H P C E A S N E E H H I S U S T B A
```

Victorian Christmas Word Search

CHRISTMAS CARDS	GARLAND	STAR	DECORATED WINDOWS
PICKLE ORNAMENT	ELABORATE	VICTORIAN TREE	AMERICAN MAGAZINE
QUEEN VICTORIA	PARLOR GAMES	SANTA CLAUS	CHRISTMAS STOCKINGS
CORNUCOPIAS	NATIVITY SCENE	ADVENT WREATH	CHRISTMAS CRACKERS
DRESDENS	HOLLY	PRINCE ALBERT	
ANGEL	WASSAILING		

Victorian Christmas Word Search

CHRISTMAS CARDS	GARLAND	STAR	DECORATED WINDOWS
PICKLE ORNAMENT	ELABORATE	VICTORIAN TREE	AMERICAN MAGAZINE
QUEEN VICTORIA	PARLOR GAMES	SANTA CLAUS	CHRISTMAS STOCKING
CORNUCOPIAS	NATIVITY SCENE	ADVENT WREATH	CHRISTMAS CRACKERS
DRESDENS	HOLLY	PRINCE ALBERT	
ANGEL	WASSAILING		

Snowman Wall Hanging

See page 6 in the color section for the finished project.
See page 270 for the pattern

Supplies needed:

3 pieces large, white, art board-
   medium weight
1 of each color (tan, black, orange)
   construction paper 8 1/2 x 11 inches
Scissors
3/4 yard green felt for the hat
1 3/4 yards multicolor felt for the scarf
2 florist sticks for back support
Tape
Thread
Glue

    This project is a little more work than most of the other projects, but we received many comments about the snowmen.

    Using the white art board make 3 circles: 1-27 inches in diameter, 1-21 inches in diameter, and 1-14 inches in diameter for the snowballs to form the snowman.

    Glue the three circles together with the smallest one at the top and working down to the largest one at the bottom.

    Tape the florist sticks on the back of the snowman, one on the right and one on the left side to give it stability.

    Cut out one 6-inch diameter circle from the black construction paper for the snowman's button that goes on the large bottom circle. Cut two 2 1/2-inch diameter circles from the black construction paper for the snowman's buttons on the middle white circle. (The top white circle of the snowman is his face.) Glue all three button circles on the two bottom white circles of

30-inch scarf with fringe cut at 3-inch slits

To draw large circles: Use a string cut half of the diameter for each circle and tie it to a pencil. Tape the string to the center of your paper and pull tight to draw a circle around with the pencil.

backside of snowman with floral sticks for support

the snowman.

Cut two more 2 1/2-inch black circles for the snowman's eyes and glue on the top white circle.

Cut the carrot nose from the orange construction paper using the pattern and glue on the snowman's face.

Cut tiny square pieces of the tan, orange, and black construction paper to make confetti. Using multi-purpose glue, glue the confetti pieces on the face of the snowman to form the mouth.

Cut two pieces of the hat pattern from the green felt. Put right sides together and sew a seam on the 17-inch side. Flip the hat so the raw edges of the felt are on the inside of the hat. Glue the hat on the snowman.

Cut out a scarf from any color felt you wish. Fringe the edges and tie around the neck of the snowman.

You can tape the snowman directly to the wall or room doors, or use a light-weight sticker hanger.

Christmas Felt Stocking

See page 7 in the color section for completed project.
See page 271 for the pattern

Supplies needed:
White felt 5 inches x 2 3/5 inches
Red felt 9 inches long
Glitter glue, or multi-purpose glue and
  various colors of glitter
Felt pen

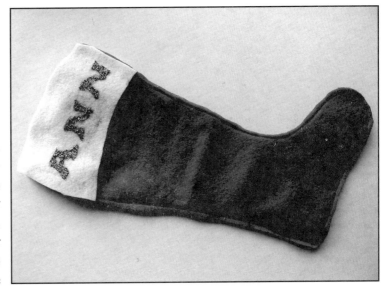

Cut two pieces of white felt and two pieces of red felt to form the stocking. Glue the white for the top of the stocking onto the red stocking body for both the front and back of the stocking.

Place wrong sides together (you're working from the right side) and glue them together around the edges.

If you wish, you can write the person's name on the white felt with the felt pen, or you can use the glitter glue and write the name on the white felt.

Be creative and make a design with the glitter glue on the stocking.

If you use glue and loose glitter, be sure to shake off the excess glitter onto a paper or into a foil pie tin so you can save and reuse.

For more durability you can stitch the stocking on the sewing machine instead of gluing the edges.

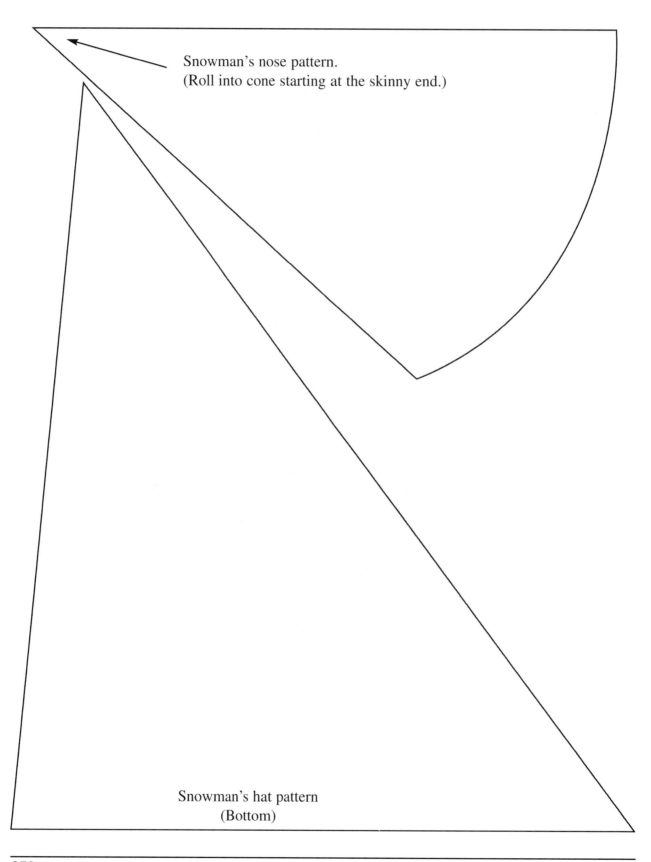

Snowman's nose pattern.
(Roll into cone starting at the skinny end.)

Snowman's hat pattern
(Bottom)

Christmas Felt Stocking pattern

Angel Candleholder

See page 6 in color section for completed project.

Supplies needed:
Small wood knob for nose
Angel hair
Soda can
Christmas ribbon 9 inches long, 2 1/2 inches wide
Acrylic paint in off white, tan, black, rose/pink
Gold pipe cleaner 6 1/2 inches long
Hot glue

Paint the soda can off-white. Paint the top end of the can tan for the angel's face. Let dry thoroughly and then glue on the wood knob for the nose. Paint the eyes and cheeks with the black and rose/pink paint (a Q-tip works well for a paint brush). Hot glue the hair around the top edge of the can for the hair. Form a halo from the pipe cleaner and glue in the middle of the hair.

Make a bow with the Christmas ribbon and glue it to the back of the can. Use as a candleholder as shown!

Singing Angel

See page 7 in color section for completed project.
See facing page for pattern.

Supplies needed:
Fun foam in white or gold for wings
White felt or lacey material for dress
1 ACT mouth wash bottle
1 ribbon 10 inches long, 2 1/2-inches wide
Gold pipe cleaner 6 1/2-inches long for the halo
Angel hair
Acrylic paint in off-white, tan, rose/pink, and black
Glue
2 Q-tips

Lay out pattern for the wings and cut two wings out of the fun foam.

Paint the entire bottle (not the lid) with off-white paint. You will need two coats of paint, and dry thoroughly between coats. Cut out the garment using the pattern on page 273. Remember to place the center front of the skirt pattern on a fold before cutting out.

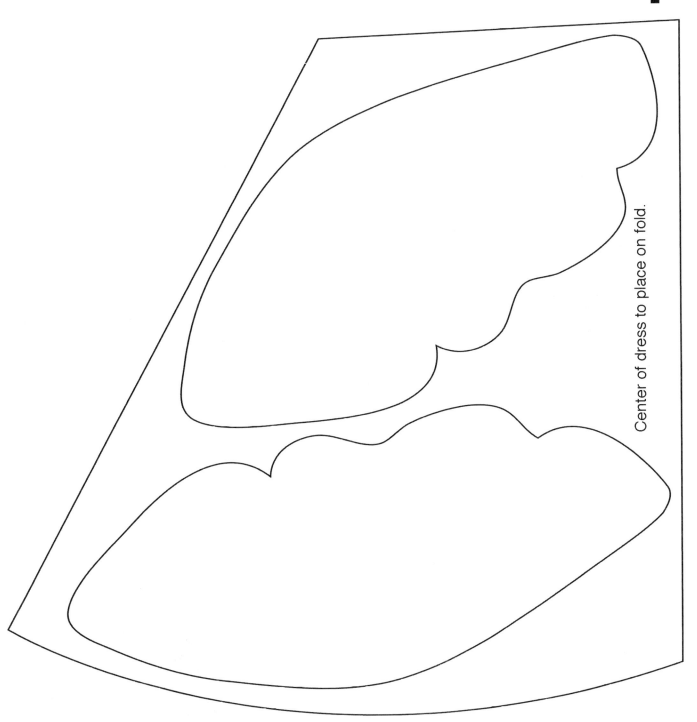

Center of dress to place on fold.

Follow the wing pattern above. The skirt piece is 7 1/2 inches long and 15 3/4 inches around so you will have to enlarge this pattern. Cut out four wing pieces. Hot glue two wings pieces together for each wing. Place the center front of the skirt pattern on the fold. Wrap the skirt piece around the bottle and glue in place. Gather as you glue the neckline. Glue on the ribbon around the bottom of the skirt, placing the seam at the back of the angel. Form the halo from the pipe cleaner. Glue on the hair and the halo. Glue the mini cotton ball on for the nose. Dab a Q-tip in the red paint and paint the rosy cheeks. Dab another Q-tip in black and paint the eyes.

Poinsettia Candle Gift

See page 7 in color section for completed project.

Supplies needed:

Glass fish bowl 6 inches high and 18 inches in diameter
3 silk leaves with berries (7 inches in length)
1/2 to 3/4 cup fresh cranberries
Floating Candle
Water to fill bowl 1/2 to 3/4 full

Place leaves with cranberries in the bowl. Place the candle in the bowl, working it into the middle of the cranberries and leaves. Fill the bowl with water—the candle will float.

Heart Shaped Santa Claus Pin

See page 5 in color section for completed project.

Supplies needed:

Wood heart blank for pin base
Acrylic paints in white, cream, red, black, pink/red
Pin back
Glue

See the picture for painting the Santa face, you can improvise any Santa face design you wish. I recommend painting the face tan first. Then you can paint the hat red, hat tassel, and beard white. Once the face is dry, dab on the eyes in black or blue, and paint the mouth red or pink.

Be sure to let your pin dry thoroughly before turning over to glue on the pin back.

Sea Shell Santa Claus Pin

See page 5 in color section for completed project.

Supplies needed:

Oyster shell half
Acrylic paints in white, red, black, tan, cream
Pin back
Glue

See the picture for painting the Santa face, you can improvise any Santa face design you wish. I recommend painting the face tan first. Then you can paint the hair, hat tassel, and beard white. Once the face is dry, dab on the eyes in black or blue, and paint the mouth red or pink.

Be sure to let your pin dry thoroughly before turning over to glue on the pin back.

Christmas Sachet

See page 7 in the color section for completed project.

Supplies needed:
Cotton fabric in Christmas pattern measuring
    7 x 8 inches
Potpourri
Christmas color ribbon of your choice

   Cut your fabric piece with a pinking shears so the edges do not unravel (this will make a nice edge). Fold your fabric in half, making a bag that is 4 x 7 inches.

   Place potpourri in center of fabric, bring corners together and tie shut with the Christmas ribbon of your choice. (See pattern on page 276.)

Rudolph Candy Cane Ornament

See page 7 in the color section for completed project.

Supplies:
Christmas candy cane, your choice of color
Animal eyes, small size
Red mini ball for nose
Red ribbon

   Glue the eyes and mini ball on the candy cane, making the face of "Rudolph". Tie the ribbon around Rudolph's neck for his necktie.

Candy Cane with Lace Decoration

See page 7 in the color section for completed project.

Supplies:
Christmas candy cane
Eyelet-type lace, you can use various Christmas colors
    if you wish
Mini present from the craft department
Small nosegay of Christmas greens

   String the candy cane through the holes in the eyelet-type lace. Hot glue the tiny Christmas greens and mini present to the candy cane between the lace eyelets.

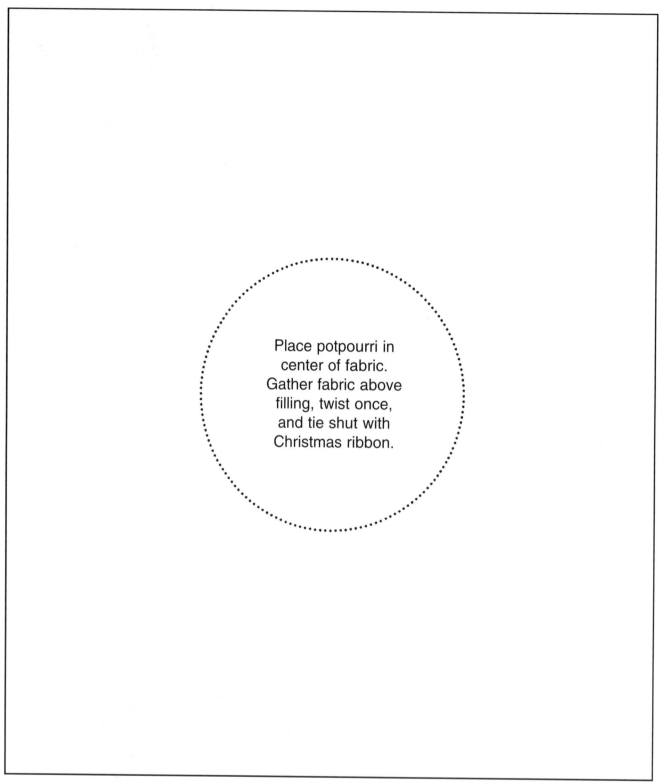

Place potpourri in
center of fabric.
Gather fabric above
filling, twist once,
and tie shut with
Christmas ribbon.

7" x 8" pattern for sachet to be cut from Christmas fabric.

New Year's Eve Celebration

Gather your residents in the lounge or dining room and serve snacks. You might make "fancy" New Year's drinks with grape juice and soda, or have punch.

Lead the discussion about the good times they remember having celebrating the New Year.

Did they go out for the evening?

Did they have friends and family at their home for a party?

What did they serve? A fancy dinner, or snacks?

What was the weather like? Snowstorm? Very Cold?

Did they go dancing? Or see a show?

Once you get the conversation going they will get involved and enjoy themselves reminiscing.

Have a great time and Happy New Year!

Index

X

Y

Z

Uncle Sam Birthday Cake from page 15.
Have an adult light it and a child blow it out!

Firecrackers from page 20.

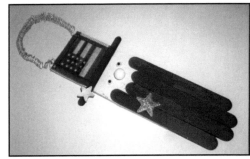

Uncle Sam Door Hanging from page 18.

Memory Butterflies from pages 31 and 32.

Dog Bone Cake from page 71.

Yarn Dogs from page 73.

Flamingo Party
from page 85.

Flamingo Pin
from page 90.

Picnic Centerpiece from page 120.

Ceiling Star Decorations from page 130.

Comfort Bears from page 164.

Color Wheel for use in scrapbooking from page 122.

Casino Centerpiece from page 140.

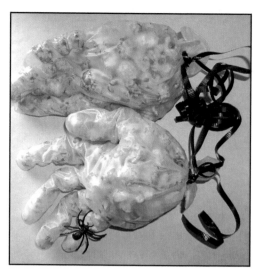

Popcorn Halloween Hands
are mentioned on page 189.

Pumpkin Pin from page 190.

Halloween Magnet from page 192.

Heart Shaped Pumpkin Pins from page 190.

Pumpkin Centerpiece from page 189.

Turkey Pin from page 226.

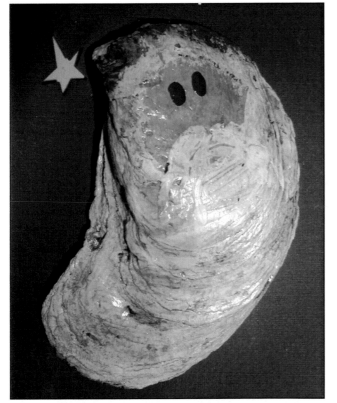

Sea Shell Santa pin from page 274.

Heart Shaped Santa Pin from page 274.

Elves from page 265.

Snowman Wall Hanging from page 268.

Can Angel Candleholder from page 272.

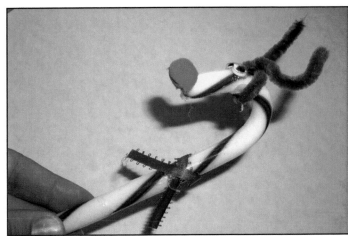

Lace Candy Cane and Rudolph Candy Cane page 275.

Christmas Stocking page 269.

Sachet and Cracker page 275.

Poinsettia Candle Gift from page 274.

Singing Angel from page 272.